The Art of Bob Dylan

Song & Dance Man

The Art of Bob Dylan

Michael Gray

St. Martin's Press
New York

From original dedication
To Linda Thomas . . . and to Sue

New edition dedication
To my son Gabriel

Thanks

To Robert Shelton for many forms of help and friendship over the last eight years; to Gerry and Carla Rafferty; Dave Laing; Nigel Fountain; Chris Perry; Gaye Goodchild; Peter Harrison; Michele Hush; Jeanne McKay; Cathy Village; Dave Willis; Sue Tyrrell; Robin Valk; Anthony Wall; Iain McLay and Jackum Brown – all of whom have given much help and/or support – and to my editor, Camilla Simmons. And special thanks to Vivienne Jez.

For much assistance with the original edition of this book, I must record my indebtedness to Bob Jones, Christine Seville, Paul & Anna Harvey and most of all to Sue Tyrrell, without whom it really would never have got written. I must also add my indebtedness to Steve MacDonogh, for allowing me to plunder his own works on links between Bob Dylan and Robert Browning, and to the published works of Alan Lomax and Paul Oliver, on which I have leant with obvious heaviness in what follows.

Photographic Acknowledgements
BBC London 95; CBS London 6, 52 top, 74, 186 bottom, 230; CBS – Don Hunstein, New York 118 top; Camera Press, London 33 top, 52 bottom, 150, 186 top; Jim Douthitt, Columbus, Ohio 16, 17, 209; Frank Driggs Collection, New York 61, 77, 91, 180; David Gahr, New York half title page, title page, 11 left, 20, 21, 26, 112, 113, 118 bottom, 125, 133, 135, 136, 164 top, 164 bottom, 175, 185 top, 189, 193, 230; Globe Photos, New York 117; Michael Gray, Tunbridge Wells 183, 204 bottom; Jim Marshall, San Francisco, California 11 right, 22, 33 bottom, 34 top, 34 bottom, 38, 41, 44, 46, 51, 69, 86, 92, 107, 115, 139, 146, 160, 203 top, 203 bottom, 204 top; National Film Archive, London 103; Rex Features, London 185 bottom; Joseph Siu, New York 108.

The publishers have made every attempt to contact the owners of the illustrations appearing in this book. In the few instances where they have been unsuccessful, they invite the copyright holders to contact them direct.

Original edition first published in Great Britain 1972
by Hart-Davis, MacGibbon Ltd and in the United States of
America 1973 by E. P. Dutton.

This new edition published in Great Britain 1981 by
The Hamlyn Publishing Group Limited, Feltham, Middlesex.
Published in the United States of America by
St Martin's Press Inc., 175 Fifth Avenue, New York, NY 10010

Library of Congress Catalog Number: 80-6305
ISBN Number: 0-312-05418-1

Composition in Apollo by
Filmtype Services Limited, Scarborough, North Yorkshire

Printed and bound in Spain
by Graficromo, S. A. – Córdoba

Contents

1 Bob Dylan's Art: Introduction   7

2 Dylan and the Folk Tradition   19

3 Dylan and the Literary Tradition   47

4 Dylan and Rock Music   88

5 Dylan's Use of Language:
Towards Complexity   123

6 Dylan's Use of Language:
Towards a New Simplicity   161

7 Lay Down Your Weary Tune:
Drugs and Mysticism   190

8 The Coming of the Slow Train   199

Acknowledgements   230

Index   232

'I think of myself as just a song & dance man.'
(Bob Dylan, 1969)

'Never trust the artist – trust the tale.'
(D.H. Lawrence, 1924)

Chapter 1
Bob Dylan's Art
Introduction

I'm a poet, and I know it.
Hope I don't blow it.
(from Dylan's *I Shall Be Free, No. 10*)

This is not a biography of Bob Dylan but a critical study of his work. I've tried to give an insight into the man not by peekabooing into what he eats for breakfast but by looking closely at what he writes in his songs.

It is more about Bob Dylan's words than his music, though it tries to take a proper account of both. After all, Dylan uses much *more* than language in his art: his words are presented not as poems but as parts of songs. His finished works of art are his *recordings*. Like his vocal performances and his music, his words are just ingredients.

This needs to be borne in mind when we analyse his lyrics – and this book makes no apology for doing that. By the beginning of the twenty-first century, and for a long time after that, those who want to understand the generations which grew up in the West in the 1960s–1980s will find it vital to study Bob Dylan's art closely.

There is a sense in which, more fully than F. Scott Fitzgerald, Dylan has created a generation. The possibilities of our inner lives have been expanded by the impingement of Dylan's art – by the impact of his consciousness on ours. And if he is not listened to much by teenagers of the 1980s (though plenty of them turned out for the London concerts of 1978 – Dylan's first in twelve years) his influence is still undeniable and primary upon the rock music they do listen to. Dylan might have been the 1960s but he never embodied the flabby hippie values that punk destroyed. He opened the way for the best of that abrasiveness. Elvis Costello, The Pretenders and so on – they did not come out of nowhere.

Whenever an artist of such real power as Dylan emerges, there is a fatalistic desire, on the part of those who appreciate it, not to analyse but to submit. But there is a collaborative process involved in art's impingement: the artist's work must be receptively approached before it can function fully.

Dylan's work has hardly been ignored on every level, of course, but much of the real impact of his art has passed unnoticed while that other impact – that of the showbiz phenomenon – has been far from ignored. Dylan has been interviewed, his concerts written up, his records reviewed, with relish and persistence; but reviews and interviews are rarely designed for analysis so much as for a kind of flippant prying. The review is as far removed from real criticism as is the interview from real dialogue.

In Dylan's case there has been plenty of this superficial Message-Hunting. It provokes, in the artist, an appropriate defensiveness:

> DYLAN: ... I do know what my songs are about.
> PLAYBOY: And what's that?
> DYLAN: Oh, some are about four minutes, some are about five minutes, and some, believe it or not, are about eleven or twelve.

What Dylan does not do – and consequently, whatever the mode of approach, the journalist's message-hunt must fail – is consciously to offer a sustained, cohesive philosophy of life, intellectually considered and checked for contradictions. What he does offer is the artistic recreation of the individual's struggle in our times. His work is truly educative, and thereby truly entertaining. Its virtue lies not in the immediacy, or pace, but in the perceptiveness of what it offers.

At its best, Dylan's work possesses much more than freshness: it has that clear integrity which is capable of 'representing the age' and competent, therefore, to go beyond it – to clarify by focusing, with a vital intelligence, on its confusions.

Even from a very basic knowledge of Dylan's art it is plain how much more there is to it than just collating a few common denominators of sentiment to which we all feel susceptible – as (say) The Beatles did – or from the rigidly formularized pop and rock of the '70s and early '80s, during which the new depression has truly become the new *re*pression: megastars, megabucks, nil risks. The whole music industry has stiffened up into its BeeGeeAbba money-babble. Real feelings don't hold much sway as ingredients. It is not a good time for artists and poets in the record business. What gets ignored, and what Dylan always deals with, is the human world as it really is.

At one time Dylan wrote songs explicitly 'about' war, exploitation and suffering. That he no longer often does so is not a mark of any lack of concern or of any retreat from responsibility.

An early Dylan song like *A Hard Rain's A-Gonna Fall*, with its clear didactic glimpses:

> I met one man who was wounded in love
> I met another man who was wounded in hatred

evinces the same kind of exploratory awareness which has matured, not disappeared, in Dylan's later work.

On a political level, his work has become more acute as it has moved beyond the early explicit rhetoric. Compare *The Times They Are A-Changin'* with *Desolation Row*. As Nigel Fountain expressed it, 'Whatever happened to all the senators and congressmen who were supposed to heed the call? Dr Filth is still around.'

There is, then, a fundamental sense in which Dylan cannot be placed alongside most heroes of the mass media; he is not selling that bland superficiality on which they depend, and which makes up what gets purveyed to the disenfranchised tribespeople of McLuhan's global village.

In this achievement, Dylan shows how right a part of McLuhan's thesis was. It *is* true that Dylan's vast audience has been attracted by the medium as well as the message; indeed that the two are bound up. And while schools, along with much else that is crumbling, stand for categorization, detachment and what Mailer calls 'the logic of the next step', so electric technology 'fosters and encourages unification and involvement'.

Dylan works in the most powerfully attractive form of electric technology yet available – since, that is, films still involve having to sit in cinemas or buy expensive video equipment, and TV is in the hands of those Dylan once called 'men and women who look like cigars – the anti-happiness committee'.

At least one wheel has come full circle. Folk-music married to poetry has been reasserted; in Dylan, as in John Bunyan before him, the sub-cultures have surfaced.

In the 1960s Dylan's generation packed together its discoveries of innumerable sub-cultures and re-formed them into chaotic, kaleidoscopic but living experience. With a free intelligence, that generation derived a dynamic vision from rock music, cinematic experiment, comic books, communal living, philosophy, existential politics, drugs, and an early tacit recognition that the cultural mainstream had done little, in our times, to combat the moral and imaginative imbecility of what was then called The Great Society.

And what changed in the 1970s? The affluence fell away, and it gave a hungry, meaner edge to the battle everybody lined up in. Nixon in the White House for a second term in '72 – that was really the beginning of the 1970s. All the vagueness and wooliness that was affordable in the '60s wasn't functional after that. The backlash concentrated people's minds wonderfully. The fad-men – the Incredible String Band, Donovan, all those people, fell away. The real artist of the times, Bob Dylan, didn't. Because he never depended on fads and the sloganizing habits of thought that fashion craves, he never became redundant. The genuine voice, if it survives at all, still speaks out; and Dylan's did.

Bob Dylan's first album came out in 1962, when anyone now in their early twenties was hardly born. So what follows, to begin with, is a guide through all *twenty-five* of Dylan's officially released albums – none of which (and this makes him unique) has been deleted.

1. Bob Dylan, 1962. This features the twenty-year-old Dylan, unique among the Greenwich Village folkies in being signed to the huge Columbia label, which had missed out on rock'n'roll altogether. But in staff-producer John Hammond they had a man who'd been involved in Bessie Smith's recordings and those of many more great blues acts besides.

He signed Dylan, spent less than 500 dollars in the studio and came out with an album which few people liked and which didn't sell. The record company was all for dropping him. It's worth remembering that in the context of Dylan's reportedly driving hard bargains when re-signing with them in the mid-1970s. There is a good reason for artists' 'greed' when they're dealing with the music business.

This first album is, in retrospect, terrific. It has such a young Dylan on it that he sounds about seventy-five. Only two of the songs are his own – one dedicated to his early idol Woody Guthrie (*Song To Woody*) and the other owing its whole format and spirit to Guthrie's own work (*Talkin' New York*).

The rest of the songs are mainly traditional and/or old blues songs by men like Jesse Fuller, Bukka White and Blind Lemon Jefferson. Dylan comes across as obsessed with the romance of dying, but the speed, energy and attack in his guitar, harmonica and voice show how fresh and excellently 'unprofessional' he was.

2. The Freewheelin' Bob Dylan, 1963. This was Dylan's first opportunity to show how fast he was to develop from one album to the next. All the songs were his own, though many were based on older folk melodies. He was better-known in 1963 as a new songwriter of weird promise than as a performer, though this album not only brought together an impressive group of songs that have since become classics – *Blowin' In The Wind*, *Girl From The North Country*, *Masters Of War* and *A Hard Rain's A-Gonna Fall* are all on one side, while the other includes *Don't Think Twice, It's All Right* – but also gained him an unstoppable cult following among people who preferred the harshness of Dylan's performances to the string-soaked cover-versions other singers released.

3. The Times They Are A-Changin', 1964. Less of a leap forward, this was again a solo album mainly of stark 'protest' songs, all written by Dylan, though often with adapted folk melodies. Like his second album, it contained songs that have achieved classic status – particularly the title track and *With God On Our Side*. It also included the love song *One Too Many Mornings*, which Dylan has subsequently included in pretty well every live performance he's ever given, taking it through many changes, from the surreal acid-rock '66 tour version to the gentle mocking of Johnny Cash of the 1969 country-duet version and on back to various rock versions in the '70s.

As it first appeared, on this third album, the song should have served notice on Dylan's early cult followers (most of whom were students and liberals who considered themselves radicals, hated pop music and wore Dylan on their sleeves like a political arm-band) that Dylan was not just going to be a graphic protest-singer. But no one seemed to notice, so that the next album, came as a shock.

4. Another Side Of Bob Dylan, 1964. Thousands screamed 'sell-out' – just as thousands more were to do later when he 'went electric', later again when he 'went country' and yet later still when he 'got religion'.

This album was much the same stark solo performance (though Dylan added piano and somehow more space and colour in the sound) but with the exception of the long *Chimes Of Freedom* there wasn't a protest song or any overtly political theme anywhere on the record. And even *Chimes Of Freedom* was, for many people, uncomfortably close to impressionism.

They were love songs – and many people felt betrayed. It must be hard now to understand how this album could so bitterly have angered so many; but it did, and perhaps that is part of why it has always been such a slow-selling album in Dylan's large catalogue. It finally 'went gold' eleven years after its release.

All that said, it was clear to plenty of people at the time, and is all the more so looking back, that the love songs Dylan offered on this album were more true and more real – and ultimately more radical – than protest songs. *All I Really Want To Do* and *It Ain't Me Babe* are important songs: they questioned the common assumptions of true love and the male-female relationship; they not only avoided possessiveness and macho strut but explained why as well. This was years before any of us understood that 'love' and politics weren't opposites – that there was such a thing as sexual politics.

This album also contained Dylan's specific recantation of the protest phase. *My Back Pages* did this, and had the celebrated chorus line 'Ah but I was so much older then/I'm younger than that now.' And Dylan's voice is actually younger-sounding than on his earlier work: he has thrown off the mantle of the old bluesmen and assumed one of his own.

If I could have only about five Bob Dylan albums, this would be one of them. *To Ramona* is an all-time great, while *Spanish Harlem Incident* is not only one of the most alive, successful of Dylan's career-spanning songs exploring his fascination with things neo-Spanish (from *Boots Of Spanish Leather* in 1963 right through via *Spanish Is The Loving Tongue* in 1970 to *Romance In Durango* in 1976 and *Senor* in '78) but also brings powerfully into play for the first time Dylan's complexity of imagery.

His writing, and control of atmosphere, on songs like this come across as the first flashes of the creative explosion that he was to go through in 1965–66. A great album, and his last solo album (so far).

5. Bringing It All Back Home, 1965. Another breakthrough album and another sudden jump to new ground. One side of the record is solo and has four long tracks, each of which has become a classic – *Mr Tambourine Man* (Dylan's first drugs song); the heavily poetry-influenced, visionary *Gates of Eden*; the original version of *It's Alright Ma (I'm Only Bleeding)* which, thanks to the special drama of Richard Nixon's criminal escapades, was to come into its own all over again on Dylan's major

Left: *1962 Carnegie Hall.*

Right: *At the 1962 recording sessions that produced the rare single* Mixed-Up Confusion. *Dylan didn't play piano on an album till 'Another Side of Bob Dylan', 1964.*

American 'come-back' tour of 1974 (caught on the album *Before The Flood*); and the beautiful *It's All Over Now, Baby Blue*.

The solo side of the album contained more than enough to justify Dylan's burgeoning popularity as a uniquely contemporary spokesman. But the other side was enough to gain him a new notoriety and to lose him even more devotees than his previous album had done.

Unprecedentedly, here was this folk-singer committing the ultimate sacrilege of singing rock'n'roll songs with electric guitars behind him. Students – serious-minded young people unaware of the social upheavals about to happen – were appalled that Dylan should resort to such triviality.

Mostly it sounds pretty thin now, a notably mediocre production job, and it was very much a dress-rehearsal/prototype for what was to come next. But it was undeniably innovative and gives us yet another collection of stand-out Dylan songs: *Subterranean Homesick Blues, She Belongs To Me, Love Minus Zero/No Limit* and *Maggie's Farm* among them.

6. Highway 61 Revisited, 1965. Dylan's first fully-fledged eagle-flight into rock. Revolutionary and stunning, not just for its energy and freshness and panache but in its fusion of new, non-pop electric music – electric music as the embodiment of our whole out-of-control nervous-energy-fuelled chaotic civilization – with lyrics that were light years ahead of anyone else's, and created a complete new politicization of the surreal and the impressionistic and the doomed.

The whole rock culture, the whole post-Beatle pop rock world, and so in an important sense the 1960s, started here. It isn't only *Like A Rolling Stone*; it's also the devastating first-time-ever 12-minute Armageddon epic *Desolation Row*, the merciless *Ballad Of A Thin Man*, the searing directness of *From A Buick 6* . . . the carving out of a new emotional correspondence with a new chaos-reality. There it all was in one bombshell of an album, for a generation who only recognized what world they were living in when Dylan illuminated it so corrosively.

7. Blonde On Blonde, 1966. To have followed up a masterpiece with another one was the history-making conquest Dylan made with this. It aims at a more limited canvas than *Highway 61 Revisited* but evokes a much richer, more multi-layered, synapse-jumping consciousness. Where *Highway 61 Revisited* has Dylan exposing and confronting like a laser-beam in surgery, descending from outside the sickness, 'Blonde On Blonde' offers a persona awash inside the chaos and speaking to others who are acceptedly in the same boat – or rather, the same ocean.

We're tossed from song to song, and they all move into each other. The feel and the music are on a grand scale, truly tidal, oceanic – and the language and delivery is a unique mixture of the visionary and the colloquial, the warm and the alert. Dylan dances like his own Mr Tambourine Man through these songs, even though tossed and blown by disorientating, desperate forces.

8. Bob Dylan's Greatest Hits, 1967. The title was offensive at the time; Dylan was no mere pop artist and his greatness had nothing to do with whether DJs loved his records or whether his singles ran up the charts. In fact never has so influential an artist had so few hit singles.

More importantly, each of the previous albums had had its own unity. They'd never been collections of isolated tracks. So a 'greatest hits' collection made no sense at all, except in money terms.

The album was put out in what was considered the disastrously long silence from Dylan between 'Blonde On Blonde' in 1966 and the next proper album in 1968. In those days, everyone made two albums a year and a long gap was supposed to be career-death.

So this was badly-selected regurgitation and provides nothing new; nor does it give an accurate picture of his progress through the earlier recordings.

9. John Wesley Harding, 1968. This quiet, authoritative masterpiece is not a rock album – it isn't categorizable at all. The back-up musicians are pared down to three: bass, drums, and, on two tracks only, pedal steel. Plus Dylan on guitar, harmonica and piano.

Economy, in fact, is the key to this huge change of direction. There could be no greater contrast between consecutive albums than that between 'Blonde On Blonde''s richness and the taut asceticism of 'John Wesley Harding'. This album is no cheap thrill.

It is, though, a most serious, darkly visionary exploration of the myths and extinct strengths of America; its calvinistic spirit gives it an eerie power in mixing the severely biblical with a surreal nineteenth-century American pioneer ethos. Dylan comes across like a man who has arisen from the final holocaust unscathed but sobered, to walk across an allegorical American landscape of small, poor communities working a dusty, fierce terrain.

The masterpieces within the masterpiece are *I Dreamed I Saw St Augustine*, *All Along The Watchtower*, *I Pity The Poor Immigrant* (of which Dylan was years later to do a triumphant flamenco-rock version with Joan Baez on the film, though not on the record, of 'Hard Rain') and *The Wicked Messenger*.

And then there are the last two tracks of the album: the à la Jerry Lee Lewis *Down Along The Cove* and the brilliant pastiche-song *I'll Be Your Baby Tonight*. With these, Dylan was serving notice of the next sharp shift in direction that was to come from him.

'John Wesley Harding' was to be Dylan's last masterpiece of the 1960s – and in spirit and artistic seriousness, it was most markedly not a part of the '60s world at all.

10. Nashville Skyline, 1969. Not Dylan's first Nashville album – 'Blonde On Blonde' had, amazingly, been recorded there – but this was his first leap into country music. Again a massive contrast to the previous album: down-home instead of visionary, warm instead of severely ascetic, optimistic instead of dark, and more under the influence of sunshine and the big sky than of catechism and nemesis.

It also offered a complete change of language – away from the impressionistic and the allegorical and the distinctive complexity of his previous work.

Dylan suddenly embraced the simplicity and clichés that are the currency of ordinary Americans' speech. A new voice went with it – gone is the husky, grating Dylan and on comes a light, melodic, almost Orbisonian tenor.

A lovely album but not a heavyweight contender, though its effects were major ones. Country music was despised, hick music when Dylan took it up. People were divided into the hip and the non-hip. The counter-culture was in full swing and riddled with its own self-importance and snobbery. 'Nashville Skyline' was a hard pill to swallow: but it did 'em good.

11. Self Portrait, 1970. A mistake. You could have got a reasonably minor album out of it if you'd cut it down to a single album from the overblown double-album it is. There was no reason why Dylan shouldn't have made this new departure – largely into pop songs and Tin Pan Alley country material written by other people – but it just wasn't all that good. At the time it was again the cue for large numbers of Dylan's followers to give up on him. Best tracks are *Days of 49*, *Early Morning Rain*, *Let It Be Me*, *Belle Isle*, *Copper Kettle* and *Wigwam*.

12. New Morning, 1970. This came a bit hastily after 'Self Portrait', and with songs like *Day Of The Locusts* and *One More Weekend* and *Three Angels*, it seemed at the time to represent a capitulation to the huge Dylan audience's demand that he return to the milieu of 'Blonde On Blonde'. Lines like 'The man standin' next to me/His head was explodin'/I was hopin' the pieces/Wouldn't fall on me' seemed a bit written-to-order. And Dylan, despite all the changes he'd gone through, had never done that before.

But in retrospect, 'New Morning' is a very individual album. A relative failure but a brave attempt to fuse the old surreal richness of feeling of the 'Blonde On Blonde' era with the recognition of a new personal desire to forge some stability out of rural-based concerns. This is all felt by Dylan in a hesitant, pessimistic, confidence-lost way, and this comes out too in the strange hesitancy with which the album also attempts a musical fusion of a sort of grown-up acid-rock with both country picking and gospel.

There is a considerable gospel feel throughout the album, created mainly by Dylan's own terrific untutored piano-work and by the use of an old-church type girl chorus.

This is a quirky album, from a Dylan not pointing a way for anyone, but from a great artist remaining at his work knowingly in the face of not being creatively on top form in the phenomenal way he had been in the period 1964–68.

13. More Bob Dylan Greatest Hits, 1971. Again inevitably a collection that rides roughshod over both the real chronology of Dylan's career and the whole-album unities of most Dylan work – but at least here there are some additional tracks not obtainable on other albums. These are: the 1971 (hit) single *Watching The River Flow*; the 1965 masterpiece of put-down *Positively 4th Street* and five previously-unissued tracks. If it sounds odd to have previously unissued material on a 'greatest hits' collection, it wasn't really in the light of what songs they were.

First there was *When I Paint My Masterpiece* (cut in '71) which was already well-known from The Band's recording of it on their 'Cahoots' album; a nigh-perfect delicate live performance of *Tomorrow Is A Long Time* done nine years earlier in 1963 – one of those love-songs of Dylan's that plenty of other people, including, to Dylan's delight, Elvis Presley, had recorded in the interim; and newly-recorded, outrageously loose versions of three songs that had long been buzzing around from the famed 1967 bootleg of The Basement Tapes: *I Shall Be Released*, *Down In The Flood* and, with playfully different lyrics, *You Ain't Goin' Nowhere*.

Which makes it an interesting album for collectors and compilers at least, although it would have been much more valuable if it had rounded up some of his other previously-only-on-singles tracks too.

They could have had *Mixed-Up Confusion* (1962), which has never had UK release; *If You Gotta Go, Go Now* (1965) ditto; the live-in-Liverpool cut of *Just Like Tom Thumb's Blues* (1966) issued only as the B-side of the *I Want You* single; the 1971 B-side *Spanish Is The Loving Tongue*; the 1966 A-side *Can You Please Crawl Out Your Window*; and the 1971 single *George Jackson*. But record-companies never do these things right.*

14. Pat Garrett & Billy The Kid, 1973. Dylan's first new album-proper since 1970 was 'only a film soundtrack'. It is a largely instrumental album, with all the characteristic roughness and lack of polish that has kept Bob Dylan less palatable to mass easy-listening taste than any of his infinitely less talented contemporaries such as Paul Simon or Paul McCartney.

Nevertheless, though a very minor collection in Dylan's catalogue, it is a finely atmospheric album quite capable of being listened to in its own right and yet far more effective as a part of the very excellent movie it was written for. There is no doubt that it was partly Dylan's significant contribution, not only in writing the score but also by his own performance and his re-writes of the script that made 'Pat Garrett & Billy The Kid' Sam Peckinpah's finest film.

15. Dylan, 1973. This was essentially a malicious record-company response to Dylan's signing with a new label, Asylum, in America. This album was a deliberate release of the worst tracks they could find lying around in their vaults. Dylan warming up before recording other things; Dylan messing about; out-takes largely from the 'New Morning' sessions; and all compounded by their apparently allowing a baboon to do a re-mix that brought the back-up vocals up horrendously high in the mix.

* The American version of this album had a slightly different tracks list.

Two ironies: despite all this malice-aforethought, the album, though for fanatics only, isn't as bad as they meant it to be; and the reason Dylan did subsequently return to Columbia/CBS had much more to do with Asylum's comparatively ineffective sales distribution system than with this shoddy bully-boy tactic of an album.

16. Planet Waves, 1974. For the first ten minutes after this came out, it was hailed – as 'New Morning' had been before it – as 'the best thing he's done since Blonde On Blonde'. Like 'New Morning', it then suffered from a disappointment backlash from which it has never fully recovered. But put in the long back-projection of Dylan's recording career it is a potent, compelling album.

Warm and emotionally rich, it comes again from a tired man without a vision but with unrivalled skills, forging a collection of songs from the inner resources of memory mixed with a determination to record faithfully his own current state of mind in spite of its tiredness, its unpopular grown-upness and its uncharismatic low-key lack of self-confidence.

Most of the songs recall, largely for the first time (except for *Winterlude* and *Went To See The Gypsy* on 'New Morning') Dylan's pre-New York years as an adolescent up in Minnesota. There is a strange tension created by this uncomfortable contrast between recollected adolescence and current father-figure weariness. The result is nostalgia-soaked but genuinely beautiful, and in this vein the stand-out tracks are *Hazel*, *Something There Is About You* and *Never Say Goodbye*, which opens with these tugging, poignant lines:

> Twilight on the frozen lake
> North wind about to break
> Footprints in the snow
> And silence down below . . .

Those lines evoke the eerie, compelling quality that marks this album as unique in Dylan's output.

The album also contains two versions of what became, for the 1970s, a perennial Dylan concert anthem, *Forever Young*.

The comparison, overall, must be with the 'New Morning' album, though 'Planet Waves' is a far greater, more cohesive success. Again it points down no new road for anyone; rather, it looks down an old one for Dylan himself. But it does so with consummate skill in avoiding the pitfalls of nostalgia and in asserting the artist's right to prefer minor work on old canvasses to doing no work at all.

17. Before The Flood, 1974. From Dylan's huge American 'come-back' tour of 1974 with The Band, on which he revisited a surprising number of his old songs, this is a double-album of confident, brash rock'n'roll Dylan; a record of an artist exhilarated by being back on stage again and in the process largely ignoring the differences between one song and another. There is an over-speedy, breakneck quality here which does little justice to the lyrics and which results in Dylan mainly just throwing back his head and yelling. Don't look to this album for any of the subtlety, nuance or understatement which have always been hall-marks of Dylan's genius.

18. Blood On The Tracks, 1975. In stunning, total contrast, this is an album from Dylan that triumphantly shows more subtlety and more nuance than anything he'd ever done, and as devastating a use of understatement as on 'John Wesley Harding'.

This was perhaps the most unexpected leap of Dylan's whole career. After years of comparatively second-rate work, years that had seen a considerable decline in 15

Acting the circus-ringmaster in his 1978 revisit to Ballad Of A Thin Man,
thirteen years on: Dayton, Ohio, October 1978.

Dylan's reputation, along came 'Blood On The Tracks', an album that stands with 'Highway 61 Revisited', 'Blonde On Blonde' and 'John Wesley Harding' – an album incontrovertibly of genius: of powerful emotional complexity, unerring fresh insight and the kind of maturity (horrible word) that manifests itself not remotely as grown-up tiredness but as pure, strong intelligence.

This was without doubt the best album of the 1970s, and may well be, so far, the best album Bob Dylan ever made.

19. The Basement Tapes, 1975. This double-album marked the official release of the world's most bootlegged bootleg – material cut by Dylan and The Band up near Woodstock in (mainly) April 1967 during the long silence between 'Blonde On Blonde' (and Dylan's motorcycle crash) in 1966 and 'John Wesley Harding' in 1968.

Its songs actually do form a very clear link between these two utterly different albums. They have the same highly serious, utterly earnest sense of a desperate, precarious quest for a personal and universal salvation which marked out the 'John

Wesley Harding' collection – yet they are soaked in the same blocked confusion and turmoil as 'Blonde On Blonde'. *Tears of Rage* on 'The Basement Tapes', for example is an exact halfway house between, say, *One Of Us Must Know* (*Sooner Or Later*) and *The Wicked Messenger* or *I Dreamed I Saw St Augustine*. Essential Stuff.

20. Desire, 1976. This was the next newly-recorded studio album after 'Blood On The Tracks', and proved to be Dylan's biggest-ever seller. With this album he found a new following among teenagers who would hardly have been toddlers when the mid-60s Dylan was so much in vogue.

After 'Blood On The Tracks' it was bound to be a disappointment but it is an important album in Dylan's catalogue nonetheless – a work with its own distinctive unity and yet with most of Dylan's traditional strengths too: not least wit, warmth and energy and a beautiful disregard for finishing things off with the professional songwriter's 'polish'. And it revealed a Dylan still wanting to experiment and still refusing to stand in one place.

The stand-out tracks are *Isis*, *Romance In Durango* and perhaps *Black Diamond Bay*.

21. Hard Rain, 1977. A generally poor selection of tracks from a concert that was far from being one of Dylan's best in the first place. After 'Dylan' and the 1967 'Greatest Hits' collection, this is Dylan's least essential album. Stand-out tracks are all inferior re-workings of 'Blood On The Tracks' material – *Idiot Wind*, *You're A Big Girl Now* and *Shelter From The Storm*.

22. Street Legal, 1978. Released around the time of Dylan's first London concerts for twelve years – at Earls Court in June of '78 – this proved to be, after 'Blood On The Tracks', Dylan's best record of the 1970s. It is a crucial album and documents a crucial period in Dylan's own life. It is of astonishing complexity and confidence, delivered in Dylan's most authoritative voice.

23. Budokan, 1978. This double-album was recorded live in concert in Japan, where Dylan took the band that appeared on the 'Street Legal' album before bringing them to Britain for the Earls Court concerts. It is Dylan's best concert recording (except for the '66 bootlegs) and includes magnificent re-workings of myriad Dylan classics, but it is a pity that it caught the band before they reached the peak form that they were to demonstrate at Earls Court. All the same, it is an essential album and a remarkable testament to the man's staying power and resourcefulness. Stand-out tracks are many, but the freshness of focus Dylan brings to these is especially dramatic: *I Want You, Ballad Of A Thin Man, Blowin' In The Wind, The Times They Are A-Changin', Don't Think Twice, It's All Right, All Along The Watchtower* and more besides.

The tour was remarkable in re-asserting Dylan's power and relevance in an entirely different decade from the one he had first emerged to shape so significantly. The album is a pale but necessary souvenir of what went down.

24. Slow Train Coming, 1979. Anyone else, riding so high as Dylan was in 1978, would have stuck with the same band and produced another 'Street Legal'-type album. Dylan did no such thing. Converted to Born Again Christianity, he gathered a different group of musicians around him and produced an album destined to be profoundly unpopular amongst almost anyone with any sense who'd ever valued him as a writer.

It is not, however, an album that can be ignored, and in some ways it is a logical direction for Dylan to take.

Beyond that, it is hard to give it a decently detached assessment at present (November 1980) because not enough time or new work from Dylan has been and gone since to allow for 'Slow Train Coming' to settle down and find its place in the overall catalogue of Dylan's achievements.

Stand-out tracks are *Precious Angel* and *When He Returns*.

25. Saved, 1980. The same remarks must apply to this as to 'Slow Train Coming'. Musically, it's very fine, and no one should have been surprised that Dylan should have chosen to add gospel to the many different modes of American popular music which he has covered (and covered so well) on his artistic travels over the last two decades. Stand-out tracks: *Pressing On, Saved, What Can I Do For You, Saving Grace* and *Solid Rock*. As I write this (April '81) a new album is in the pipeline and there is every reason to expect from it yet another shift in direction.

These, then, are the albums on which Dylan's reputation as an artist has been constructed. This book examines the work within them.

Chapter 2
Dylan and the Folk Tradition

Strap yourself to a tree with roots
You ain't goin nowhere.
(from Dylan's *You Ain't Goin Nowhere*)

When Dylan first went East and arrived in New York, at the start of the 1960s, the repertoire and styles of delivery he brought with him provided a culture-shock not only to Sinatra-tuned audiences but also to the patrons of the many small 'folk clubs' then in bloom around Greenwich Village. As he recalls the latter's reaction, it ran as follows:

> You sound like a hillbilly:
> We want folk-singers here . . .

The point, made here with a characteristic lightness of irony, is of course that Dylan *was* a folk-singer; and to learn how his early work was received is to understand the various misconceptions that obtained in New York at that time and which, from New York, spread (though not back into the Appalachians) via college circuits and out across the Atlantic.

To sound like a 'folk singer' you were supposed to be smoothly ingenuous, Angry and, above all, Sensitive. It is hard to pin down precise criteria but it's enough to say that Peter, Paul & Mary fitted the bill. With a name like that, how could they fail? They were the Greenwich Village ideal – white, clean and middle-class to the point of cultivated preciousness. They had all the essentials required: a coyness and a bourgeois gentility that functioned as marketable post-adolescent reproach.

Young, white, middle-class Americans were thus provided with a handy collective psyche that was a palliative to all kinds of inadequacy. This was encouraged and strengthened by the arid folk preservation movement, which judged its music on 'purity of style', regardless of quality of content. A formidable alliance. If you could only keep away the hillbillies, you could fill out life amiably enough with an indulgent, deadening orthodoxy.

This did not suit Dylan. His first album consisted mainly of his own impressionistic arrangements of modern-traditional songs (songs like Blind Lemon Jefferson's *See That My Grave Is Kept Clean**) performed without any 'gentility' and with a voice that, far from suggesting a soul-mate for Peter, Paul or Mary, suggested some black octogenarian singing personal blues at the back of his shack. The blurb that went out on the album could quite plausibly call Dylan the newest voice in country blues.

---

* Blind Lemon Jefferson: a great Negro blues singer, also a guitarist and composer, born in the 1890s in Texas, and contemporary with Lonnie Johnson. He shaped the Texas blues and put it on record, though his recording career was, typically, very short (1926–1930). He was the main blues influence on Leadbelly and, through Leadbelly, an important tutor to many, many others. He wrote the line 'I'm standin' here wonderin' will a matchbox hol' my clothes' which crops up twenty-five years after Jefferson's death in Carl Perkins' song *Matchbox* and (around the same time as Dylan's arrival in New York) in Sam Cooke's *Somebody Have Mercy*.

19

Left: *1961, in front of Israel Young's Folklore Center, Greenwich Village.*

Right: *Dylan at the event in which he launched his electric music: Newport Folk Festival, 1965. Behind him (in more senses than one) – Donovan and Mary Travers of Peter, Paul & Mary.*

In fact Dylan's recordings of folk material are very much more extensive than those officially released suggest, but this first official album is a unit, a collection which stands up by itself.

There are tracks that ring a little false. On Dylan's rendition of the spiritual *Gospel Plow*, for instance, the death-wish of the young man (Dylan was twenty) may be genuine but the evocation is not: wrongly, it relies on a pretence at the experience of age to 'justify' that death-wish. So that what comes through is a clumsiness of understanding as to what the artist requires of himself.

Yet what comes through from the album as a whole is a remarkable skill and more than a hint of a highly distinctive vision. In the context of what was happening at the time – American folk culture all but obliterated and a stagnating 'folk' cult established as if in its place – Dylan's first album can hardly be faulted.

It is a brilliant début – a performer's tour de force – and served as a fine corrective for Greenwich Village: it was the opposite of effete.

The same asset of irony appears again, and to greater effect, in the other self-composed song on the album, the reflective *Song To Woody*. Here, the irony closes the lyric:

> Here's to Cisco and Sonny and Leadbelly too*
> And to all the good people that travelled with you
> Here's to the hearts and the hands of the men
> That come with the dust and are gone with the wind.
>
> I'm a-leavin' tomorrow but I could leave today
> Somewhere down the road someday . . .
> The very last thing that I'd want to do
> Is to say I bin hittin' some hard travellin' too.

Clearly, to say he'd been hitting some hard travelling too is not the last thing Dylan would like to be *able* to do.

It is with those final lines – which get their special strength not just from the understatement but from the carefully clipped reluctance of the cadence – that we get a fresh focus on the whole theme of the song. At the same time, we still hear the echoes of all those delicate rushes of confidentiality which, throughout the lyric, establish its tone.

There are other aspects of the song which contribute to its appeal. There is the frank if implicit statement of what is, on Dylan's part, a plea for an innocent drop-out and the concern to find a new allegiance in the 'hard travellin'' ethos. Again, there is a delicacy in handling this – a balance struck in perceiving both the harsh reality and the romantic flavour of this ethos. The song not only reflects Guthrie faithfully but

---

*Guthrie travelled around with Leadbelly, Sonny Terry and Cisco Houston during the Second World War. Their recordings include a Leadbelly song, *We Shall Be Free*, on which Dylan based his own *I Shall Be Free* and *I Shall Be Free No. 10*. (The tune is the same in all three songs.) Part of the Leadbelly song runs:

> I was down in the henhouse on my knees
> Thought I heard a chicken sneeze
> It was only a rooster saying his prayers
> Thanking his God for the pullets upstairs.

Dylan sings, among much else of precisely the same tone;

> Well I took me a woman late last night
> I was three-fourths drunk, she looked all right
> Till she started peelin' off her onion-gook
> She took off her wig said how do I look? . . .

21

assesses his real but disappearing America from Dylan's, the young man's, perspective. We are offered a highly intelligent understanding of the subject.

This comes over, equally, in the rhythmic balance of the lyric – look at the third and fourth lines, the seventh and eighth, and so on; and likewise, the wind and the dust are there in the song's construction. Lines and syllables take the form of a list: the suggestion is one of restless movement within a preordained pattern of repetition. The share-cropper's life rhythm.

In Guthrie's triumphant autobiography, *Bound For Glory*, we see him travelling around with the homeless families who are also the heroes of Steinbeck's *Grapes of Wrath*; and while recalling one particular encounter, Guthrie quotes one of his own songs, *Pastures of Plenty*. Dylan's tribute reworks this. One of Guthrie's verses runs:

> I work in your orchards of peaches and prunes
> Sleep on the ground 'neath the light of the moon
> On the edge of your city you see us and then
> We come with the dust and we go with the wind.

Dylan's alteration of that last verb, from 'go' to 'are gone', shows his awareness that the era which produces such men is all but over.

Elsewhere, Dylan can use the *tone* of Guthrie's autobiographical writing unaltered, can capture it exactly, in song. The chaotic scurrying around of cram-jam-packed humanity which Guthrie describes so well (particularly in the sequence on the box-car ride that opens and closes his book) is done *precisely* in this way (from Dylan's unreleased 1962 song *Talking Bear Mountain Picnic Massacre Blues*):

> Dogs a-barkin', cats a-meowin'
> Women screamin', fists a-flyin', babies cryin'
> Cops a-comin', me a-runnin'
> Maybe we just better call off the picnic.

That is Woody Guthrie's voice.

Alan Lomax wrote of Guthrie that '. . . he inherited the folk tradition of the last American frontier (western Oklahoma) and during his incessant wandering across the US he has recomposed this tradition into contemporary folky ballads about the

22

lives of the American working class. . . No modern American poet or folk singer has made a more significant contribution to our culture.'

If Dylan's debt to Guthrie is, as he admits, substantial it is not in essence just derivative. Few people can have gained so much from Guthrie's work even though that work is among the best of the American folk-art accessible to us from the pre-1960s. When Dylan sings that 'I'm seein' y'r world of people and things' he is too modest: he has not so much seen as re-created.

Nevertheless, Guthrie's influence can be traced much further through Dylan's work than simply to tribute-songs. Elsewhere on the latter's first album we recognize Guthrie's subject-matter – the hobo's America – and Guthrie's humour. In the famous Dylan 'protest songs' of his second and third LPs (*Blowin' In The Wind*; *Masters of War*; *The Times They Are A-Changin'*; *Oxford Town*; and others) it is largely Guthrie's idealism. And it must have been Guthrie, rather than Dylan's 'first idol', Hank Williams, who impressed upon Dylan, by his example, the need of the artist to stand alone, true to his individual vision.*

Like his early 'hillbilly sound', this sense of responsibility to oneself and to one's art was not understood (it is not surprising) by the Greenwich Village/Newport Folk Festival devotees. Even when the protest phase was rampant, most of its fans preferred it with jam: preferred the sweeter versions of the *Blowin' In The Wind* kind of song, by – the example is inevitable – Peter, Paul & Mary. There were, in fact, over sixty different recorded versions of that song, all performing the same function: anaesthetizing the Dylan message. Columbia Records (CBS), being in it for the money, were caught both ways: on the one hand they forced the suppression of his *Talking John Birch Society Blues* and then they mounted a campaign with the somewhat mournful slogan 'Nobody Sings Dylan Like Dylan'.

In fact, of course, the 'protest' group of songs is not of outstanding quality: Dylan's performances of them can do little more than partly compensate, as it were, for the lack of anything in them but 'messages'. It is not just the clichés that mar these songs but – along with their obviousness – the assumption that cliché is necessary for emphasis: the assumption that the listener must be spoon-fed, if not force-fed. Dylan is giving us rhetoric, not art. In contrast, where societal comment is present in his later work – as for instance in the 12-minute *Desolation Row* on the 'Highway 61 Revisited' album – Dylan's critique is always offered in a form dictated by a most formidable art and not by an anxiety based on lack of trust in the listener.

We have already seen from *Song To Woody* that the early Dylan was aware of such criteria; his early folk-protest-conservationist audiences were not. Here was a folk singer, by any sane definition of the term, who was first upbraided with the hillbilly tag and then, because he had written *Blowin' In The Wind*, made the victim of a public idolatry, which demanded that he keep on writing that song, again and again, for the rest of his artistic life. When he broke away from this, the response was again an upbraiding: you sound like a pop-star: we still want folk-singers here.

---

* Guthrie's impact on Dylan was not only direct – it also came via Ramblin' Jack Elliott, whom Dylan met and befriended early on in his time in New York City in the very early sixties. Ramblin' Jack Elliott was the singer-guitarist of whom Guthrie once remarked, 'He sounds more like me than I do.'
In 1975, Dylan popped up again with Elliott at a gig by the latter back at Greenwich Village's Other End Club – at which they duetted on Guthrie's *Pretty Boy Floyd* and the old *How Long?*, and then Dylan debuted, solo, a brilliant new song (called, perhaps, 'My Heart Is Telling Me') which he has unfortunately not put on record.
Ramblin' Jack Elliott was subsequently one of Dylan's guests on the Rolling Thunder Revue tours and so can be seen in Dylan's 1977 film 'Renaldo & Clara'.

The blankness of such a response was made clear at the 1965 Newport Folk Festival. By this time exploring an electric sound, Dylan appeared with his electric guitar. The audience took this as a 'sell out'. The songs he sang, which did not include the 'protest' group, were at first greeted by hostile silence. Eventually, the audience shouted its objections and Dylan walked off the stage. He was, in the end, persuaded to return and reappeared, this time with his old, acoustic guitar. The audience assumed that they had disciplined their idol into submission – and it condemns their intentions that this pleased them. Dylan sang only one more song – the aptly-titled *It's All Over Now, Baby Blue*.

Such an explicit lesson should not have been necessary. The whole controversy about Dylan's songs and styles reveals a fundamental misunderstanding of his claim to be an artist, and an almost total failure to appreciate the traditions of folk culture which Dylan's work has, with varying degrees of prominence, always displayed.

It isn't necessary to spend long on defining what American folk music is and is not. Traditionally, it has been that day-to-day music created by the people and for the people. It gives form to the democratic ideal. It moves below the mainstream of culture, the flow of which is sustained and altered by small elites.

In the present century, this music of the ordinary American people has become radically less regionalized. The slump and dust-bowl times provided a focus on this inevitable shift. As the people moved from the farms and small communities, folk music moved to the media.

On the other hand, though the way of life from which folk music flowed naturally has essentially disappeared, the changes of environment forced upon millions of Americans by an ailing capitalist system have acted as stimuli to self-expression – however defensive that impulse must now be – and so as a regenerative influence on the creativity of ordinary people. Urbanized life still provokes a means of invention of music and song undreamt of in the Cole Porter philosophy.

Alan Lomax wrote (in noting the effects of such environmental changes) that

> ...there are aesthetic needs that Hollywood and Tin Pan Alley do not yet know how to satisfy. Tomorrow the Holy Rollers, the hillbillies, the blues shouters, the gospel singers – the Leadbellies, the Guthries ... who have formed our twentieth-century folk-music, will be replaced by other folk artists ... [who] will give voice to the deep feelings and unspoken needs of their own time, as have all the folk-singers of the past.

Future or past, folk music must flow naturally from peoples' lives. When such lives were eked out traditionally, in country communities, the primary material – to shelter in and to work with – was wood. This was the simple reason for the centrality of the acoustic guitar in folk music. Now that people buy their environments in units of electric technology, folk culture has new material to work with. The serious contemporary artist cannot ignore the technology that surrounds him and shapes his life-style; and he has every reason to utilize it not only for his art but also in the interests of the clear duty to reach an audience. The black folk artists of twentieth-century America have always understood this.

Disputing the validity of 'going electric' in folk music disregards the responsible resources of artistic work; and the attempts of the 'purists' to 'preserve' folk music from such moves can only, where successful, act to the detriment of folk music's potential for growth.

Two final observations here: firstly that to insist on all this is not to argue that the issue at stake is one of trendiness versus the old-fashioned; and secondly that other issues raised here – for instance, that of the borderline area between folk art and 'art proper' (between the sub-culture and the mainstream) – are returned to at a later point. It seems more appropriate here and now to concentrate on the specific folk music roots, traditional and modern, in Dylan's work.

When American life was wholly localized and regional, there were four main types of American folk music (apart from the traditions preserved by foreign-language immigrants). These four were: Yankee, Southern Poor White, Cowboy and Black. All four figure strongly in Dylan's art, if in very different guises as that art has matured.

The Yankee, who first sang on packet ships and there revived the sea-shanties that had dropped out of circulation in the British Navy, adapted his songs to the newer environment when working in the forests that stretch from Maine to Dylan's home-state of Minnesota. The nature of this life and work produced a tradition of song in which the workman was a hard and grimly realistic hero. A less 'reflective' Hemingway ideal.

The Yankee backwoodsman sang in a hard, monotonous, high-pitched, nasal voice; his songs used decorated melodies in gapped scale structures; and words mattered more than tunes.* Those familiar with Dylan's early work will recognize aspects of it, both of style and content, in that description. Indeed, the close relation much of the early Dylan output keeps with this Yankee tradition is what makes that output difficult to attune to, not only for those trained by Gilbert and Sullivan (in which the words are nonsense and a-tune-you-can-hum is the main ingredient) but also for the pop-orientated.

There is perhaps little more in the Yankee tradition that claims Dylan as its modern voice. Although a song such as his *Lonesome Death of Hattie Carroll* makes 'an ordinary worker' into a kind of heroine, Dylan makes this happen as a device, not an end in itself: a device for strengthening an essentially political and social polemic. He does the same with Medgar Evers and his killers in *Only A Pawn In Their Game*: the two men are just pawns in Dylan's 'game'. On the other hand, *North Country Blues* much more nearly exhibits a traditional Yankee perspective, in that it deals very consciously with a working community's suffering, treated through the story of one family's misfortunes, and with that community's annihilation. The song provides a timely epitaph to the destruction of the folk culture such a community produced, while getting the dynamics of its construction from that kind of culture. When, on the much later album, 'Self Portrait', Dylan returns to a Yankee song, *Days of '49*, he offers it quite rightly as a museum-piece even as he breathes new life into it.

Southern Poor White folk music, hillbilly mountain music, the music of the settlers – which was the second of the four main American folk traditions – consisted of hybrids. Its songs fused Scots, Irish and English influences and yet expressed a new-world pioneer milieu. Songs like *Come All You Virginia Girls*; *Old Blue*; *I Love My Love*; *Went Up On The Mountain*; and *Pretty Saro* reflected normal life all across the southern backwoods, and testified to the cultural bonds between poor whites as far west as Texas and Oklahoma.

It was a tradition linked fundamentally to Calvinist precepts: to the passionate belief in sin, the concern for individual salvation and the surety of a God On Our Side. Uncle John, from Oklahoma, in *Grapes of Wrath*, is in this sense the complete descendant of the pioneers who constructed the tradition.

* Lasting, well-known traditional Yankee songs include – many remaining quite close to their English antecedents – *The Erie Canal*; *The Bay of Mexico*; *The Foggy Dew*; *Weary of the Railway*; *Katy Cruel*; and of course *Yankee Doodle*.

At the Newport Folk Festival, 1963 – at which Dylan arrived as a promising newcomer and left as a star.

Whether this tradition impinged on Dylan in childhood – his was a suitably small-town community – or in adolescent travelling or even simply in listening to the radio, one doesn't know; but at any rate, its eccentric and fascinating hybrid songs certainly did reach him somehow.

With its vital mixing of ancient and fresh vocabulary and its truly pioneering grammatical freedom, this tradition offered what is the real core of folk song, a conserving process which is at the same time creative; and in his use today of that fundamental life-force, Dylan is the great white folk singer. He has drawn on this tradition in two ways; he has used its established characteristics for some of his song-structures, and he has used its very lively inventiveness as a source of strength for his own.

His adaptation of the traditional Scottish song *Pretty Peggy-O*, on his first album, gives a Texas accent a central rhythmic purpose. The guitar-work and melodic structuring on *Ballad of Hollis Brown* are straight from the Appalachians, where such forms and modes had evolved, in comparative isolation,* over a period of almost two hundred years. And a traditional song such as *East Virginia* reflects the brooding about death which Dylan echoes throughout his first album (and sometimes in later

*It is all too easy to oversimplify questions of cultural isolation in the Appalachian mountains. On the one hand we have clear evidence of its survival up to the First World War; on the other hand, there is this note by Paul Oliver, offered in his invaluable book *The Story Of The Blues*: 'Although the Appalachians divide North Carolina from Tennessee, the mountains provide no physical barrier and . . . numerous roads . . . break across them which . . . circulating singers used. Highway 70 was the most popular, linking the Atlantic coast by way of Raleigh, Ashville and Knoxville with Nashville and Memphis.'

work) and which is rooted as much in the orthodoxy of Calvinism as in black folk culture.

The Calvinist precepts are not, of course, taken up wholesale by Dylan: rather, he takes up the challenge, the encapsulating threat, of these ideas. In *With God On Our Side*, which appeared on his 'Times They Are A-Changin'' album towards the end of his flirtation with the protest movement, it is the early part of the song, and not the later homilies on world wars and atom bombs, that is of real and lasting interest. It gives us Dylan assessing the inroads of pioneer religiosity on his own sensibility:

> O my name it means nothing
> My age it means less:
> The country I come from
> Is called the Mid-West.
> I was taught an' brought up there
> The laws to abide
> And that the land that I live in
> Has God On Its Side . . .

There is an extraordinary sweep of implicit experience in those first four lines. The sense of the narrator's context – his sense of history and therefore of identity – makes itself felt quietly and yet has impact. The careful omission of any 'but' or 'yet' or 'and' between the second and third lines has a striking and forceful effect. This creation of effect by what is lacking, not by what is there, is characteristic of much Dylan material, and gets a fuller discussion later in this book.

The verse just quoted also provides an obvious dismantling of the Calvinist doctrine contained in the song's title: and it is a pity that as the later verses draw nearer and nearer to the 'protest' formula, this dismantling becomes correspondingly heavy-handed. In contrast, this first verse has a truly compelling delicacy. And it is able to give us very finely the narrator's sense of the intellectual and moral pressure of his upbringing in terms of 'folk education'. The third and fourth lines refer the listener, again with a considerable poise of implication, to the seeds of folk lore blown over by travel and by time from New England and its neighbours. Clearly, those two lines do not provide a mechanically-inserted or merely peripheral piece of information. Dylan is stating his awareness that the country he comes from has its claims upon him, and upon his art, for both good and bad. (He nowhere draws more on his background familiarity with Calvinistic folk life than in his beautifully poised, pinched delivery on the unreleased *Quit Your Low Down Ways* – a definitive cameo, as he does it – or the very much later *You Gotta Serve Somebody*.)

Lastly, Dylan returns to Appalachian music on his 1970 double-album, 'Self Portrait', to give us an odd but effectively atmospheric version of the traditional song *Copper Kettle*. As with all the music he touches on this collection, he brings back to life the spirit of the age that the song is all about, and does it immeasurably better than those purists to whom his version (it has violins and women on it) is anathema. And as if to emphasize further his ability to do this sort of thing, the same album offers a Dylan composition, *Belle Isle*, which reaches back even further into the traditional folk past, invoking those purely Gallic origins which are part of the founding ingredients of America's Southern Poor White music.

The Cowboy music tradition was, like the Southern Poor White, a hybrid, though of a different and more simple kind: it was basically an amalgam of Southern and Yankee brands of folk. In Lomax's phrase, 'the cowboy singer was a Yankee balladeer with a southern accent'.

As with the hillbilly genre, Dylan uses the cowboy tradition in two ways. He uses the structures and conventions, and he uses the atmospheric essence. This essence is the lyric magic that first takes its being from the 'noble' struggle of hard-living men in a hostile work environment (and later, much more famously, from the communion of the individual with his own loneliness in the environment of the great western plains). A traditional sample of the hard-struggle song is this:

> Our hearts were made of iron, our souls were cased with steel,
> The hardships of that winter could never make us yield,
> Our food, the dogs would snarl at it, our beds were in the snow,
> We suffered worse than murderers up in Michigan-i-o.

That recalls, in Dylan's output, more than his delighted use of that last rhyming device in his version of *Pretty Peggy-O* ('He died somewheres in Loos-i-ana-o'). We can easily envisage Dylan singing – say, on 'Self Portrait' – the lines just quoted. Phrases like 'our food, the dogs would snarl at it' are well within what we've come to know as Dylan's scope. And to think back to *Song To Woody* is to recognize a rhythmic effect similar to that achieved in the above, on phrases like 'Here's to the hearts and the hands of the men'.

This same flavour is prominent again in Dylan's *Ballad of Hollis Brown* – even though there the sense of community is taken outside the song's characters and exists solely between the narrator and his subjects (and is only a one-way awareness, for the narrator's sympathy cannot reach their loneliness):

> There are seven breezes blowin' all around the cabin door
> Seven breezes blowin' all around the cabin door
> And somewhere in the distance a cold coyote calls.

A very different song, from the same Dylan album, draws just as firmly on the idea of the hard struggle of good-hearted men to overcome adversity. The song is *When The Ship Comes In*, and it is a tribute to Dylan's intelligence and artistry that he can use the strengths of this theme from this tradition in the utterly different context, in this song, of a moral struggle, without any loss of poise. It is a much underrated song.

Part of its appeal comes from its tune and from Dylan's performance. These two elements combine, and combine with the words, to sustain a maximum effect and energy (as, for instance, when we come to that simple word 'shout' in the last verse: the voice does indeed break into a shout, a celebratory exclamation, and hits the word as the tune hits the highest note in the verse).

Even as mere words-on-the-page, though, the song has a distinctive and distinguished charm, very much its own – like a glimpse into a world both real and unreal: morally mature (if severe) yet childlike in conception.

The internal rhyming is so effective, driving the vision along in the rhythm of the oncoming ship as it meets, again and again, relentlessly, the swell of the sea:

> And the song, will, lift, as the main, sail, shifts
> And the boat, drifts . . .

Moreover, this internal rhyming collaborates perfectly with the alliterative effects (as well, of course, as with the tune):

> Then the sands will roll out a carpet of gold
> For your weary toes to be a-touchin' . . .

Never once does this immense charm come across as simplistic or faulty, and this is a more than merely technical achievement. The childlike allegory offered comes over as a quite unexceptional moral cleanliness – a convincing wisdom.

This not only redresses anger; it yields a positive and spirited apprehension of the new age's possibilities:

> Oh the fishes will laugh as they swim out of the path
> And the seagulls, they'll be smiling . . .
> And the sun will respect every face on the deck
> The hour when the ship comes in.

Political yearnings do not sweep aside more ordinary joys: to talk of having sand between your toes, to feel glad of the imagined sympathy of fishes as well as of the overseeing of 'the ship's wise men', and to conceive, in the midst of creating a mood of general anticipation, such a particular image as that of a smiling seagull face – this is to encompass a wise and a salutary statement of hope.

It accords with this achievement – this sustained control – that Dylan avoids painting 'the foes' as demons or fools. They are big enough to hold on to a certain dignity where the allegory goes biblical; and yet, beyond this, the apparently childlike vision applies to them too, humanizing them even as it condemns:

> Oh the foes will rise with the sleep still in their eyes
> And they'll jerk from their beds and think they're dreamin'
> But they'll pinch themselves and squeal and they'll know that its for real
> The hour when the ship comes in.

As even this perfunctory glance shows, Dylan has taken us a long way, in *When The Ship Comes In*, beyond the cowboy tradition on which the song is based; and in any case, its basis is in the less recognizable of the two cowboy types. What needs to be considered now is Dylan's relation to the other type: that which corresponds to our image of the cowboy hero, that which is bathed in the romantic lyricism of saddle-sore silent men set against lonesome prairies and plains.

The traditional song *I'm A-Ridin' Old Paint* well represents the genre:

> Now when I die don't bury me at all
> Just saddle my pony, lead him out of the stall
> Tie my bones in the saddle, turn our faces to the west
> And we'll ride the prairie that we love best.

The cowboy nurtured an internal restlessness into something bigger than himself. His home became the Big Wide West – and he always felt compelled to be 'movin' on'. And how easy it was for this spirit to pass from the nineteenth-century cowboy to the twentieth-century professional hobo.

Dylan takes this up, sometimes comically, more often with a plausible earnestness. The comical example that springs to mind is from *Country Pie*, on the 'Nashville Skyline' album:

> Saddle me up a big white goose!
> Tie me on her and turn her loose!
> Oh! me, oh! my –
> Love that Country Pie!

– a sympathetic send-up of the traditional song just quoted.

Dylan's more serious expressions of this compulsion to move on, to not get entangled, are numerous. On 'Self Portrait' he relaxes (as he does more conspicuously and perhaps less wholeheartedly on *Country Pie*) and handles Clayton's famous *Gotta Travel On* as the archetypal statement it is – in other words, he lets the words remain as simple as they are and puts the song across as music: and that music rides on beautifully. In contrast, he gives voice to the same roving compulsion in the disarming aphorism that brings his *Ballad Of Frankie Lee And Judas Priest* to a close on the 'John Wesley Harding' album: '. . . don't go mistaking Paradise/For that home across the road.'

In Dylan's more concentrated and sustained expressions of this same theme, of this negative-positive moral, their plausibility derives from their being always addressed to a particular woman or specific entanglements of which the narrator understands the full worth. It is never, in Dylan's hands, a merely boastful theme – never a Papa Hemingway conceit, an I'm-too-hot-to-hold bravado. The opposite impulse, the desire to stay and be entangled, is always felt to be present, though it cannot (until 'Nashville Skyline') win.

Later still, on *You're Gonna Make Me Lonesome When You Go* (from 'Blood On The Tracks', 1975) things have progressed further – to the point where it is the *woman* who has the gotta-travel-on urge, and the male narrator who must accept this philosophically. Later still, on 'Street Legal', the album that prepares us for the Born-Again Christian albums 'Slow Train Coming' and 'Saved', Dylan takes a further step – to the point where he again feels he has to move on and abandon love: but this time it is in order to embrace Jesus instead of 'the road'; to find a specific salvation rather than a nebulous, wandering 'freedom'.

We have one moving-on theme in *Don't Think Twice, It's All Right*, from the second Dylan album, a song based, for its tune, on Johnny Cash's composition *Understand Your Man*:

> I'm a-thinkin' and a-wond'rin', all the way down the road,
> I once loved a woman – a child, I am told:
> I gave her my heart but she wanted my soul
> But don't think twice, it's all right.

The same integrity of spirit underlies the 1964 song *It Ain't Me, Babe*:

> You say you're looking for someone
> Who'll pick you up each time you fall,
> To gather flowers constantly
> An' to come each time you call:
> A lover for your life an' nothing more –
> But it ain't me, babe.

There are many more instances of Dylan's using this 'gotta travel on' spirit. Perhaps his most directly autobiographical statement of it comes in the hastily-composed yet excellent *Restless Farewell*, with which he closes his 'Times They Are A-Changin'' album. Within the same collection, that word 'restless' is taken up again in a song Dylan has revisited often since, the lovely *One Too Many Mornings*:

> It's a restless, hungry feeling that don't mean no one no good*
> When ev'rything I'm sayin' you can say it just as good
> You're right from your side. I'm right from mine:
> We're both just one too many mornings
> An' a thousand miles
> Behind.

Often, then, this restlessness runs into what is for Dylan a search for the ideal, for nothing less than the perfect. It is only when we reach as far through his career as the

---

* A fine example, this, of the hillbilly traditions of grammar construction. Dylan's multiple negatives in this line are a direct inheritance from those traditions.

'Nashville Skyline' album that we find this search largely discarded. Consciously, at last, an imperfect love can be accepted as salvation.

The last song on the album brings this out most explicitly: *Tonight I'll Be Staying Here With You*. As its title suggests, it's a deliberate announcement of the fall from restlessness. The habit of always moving on has been kicked and the impulse to stay has at last succeeded:

> Throw my ticket out the window
> Throw my suitcase out there too
> Throw my troubles out the door
> I don't need them any more
> 'Cause tonight I'll be staying here with you
>
> I should have left this town this morning
> But it was more than I could do
> Oh your love comes on so strong
> And I've waited all day long
> For tonight, when I'll be staying here with you.

In the first of those verses, we get the direct announcement; and the first three lines give us the gestures that go with it.

Similarly, that 'should have left this town this morning', in the second verse, is a reference to the old travelling compunction now renounced, not to some particular journey's schedule. The point of the title line is that it isn't just tonight; the narrator has come to rest. Not even the train whistle heard in the distance can lure him back to homeless sojourns now.

When I first heard *It Ain't Me Babe* I specially liked that line 'A lover for your life and nothing more' because in pop songs there never was anything more: to be 'a lover for your life' was the ultimate ideal. For me, then, *It Ain't Me Babe* was good in the context of this contrast: and five years of Dylan output later, *Tonight I'll Be Staying Here With You* is good in that it can make use of its contrast to *It Ain't Me Babe*. It's not a step back, it's another step beyond (and it is in this same spirit of achievement that Dylan can reintroduce that 'I bless the day I found you' in *Let It Be Me*, so that despite its being an old pop song it too, under Dylan's auspices, shows the same progressive second step. It parallels 'Throw my ticket out the window'.)

Love doesn't always come Dylan's way on 'Nashville Skyline', but it does provide the focus of his desire. The second verse of the quiet *I Threw It All Away* – the 'it' being love – echoes the cowboy ethos succinctly by using, as his image for the discarded love's value, the scenery the lonesome traveller has around him (though it acts also as sexual imagery):

> Once I had mountains in the palm of my hand
> And rivers that ran through every day –
> I must have been mad, I never knew what I had
> Until I threw it all away.

The emphasis there is on the problem of choice, but the choice propounded is again that between loving and moving on.

It may be said that there are much stronger influences in all this from modern country music (country-'n'-western, as it was once called in England) than from the older traditional material. Let's not quibble too much about that: it is from the traditions that the modern amalgam derives, and in any case it is hardly possible to draw a line through some year in American history and say that behind the line stands virginal tradition, and in front the whore of Nashville. There is more in

Dylan's country pie than cowboy classics revisited (as we have seen) and more, equally, than the bland successors of Hank Williams can match. More too than modern voices with styles or techniques of their own – the Roger Millers, Glen Campbells, Buck Owenses and Jerry Lee Lewises.

At the same time, one of the many things that 'Self Portrait' and the like can send us back to with a heightened appreciation is certainly Jerry Lee Lewis's old country B-side material – material like Hank Williams' *Cold, Cold Heart* cut for the legendary Sun label in Memphis and issued as the flip of *It Won't Happen With Me* in 1961.

As for the Dylan song that most clearly registers Hank Williams himself – *One More Night*, from 'Nashville Skyline' – the tune of the verses is that of an old English popular song. Correspondingly, the lyric is not only consciously 'unoriginal' but actually recalls other lyrics:

> Oh it's shameful and it's sad
> I lost the only pal I had
> I just could not be what she wanted me to be
> I will turn my head up high
> To that dark an' rollin' sky
> For tonight no light will shine on me
>
> I was so mistaken when I thought that she'd be true
> I had no idea what a woman in love would do:

That couplet beginning 'I will turn my head up high' comes straight from the traditional cowboy song *Lonesome Prairie*. There is a less exact but none the less striking resemblance also between Dylan's last verse and a part of the famous oldie *Blue Moon Of Kentucky* – and this is a resemblance that goes further than the lyric. Dylan's use of the tune at this point, and the whole tone of his delivery, suggest that Dylan has a copy of the very early Elvis recording of the *Blue Moon Of Kentucky* song.

Another aspect of the cowboy tradition is its special fondness for heroes, and Dylan comes to this on the 'John Wesley Harding' album, as he reaches back into America's past for the secret strengths of her myths. The album is a 'retreat' – a turning away – from the chaos of the modern urban intellectual's burden; yet clearly it is a regenerative spirit that drives Dylan to search back as he does. He engages, in this album, in a desperately serious struggle to free himself – and subsequently to free us – from the debilitating predicament our fragmented sensibility has placed us in; the predicament Dylan defined on his previous album, the druggy, urban, chaotic, compelling 'Blonde On Blonde'. *Visions of Johanna* summed up this mess:

> We sit here stranded
> Though we're all doin' our best
> To deny it . . .

As Dylan comes, in 'John Wesley Harding', to the myths and extinct strengths of America, he explores the world of the cowboy as well as the pioneer. The man in the title song is a cowboy, and, indeed, a hero.

It is a modest exploration, in that the cowboy-outlaw is not an unusual subject for hero-treatment; but what a delicate, subtle portrait the song offers. It is all so simple, so straight-forward (like the system of values we have come to associate with the cowboy world): a ballad that tells the story of its hero's exploits. Yet at the end one still has no idea what actually happened, nor any clear indication of the narrator's attitude. One is given clues but no bearings. It was never like this when Tennessee Ernie Ford sang *The Ballad of Davy Crockett*.

The song's economy of organization and language is noticeable at once. There is no

Above: *This would suggest that Dylan is as eccentric at chess as he is inside the music business.*

Left: *Love is all there is, it makes the world go round. . . another new Bob Dylan emerges, 1969. Asked how he'd changed his voice to a smooth, Roy Orbisonish tenor, he said 'I quit smoking cigarettes.'*

Left: *1969 on the Johnny Cash TV Show. The BBC declined this. Bill Cotton Jnr. considered that Dylan 'gave an inferior performance'*...

Below: *Newport Folk Festival, 1963.*

use of simile and no reliance on images or symbolism. Following that, we notice a corresponding lack of what may be called 'moral centre'. Nine of the twelve lines provide what could be taken, at first glance, as testaments to the hero's worth and virtue: yet actually none is free from significant ambiguity – and these equivocations, collectively, have a piercing eloquence to offer.

> John Wesley Harding was a friend to the poor

In what way? To what extent? The claim has, deliberately, no core behind its apparent bluntness. It refrains from contradicting the suspicion that Harding's name could be added to a long list of men whose lives and interests are spent in opposition, effectively, to the lives and interests of the poor but to whom it is advantageous to seem to appeal. Plenty of hero-reputations depend upon this pretence.

As for those two very reasonable questions raised by that first line of *John Wesley Harding* – a friend in what way? and to what extent? – they are in no way answered by the rest of the song.

> All along this countryside he opened many a door

We could put similar questions in response to that, and be met by a similar blank. The line opens no doors for us.

It works, as intended, by yielding an echo which lingers throughout the song: the echo of a second empty claim. To it must be added the corresponding echoes of the other claims that confront us. As we meet them, the next is this:

> But he was never known to hurt an honest man.

Dylan chooses the negative form of expression; and the consciously reductive intention this reveals gets reinforcement from further negatives in the song; and it ends by giving us a pile-up of three of them:

> But no charge held against him could they prove
> And there was no man around who could track or chain 'im down
> He was never known to make a foolish move.

Not only is all this presented carefully in the negative, but it all serves to emphasize the deliberate vicariousness of the testimony we're given: 'He was never known to . . . ; He was never known to . . .'

Back in the first verse again, the fourth line is linked to the third in such a way as to discredit any inference of virtue from either when they are considered together. He opened many a door but he was never known to hurt an honest man. That word 'but' gives the statements either side of it a cynical focus which the substitution of 'and' could have avoided had Dylan's intention been different (had Dylan's approach, for instance, been Hollywood's).

The following lines add precisely nothing to our picture of the hero's character:

> 'Twas down in Caynee Coun'y, the time they talk about . . .
> And soon the situation there was all but straightened out . . .
> All across the telegraph his name it did resound;

and the inferences to be made do not concern his heroism, his virtue or his good deeds. They concern the far less earth-bound strengths of his fame and reputation. There is, again, a consciously reductive intention on Dylan's part: the intention of repeating, and giving a collective weight to, the idea that Harding had a reputation for . . . and then the vague list: lending help, opening doors, refraining from injuring the honest, almost straightening out some utterly unspecified 'situation', not getting tracked down, and, lastly, looking after himself cleverly. Moreover, this repeated insistence on Harding's reputation casts a doubt on the veracity of what is being insisted upon. Thus Dylan trades on our methinks-he-doth-protest-too-much reaction, in order to increase further our sense of the empty centre of the story.

Two of the lines – but only two – work in a different way. One – 'With his lady by his side he took a stand' – adds to those echoes of the unspecific in the way that other lines do, by that flamboyantly vague phrase 'he took a stand'; but it creates, with the other half of the line, an almost explicit condemnation. Within the cowboy ethic, the hero should neither have needed his lady by his side to give him his courage nor have placed her inside the danger-zone.

The other line – 'He travelled with a gun in every hand' – goes further. The wit of that phrase 'in every hand' serves quietly to highlight Harding's inadequacy. Such a reliance on his weapons suggests something discreditable. And in support of this, the phrase acts as a reference back to Dylan's earlier song *With God On Our Side*.

> And the names of the heroes
> I's made to memorize
> With guns in their hands
> And God on their side.

It is not, however, from these two lines of near-explicit criticism that *John Wesley Harding* gets its power. This comes emphatically from Dylan's carefully constructed 'echoes of the unspecific', as I have called them – and these are indeed eloquent. In its three short verses, the song offers a keen critique of values pertinent not only to the nineteenth-century cowboy's world but to the heirs of that bygone civilization in contemporary America. The clichés of thought exploded so precisely in the song are still in the way today; but Dylan has done battle with them. *John Wesley Harding* joins with the rest of the album of that name to give us, through this 'battling', Dylan successfully engaged in the mature artistic attainment of reconstruction and revaluation: Dylan at his most seriously and intelligently creative.

Dylan's relation to the black folk music tradition is at least as strong and clear.

Black folk music began by reflecting the basic dream of release – yet it first impinged upon white America as a novel, engaging entertainment (which is as telling an introduction to the history of race relations on that continent as the attempt to wipe out the Red Indian). The distinctive, animated dancing of the slave won the attention and applause of his owner. Then enforced initiation into the prosaic mysteries of the Protestant tradition gave rise to spirituals which reflected a double burden: chains plus original sin.

These spirituals were first studied and collected by campaigners for the abolition of slavery, whose aim was to prove that the black man had a soul and should therefore be set free. Since then, the influence of white and black folk music on each other has been substantial. The black, although preserving African modes of tune and rhythm, has adopted many Celtic musical conventions even while retaining the habits of improvization and adaptation and the endless repetition of short, sharp phrases. Owing to African influence, correspondingly, white folk music has become increasingly more polyphonic and polyrhythmic.

The blues, which emerged in the present century, relied on newly-found Afro-American dialects, 'spoken' through the guitar as well as the voice, latterly (but not always) in a 3-line, 12-bar verse pattern.

A song such as the old *Blowin' Down The Road* illustrates the common ground which developed both musically and socially between blacks and poor whites. This was the seminal folk song of the depression and New Deal period. In form and origin a blues number, it became of expressive importance to millions of displaced whites. The *Grapes Of Wrath* people understood the blues.

Woody Guthrie, anyhow, in his autobiography, describes the experience of those times in a noticeably duo-racial way. The box-car ride of the opening and closing chapters is one in which blacks and whites are so jumbled together as to disarm any racial distinctions: they are all men who share the same nomadic discomforts: they are all looking unsuccessfully for a living; they are all outside the cop-protected communities:

> 'And remember – take an old 'bo's word for it, and
> stay th' hell out of the city limits of Tucson.'
> 'What kind of a damn town is this, anyhow?'
> 'Tucson – she's a rich man's bitch, that's what she is,
> and nothin' else but.'

This same situation is handled again in the Guthrie song quoted earlier in this chapter. 'On the edge of your city, you see us and then/We come with the dust and we go with the wind.'

Both white and black are hungry, poor, 'a problem', the pawns of an economic game that demands unemployment for flexibility of labour – and therefore high profits – yet attacks, economically and socially, the people who have to provide its unemployment pool.

This kind of common ground reduces the difference between black and white perception. Guthrie's pen-and-ink sketches, included in his autobiography, feature people not easily classifiable by race – and indeed his sketches of himself make him look, if anything, more black than Caucasian. In the text he cites only one instance of racial prejudice amongst the hobo community.

Dylan, then, inherited black folk traditions not entirely from the outside – not as a separate form but as ever-present influences on other hybrid forms. This inheritance shows clearly right from the start. As Wilfred Mellers has expressed it:

> In the first phase of his career . . . [his] musical materials were primitive:
> modal white blues, hillbilly, shaker songs and hymns, with an interfusion
> of (pentatonic) black holler, relating the young white outcast to the Negro's
> alienation.

Artistically, Dylan the middle-class white Minnesotan anticipated the (uneasy) attempts of the militant hippies to hold hands with Black Power, at the start of the 1970s.

The strands for Dylan are pulled together by his *Only A Pawn In Their Game*, a song written after the murder of Medgar Evers. The poor white is the pawn:

> From the poverty shacks he looks
> from the cracks to the tracks
> and the hoofbeats pound in his brain
> and he's taught how to walk in a pack, shoot in the back,
> with his fist in a clinch,
> to hang and to lynch,
> to hide 'neath a hood,
> to kill with no pain;
> like a dog on a chain,
> he ain't got no name,
> but it ain't him to blame:
> he's only a pawn in their game.

The old king of the new left, and the heir-apparent/pretender: Pete Seeger and Bob Dylan at the Newport Folk Festival, 1963.

Dylan, however, comes closer to black culture than is suggested by this 'holding hands'; closer than he comes by singing to civil rights workers in Greenwood, Mississippi, at the start of his career.

What the blues encompasses is summed up succinctly in Paul Oliver's book *Conversation With The Blues*:

> The narrative and folk tales, the telling of 'lies' or competitive tall tales, the healthily obscene 'putting in the dozens', the long and witty 'toasts' and the epigrammatic rhyming couplets which enliven the conversation of folk negro and Harlem hipster alike, have their reflections in the blues. They are evident in the earthy vulgarity, the unexpected and paradoxical images, the appeal of unlikely metaphors, the endless story that makes all blues one . . .

For all this, Dylan's work shows an affinity that is often blatant and forceful. He has absorbed its characteristics into his thinking and thereby his vocabulary.

Another point made by Oliver is worth noting here too: namely, that

38

. . . if the blues, like any folk art or indeed almost any art form, is illuminating in terms of a whole group it is still sung and played by individuals . . . the individual tends to become submerged . . . and even when the assessment of the major figures is made, the minor blues singer is forgotten.

To listen to much of Dylan's work – which at least between his break with 'protest' and his conversion to Christianity has in every sense put a consistent emphasis on the importance of the individual rather than the mass – is to feel that Dylan has not forgotten the minor blues singer at all. One guesses that he has listened to the minor figures wherever the somewhat random process of recording folk artists has allowed. He must have learnt and assimilated experience from the older songs and the older singers – singers who, in some cases, have been 'discovered' or 're-discovered' in recent years. Mississippi John Hurt is one example, Mance Lipscomb another.

Lipscomb was 'discovered' in July 1960 by Mack McCormick and Chris Strachwitz and recorded – for the first time – a few weeks later in his two-room cabin. Dylan met Lipscomb at about this period, and we can get an idea of the aura of the man, and thus a hint of the insights he could have given Dylan, from the description of Lipscomb, and a transcribed conversational fragment, in Paul Oliver's book. He was a

Texas sharecropper and songster with a reputation that extends widely in Grimes, Washington and Brazos counties . . . A man of great dignity and natural culture . . . a veritable storehouse of blues, ballads and songs of more than half a century . . . He was born on 9 April 1895.

This is Mance Lipscomb talking (the spelling is as in Oliver's transcript):

I been playin' the git-tar now 'bout forty-nine years, and then I started out by myself, just heard it and learned it. Ear music . . . My pa was a fiddler; he was an old perfessional fiddler. All my people can play some kind of music. Well, my daddy . . . he played way back in olden days. You know, he played at breakdowns, waltzes, shottishes and all like that and music just come from me . . . Papa were playing for dances out, for white folks and coloured. He played Missouri Waltz, Casey Jones, just anything you name he played it like I'm playin'. He was just a self player until I was big enough to play behind him, then we played together . . . 'Sugar Babe' was the first piece I learned, when I was a li'l boy about thirteen years old. Reason I know this so good, I got a whippin' about it. Come out of the cotton-patch to get some water and I was up at the house playin' the git-tar and my mother came in; whopped me 'cause I didn't come back – I was playin' the git-tar:

> Sugar babe I'm tired of you,
> Ain't your honey but the way you do,
> Sugar babe, it's all over now. . . .

Lipscomb must have been an invaluable contact for Dylan – the one a black Texan with a personal repertoire stretching back to 1908, the other a white Minnesotan would-be artist of the whole American people born in 1941. Not only could Dylan have gained a knowledge ready to work for him but also, in a specific and personalized testimony, a feeling for the intimacy of connection of words and music in the expression of a spirit and a theme.

Song, speech and music are frequently one in the blues . . . the piano, guitar, even harmonica is a complement to the voice. Though he may play instrumental solos, the most characteristic blues artist sings through both voice and instrument(s). (Paul Oliver)

How striking is the pertinence of that passage to Dylan's work. Dylan plays piano, guitar and harmonica – three of the commonest blues instruments – plays instrumental solos on each and emphatically uses each as a complement to his voice.

This is evident even in such a 'white' protest song as *The Lonesome Death of Hattie Carroll*, where, in the final refrain, the irregular strum of the guitar rises and falls, quickens and slows again, conveying the heartbeats of the narrator, while the harmonica phrases between the vocal lines act as graphs of his anger, shame and sympathy.

The huge instance in Dylan's work where this fusion shows vividly its creative force is in his wide-ranging, flexible, recurrent treatment of the classic Railroad Theme.

Just as the heroic-outlaw-of-the-West myth was, despite having European antecedents, significantly the product of the frontier social situation, so too the railroadmen, the hobo and the railroad itself became folk heroes as a result of environmental circumstances. The railroad meant, or was at least seen to mean, freedom, opportunity, rebirth. It became, as in Guthrie's autobiography, a duo-racial symbol and experience. It is only natural and appropriate that a duo-racial consciousness is required to deal with such a theme in modern folk art. Dylan applies just such a consciousness to this focus.

It isn't altogether possible, however, to isolate or point to specific pieces of vocabulary or whatever and say there, precisely there, is the black ingredient; and that it is an ingredient – subservient to the art as a whole – argues against the value of any protected isolation of that sort. In his songs explicitly 'about' contemporary America – the protest songs, in the main – one of the aims is, as Mellers suggests, to express the relation of the spirit of the young white outcast to that of the alienated black. In Dylan's later work his encompassing of black traditions serves more subtly to enhance the expression of many different perceptions.

Musically, of course, this is often obvious. Beyond examples like the one already cited – *Hattie Carroll* – in which part of the impact comes from a blues-derived feeling for voice, words and instruments as complements, there are plenty of examples in Dylan's work of songs with the conventional 3-line, 12-bar verse structure, including, from his more recent work, the outstanding *Buckets of Rain*, *Meet Me In The Morning*, *New Pony*, *Trouble In Mind* and *Gonna Change My Way Of Thinking*. Others use similar structures to similar effect.

One such song is the underrated *Pledging My Time*, from 'Blonde On Blonde':

> Well they sent for the ambulance, and one was sent
> Somebody got lucky, but it was an accident
> Now I'm pledging my time to you
> Hopin' you'll come through, too.

In that verse the black influence is strong. It goes beyond the music – the coiled insistence of guitar, harmonica, drums and voice – and beyond that characteristic bending of 'ambulance' in the pronunciation. There is also the curious ominous quality of those first two lines. They recall dramatically those stories of the legendary Beale Street in the Memphis of the '30s, where Saturday night razor fights

Opposite: *In Greenwich Village, 1963.*

between blind-drunk blacks were so frequent that a fleet of ambulances waited like taxis at one end of the street. Killer ambulances, apparently, with drivers who made sure that if you weren't dead when they got to you, you were before they'd finished their night's work. (As these stories have blown up into myth, they provide a curious corollary to the stories about hospitals and doctors, and particularly surgeons, widely current in nineteenth-century England – and passed into upper- and middle-class consciousness by terrifying children's nannies. The subject is aired in George Orwell's grim essay, 'How The Poor Die'.)

But it is Dylan's treatment of the railroad theme that merits a closer consideration. If it is a standard American symbol of freedom, the railroad also represents 'home' for the professional tramp of the dust-bowl years; the railroad symbolizes other things too, from the real as well as from the dream world. The traditional black folk song which includes these lines:

> When a woman blue, she hang her little head an' cry,
> When a man get blue, he grab that train an' ride

– makes the railroad a symbol of masculine social virility. Dylan, singing in the 1960s, emancipates contemporary woman. The song is *It Takes A Lot To Laugh, It Takes A Train To Cry*:

> Don't the moon look good, mama, shinin' through the trees?
> Don't the brakeman look good, mama, flagging down the double-E's!
> Don't the sun look good goin' down over the sea –
> Don't my gal look fine when she's comin' after me! . . .

[These lines are an adaptation of several things – including parts of Presley's version of 'Milk Cow Blues Boogie' and from an older blues song, which runs:

> Don't the clouds look lonesome 'cross the deep blue sea
> Don't the clouds look lonesome 'cross the deep blue sea
> Don't my gal look good when she's comin' after me

– but the Dylan version in *It Takes A Lot To Laugh, It Takes A Train To Cry* is also adapted from his own earlier song *Rocks and Gravel* (unreleased):

> Don't the clouds look lonesome shinin' across the sea
> Don't the clouds look lonesome shinin' across the sea
> Don't my gal look good when she's comin' after me.

Ten years after *It Takes A Lot To Laugh*, Dylan gives us another variant on those same lines, in *Meet Me In The Morning*, from 'Blood On The Tracks':

> Look at the sun, sinkin' like a ship
> Look at that sun, sinkin' like a ship
> Ain't that just like my heart babe, when you kiss my lips.

Dylan often does this – often preserves a phrase and, with perhaps some alteration, uses it again in a later song. In his unreleased Civil Rights song *Ain't Gonna Grieve*, he uses 'notify your next of kin' which, almost unchanged, crops up years later in his *This Wheel's On Fire*. The verse of *Just Like Tom Thumb's Blues* which deals with 'my best friend my doctor' – who 'won't even say what it is I got' is revisited in another song of the same time, the unreleased *Barbed Wire Fence*:

> The Arabian doctor comes in 'n' gives me a shot
> But he wouldn't tell me what it was that I got.

42   And the whole of the *Outlaw Blues* verse beginning 'I got my dark sunglasses' is

repeated in an unreleased song of Dylan's called *Going Down South*.

Similarly, the plaintive line 'where are you tonight?' which gets the stress of repetition, with variants, all the way through *Absolutely Sweet Marie* (1966) is resuscitated twelve years later on *Where Are You Tonight (Journey Through Dark Heat)*.

Again, fifteen years after the film 'Don't Look Back', Dylan quotes its title line in one of the best songs on 'Saved', *Pressing On*:

> Kick the dust off of your feet
> Don't look back

There is a noticeable parallel, too, between this joke from *Day Of The Locusts* (1970):

> The man standin' next to me
> His head was exploding
> I was prayin' the pieces wouldn't fall on me

and this one from *Isis* (1976):

> The wind it was howling
> And the snow was outrageous . . .
> When he died I was hopin'
> That it wasn't contagious

And one of the very best instances of Dylan quoting himself occurs on the 'Planet Waves' album, where, in *Never Say Goodbye*, he delivers a devastating punch by singing the line 'Ah! Baby, baby, baby blue' in back-reference to his 1965 classic *It's All Over Now, Baby Blue*.

Finally, it is a striking feature of the 'Slow Train Coming' album that *Do Right To Me Baby (Do Unto Others)* is just a re-write of *All I Really Want To Do* from fifteen years earlier.]

Back again on the railroad it is, paradoxically, the repetitive framework that helps a notable economy in the evocation of railroad feeling in those four lines. In the music – of which the vocal tone and phrasing are parts – the drums and piano suggest not only the rattle of the train, and, as such, a measure of its speed and mechanic vitality, but also the elation of the traveller who identifies with the locomotive's performance. The lyric's economy on adjectives and its emphasis of nouns – the moon, the sun, the brakeman, the trees, the sea, 'my gal' – makes for an exciting balance between the romantic and the concrete. Symbol and reality are fused.

This fusion, in context, recalls a passage from one of those autobiographical Dylan poems which got into print from time to time on the back of LP covers and in old underground magazines:

> An' my first idol was Hank Williams
> For he sang about the railroad lines
> An' the iron bars an' rattlin' wheels
> Left no doubt that they were real . . .
> An' I'll walk my road somewhere between
> The unseen green an' the jet black train

Dylan can not only give the railroad the importance a hard-travellin' hobo might give it but can also use it as an axis round which to spin his ideas of what is real and thus pursue his quest for the concrete.

The railroad appears in many other songs – *Freight Train Blues* among them – and in several an essential ingredient is the railroad's importance where some

fundamental choice is involved, related to the real or the true. In the poem just quoted from, the 'iron bars an' rattlin' wheels' provide a yardstick, albeit simplistic, of reality, against which are contrasted smoother kinds of beauty – the nightingale sound of Joan Baez's voice is an instance he gives – and against which is balanced Dylan's consciousness of 'the unseen green'. In *Tonight I'll Be Staying Here With You* (as already noted) the choice is between two life-styles, with the railroad as the symbol of the one Dylan at last renounces. It calls to him on behalf of the 'keep travelling' spirit and it loses to new-found love:

> I find it so difficult to leave –
> I can hear that whistle blowin'
> I see that station-master too . . .
> . . . tonight I'll be staying here with you.

He hears, but this time, at last, he doesn't follow.

In direct contrast, there is Dylan's first-album adaptation of the traditional *Man of Constant Sorrow*, which equally relates to this particular choice. In this song, he wants the girl but cannot have her. He has travelled a long way to make the attempt to win her, and so the railroad becomes the symbol of a nomadic no-man's-land:

> Through this open world I'm bound to ramble
> Through ice and snow, sleet and rain
> I'm bound to ride that mornin' railroad
> P'raps I'll die on that train

With this, of course, Dylan has come away from the concrete – despite the 'realism' of that wintry weather – and into the realms of romance. What could be more splendid, granted the imagined death-wish, than dying on that train?

Even though *Bob Dylan's Dream*, with all its ponderous nostalgia, is launched with these lines –

> While riding on a train goin' west
> I fell asleep for to take my rest
> I dreamed a dream . . .

– Dylan never quite returns to the dream mood given us by the *Man of Constant Sorrow* railroad. There is a parallel of sorts on the 'Blonde On Blonde' album, in the surrealistic symbolism of *Absolutely Sweet Marie*, but the mood is very different. The solemnity is replaced by a good-natured if double-edged mockery:

> Well your railroad gate, you know I just can't jump it
> Sometimes it gets so hard, you see
> I'm just sitting here beating on my trumpet
> With all these promises you left for me
> But where are you tonight, sweet Marie? . . .
>
> And now I stand here lookin' at your yellow railroad
> In the ruins of your balcony . . .

but the symbol there, though used at both the beginning and the end of the song, is incidental. It is not a song that has much to do with trains.

The romance returns, but more respectably than in *Bob Dylan's Dream*, or even *Man of Constant Sorrow*, in another part of *It Takes A Lot To Laugh, It Takes A Train*

1963, in a New York City coffee-shop with cat.

Lower West Side, New York City, 1963, with Susie Rotolo and folksinger Dave Van Ronk.

To Cry, where the narrator grows lyrically expansive:

> Well I ride on the mailtrain baby; can't buy a thrill
> Well I've been up all night, leanin' on the windowsill
> Well if I die on top of the hill –
> Well if I don't make it, you know my baby will.

That last line provides the ballast, taking the railroad romance away from narcissism and into a wider context – that of a more selfless and universal celebration of life. The goal here is to 'make it', not to die in glory on the train (although paradoxically, that conjectured dying 'on top of the hill' brings in by allusion a picture of history's most celebrated martyrdom, that of Christ on the cross on Calvary).*

Such celebration of life is, naturally, the business of any artist, but the use of the railroad theme, as of the highway theme, is the province very largely of the folk artist.† Dylan is more than a folk artist – his creative insight and integrity set him beyond that sphere – but his work has been gorged on the folk culture of America. It has provided a basis for his creativity, has literally been fundamental. In both senses, folk music is behind him.

---

* And of course it is precisely *this* use of the train symbol that Dylan finally comes to on the 'Slow Train Coming' album, and in a couple of instances just prior to it – he sings the Staple Singers' *People Get Ready* on the 'Renaldo & Clara' soundtrack, and the glory-train image runs through that, and the last track on the album leading up to 'Slow Train Coming' – 'Street Legal' – opens by forewarning us:

> There's a long-distance train
> Pulling through the rain

and has Dylan riding that train to his new-found salvation.

† Like railroads, highways (and indeed some rivers, particularly the Mississippi), are main arteries in the body of American folk culture. It is the folk-spokesman, the Preacher Casy, in Dylan who relishes lines like 'I know this highway like I know my hand' (From *Highway 51 Blues* on the album 'Bob Dylan').

Chapter 3
Dylan and the Literary Tradition

It's all bin done before
It's all bin written in a book
(from Dylan's *Too Much Of Nothing*)

PART ONE

We talk nowadays as though the relationship between ... [words and
music] ... constituted a problem; even as though there were a natural
antipathy between them which composer and poet must overcome as best
they may. Yet the separation of the two arts is comparatively recent, and
the link between them would seem to be rooted deep in human nature.
(Wilfred Mellers, professor of music and formerly a *Scrutiny* literary critic.)

The folk tradition ... the English literary tradition ... it sounds like pigeon-holing
but everything connects. A very intricate chain links the two and runs from pre-
Aelfredian England through to contemporary America.

Because we have forgotten this, we find it hard to accept Dylan as a serious artist.
He has chosen a medium we are unused to taking seriously: an inseparable mixture
of music and words – and we grew up finding this a cheap and trivial formula. Thank
you Gilbert and Sullivan, Rogers and Hammerstein.

We should look back beyond the Elizabethan Age to the time when troubadours
were an important part of our culture, when that culture was orally-dominated and
when sophisticated art was the same in kind as the heritage 'of the people'.

If Marshall McLuhan is right, if our electric technology is pushing us forward into
another orally-dominated age, then it shouldn't be surprising to find a serious artist
once again at work in the medium Dylan has chosen. Nor should it astonish us that
such an artist can have re-forged the links between folk and sophisticated culture.

Dylan's work needs this wide historical context. It is no good just looking at it
against a background of Coca Cola: no good making vague references to kids in the
'50s having increased spending-power, or their cousins in the '60s getting tired of
the stars and stripes. To go back further, beyond Presley, Guthrie or Ginsberg, and
see Dylan's art also in relation to the English literary tradition, makes more sense
than simply to fool about with a few sociological guesses about what's made America
tick for the last quarter of a century.

Those who feel, like Nik Cohn, that the significance of anyone with an electric
guitar can be summed up as 'Awopbopaloobop Alopbamboom!' had better skip
straight to chapter 4.

It is only comparatively recently, too, that folk and sophisticated culture have
been separate. The gulf was not complete in England until the emergence of the
Augustans, with their classicists and coffee-house smart-sets, although it had started
with Chaucer, who brought to dominance an East Midlands dialect which became
what we call 'standard English'.

With only a few exceptions, pre-Elizabethan poetry was 'of the people'. Pre-
Aelfredian poetry was all vernacular and all, in essence, orally disciplined, including
Beowulf. It was sung, and its development was the responsibility of its singers; and
so, roughly, things continued until the Norman Conquest. And in the long run, the 47

English absorbed the Normans and the English language rose in importance.

The poetical literature which grew with it was again emphatically 'of the people' from Orm's *Ormulum* to Langland's *Vision of Piers Plowman* in 1362. *Piers Plowman* might now be the province of University English Departments, but in its own time it appealed to everyone. Written in the Old English manner, in alliterative verse, it had an equal impact on those who wanted a reform of the Church and those labourers and serfs to whom Wat Tyler offered himself as a symbol of progress and hope.

Throughout the entire fifteenth century the divisive power of Chaucer's influence was fought by the ingredients of English life which worked towards keeping up the old cultural unity. In this transitional period, the ballad, lays and so on, blossomed alongside a renewed concern with classical literature. So the Elizabethan age that followed grew out of a cultural turmoil never equalled before or since, until our own times. Folk culture was intimately and creatively linked with literary culture in the age that has given us an unmatched richness of artistic achievement.

The links are clear enough in Shakespeare. He might have amused the cockneys and the refined with his rustic caricatures – Bottom doing battle with Pyramus and Thisbe – yet in his poetry he builds upon rural thought and metaphor, upon imagery springing naturally from a traditionally agricultural society. And so do the best of his contemporaries. As drama abandoned these folk foundations, and country communities went under to puritanism, so that drama declined.

All English literature lost out as a result, and the more recent onslaught of the Industrial Revolution made the loss irretrievable. As F. R. Leavis describes it, what was involved was

> not merely an idiomatic raciness of speech, expressing a strong vitality, but
> an art of social living, with its mature habits of valuation. We must beware
> of idealizing, but the fact is plain. There would have been no Shakespeare
> ... if ... with all its disadvantages by present standards, there had not
> been, living in the daily life of the people, a positive culture which has
> disappeared.

At this stage in the narrative, enter John Bunyan, precursor in achievement of Bob Dylan. Although he was the worst, the least Miltonic, kind of puritan, epitomizing narrow sectarianism, Bunyan restored the strengths of popular culture to main-stream literary culture after the two had gone their largely separate ways. He was thus Elizabethan in spirit, and he helped stave off the disappearance Leavis laments.

Granted the new conditions, it is reasonable to say that what Bunyan did then, Dylan has done again: put the dynamics of folk culture back into sophisticated art, exalting the one to the level of the other's greatness.

The parallel between the two writers is worth pursuing: and to do so, it has to be said that *Pilgrim's Progress* is, in the best sense, a classic. Overriding its reductive intention – the disease of Calvinism trying to lacerate life with the stick of hell-fire – it offers an enriching humanitarianism.

Its humanity comes across with that Biblical dignity of expression which graces the language of all folk culture. Bunyan's work is a reminder of the powerful influence of the various English-language translations of the Bible, from Wyclif's version to the Authorized of 1611 – an influence that still operates on folk idiom both in England and America, as, indeed, Dylan's work testifies. The Authorized version has been the most important: has been, for hundreds of years, the countryman's only book. In imagery and rhythm, it is popular, not classical; it harks back to and reflects the language of medieval England.

Bunyan therefore harks back also to the language of medieval England – and so does Dylan. It is not mere coincidence—it is a question of common roots: shared cultural history. The Bible's linguistic influence is clear in all the kinds of American folk music dealt with in the previous chapter which have affected Dylan's work.

As if to prove the point, Cecil Sharpe discovered the popular culture Bunyan represented, not fossilized but vitally alive, in the remoter valleys of the Southern Appalachians during the First World War. And if anyone doubts that this has impinged on Dylan, the guitar-work on his *Ballad Of Hollis Brown* should alone prove the point.

Bunyan, then, is very much Dylan's forebear; and there are many and noticeable similarities of language in their work. It is from Bunyan, and certainly not from any rock'n'roll vocabulary, that Dylan gets this great, and typical, phrase from *Joey* on the 'Desire' album:

> . . . God's in heaven
> overlooking his preserve

And isn't this, for example, instantly recognizable as a Dylan line (say, from the 'John Wesley Harding' album)?:

> Pray who are your kindred there, if a man may be so bold?

But it is not Bob Dylan, it is Christian in *Pilgrim's Progress*. And doesn't this comply almost exactly in rhythm and vocabularitive tone?:

> Oh what dear daughter beneath the sun could treat a father so:
> To wait upon him hand and foot and always answer no?

Thus Dylan's *Tears Of Rage* which also illustrates, as do so many other Dylan songs, its creator's concern for salvation. In terms of the parallels with Bunyan, this is the nearest to a merely coincidental one: and yet even here, coincidence is perhaps not the right word.

'Salvation' exposes universal predicaments which no serious writer ignores. Only the ideal behind the term has changed as succeeding philosophies have shifted it from generation to generation. Consequently, Dylan's idea of it was for a long time far from Bunyan's—though noticeably not very different from Lawrence's. When Bunyan was writing, of course, God existed. To his contemporary pamphleteers, salvation was a narrowly Christian matter (either you got there or you didn't) and it was a wider thing to Bunyan himself in spite of, not because of, his Calvinism. Since then, God has been through many changes, all reducing His omnipotence. He has been through a career as Watchmaker Extraordinary in a Newtonian world—a career already made redundant by David Hume by the time that Paley crystallized it—and on through Victorian loss of faith ('Oh God, if there is a God, Save my soul, if I have a soul!'), to twentieth-century oblivion and beyond. The Dylan of the mid-60s to mid-70s showed us our world too plagued and helpless easily to countenance that God was really dead. We identified with the tortured vision of the medieval Hieronymus Bosch. There was a serious anguish behind our trivia—hence the power of a book like *Catch 22*. With 'Slow Train Coming' and 'Saved', in 1979 and 1980, Dylan demands that we re-examine all this—and indeed that we re-examine Bunyan's vision and our notion of what our quest for salvation requires of us.

What comes to mind on the impulse of Dylan's concern for salvation is a consciousness, modern yet universal, of how spiritual sickness damages the individual psyche. This is manifest in both Dylan's secular and (recent) religious work. It is a delicate thing, unspecific: a religious concern for life that need have nothing to do with theology. And in this sense, a Laurentian consciousness. Dylan points to this by projecting himself as spiritually healthy in a world that is patently not so; and confirming a sense of need, he attributes a similar quality to the women his songs celebrate:

> My love she speaks like silence,
> Without ideals or violence,
> She doesn't have to say she's faithful
> Yet she's true like ice, like fire.

There is more involved in that 'faithful' than a pop-writer would be conscious of, and the clarifying 'like ice, like fire' suggests (with succinct understatement) just how much more. Again, the echo is of Lawrence: Lawrence deploring the merely lovable and trying to restore the elemental, asking us to go beyond a simplistic use of our senses, to be more real. Part of Lawrence's poem *Elemental* runs:

> Why don't people leave off being lovable
> or thinking they are lovable, or wanting to be lovable,
> and be a bit elemental instead? . . .

> I wish men would get back their balance among the elements
> and be a bit more fiery, as incapable of telling lies as fire is.

Dylan's 'she's true' plainly encompasses all this. Being true involves being true to yourself. True 'like ice, like fire'.

This sense of elemental tension comes up again and again in Dylan's work. In *Gates of Eden* we are given this image: 'With his candle lit into the sun/Though its glow is waxed and black' and in *It's All Over Now, Baby Blue* there comes the powerful 'Crying like a fire in the sun'.

At least as elemental, in *Wedding Song*, from the 1974 album 'Planet Waves', is this:

> Eye for eye and tooth for tooth
> Your love cuts like a knife

where the *Old Testament* is invoked for its fierce, fundamental Jehovah-power. And again, from the same song:

> What's lost is lost, we can't regain
> What went down in the flood . . .
> And I love you more than blood.

Lawrence would have loved that one.

All this search for the quintessential man comes into an intelligent concern for salvation, a concern Dylan stands by in much of his work. It is there in *Don't Think Twice, It's All Right* in the simple line (it is almost just a passing remark): 'Gave her my heart but she wanted my soul' and in his tender, appreciative *To Ramona*:

> Your cracked country lips I still wish to kiss
> As to be by the strength of your skin,
> Your magnetic movements still capture the minutes
> I'm in . . .

That 'strength' is felt by him, it implies a given moral strength, a Laurentian awareness of the real derived from an alertness of the physical senses.

Through the abrasive intelligence of work invested with such values, Dylan has changed a generation – has made it more sensitive to what is enhancing and what is impoverishing. It is as much as the artist can do.

Opposite: *Newport Folk Festival with Pete Seeger seated, 1964.*

It is to 'words' I now return. I was tracing the historical links between, among other things, the language of folk culture and of literature. The creative links are worth examining too.

Why is it that there is such a marked similarity of impulse between idiom and poetic expression? How come the 'uneducated' countryman, whose life has been traditionally agricultural and whose vocabulary is limited, apparently carelessly produces those terse, ellipsed phrases which 'educated' people find unreachably admirable and evocative? Why is it that the unschooled Englishman or American with a rural background is closer to the poet than are most 'educated' men?

There are answers to these questions, and many a missing link thrown in as well, in an essay written by Adrian Bell* and published nearly fifty years ago. It's an exciting essay (at least, it excited me).

Bell argues:

> To understand how language is still reborn out of tradition in the unlettered mind . . . it is necessary to be immersed in the life until one thinks, as well as talks, in local usage. The countryman kindles as he speaks, assumes the authority of one rooted in his life, and that emotional quickening is the same in essence as the artist's – creative. In the glow of it he coins words. Linguistically, there is a kind of half-light in his brain, and on the impulse of an emotion, words get confused with one another and fused into something new – a new shade of meaning is expressed . . . [and the result is] not traditional words, but words born of momentary need out of tradition.

Bell concludes:

> The countryman's speech is only roundabout to that superficial view which regards a poem as going a long way round to say what could be conveyed in a few words. Sustainedly, the emotional and muscular content of his idiom is almost equal to that of poetry, *for he possesses the same instinct by which the poet places words in striking propinquity: the urgency of his feeling causing his mind to leap intermediate associations, coining many a 'quaint' phrase, imaginatively just, though superficially bizarre.*

That phrase 'almost equal to poetry' stays in the mind – because isn't it exactly the half-praising half-damning judgement that the work of a really good folk artist, a Guthrie, inevitably receives? Thus such work is locked forever within the labyrinth of its popular roots and fails to reach the notice of a literary public. Or much of a musical public, for that matter. Yet Bell's 'almost', coming after his other observations, shows again, I think, how natural and logical it is that a Dylan figure, like Bunyan before him, should have broken through the barriers to achieve recognized greatness by making the cultural mainstream from a folk source.

More than this, the section quoted above in italics gives a striking insight, in effect, into the kind of poetry on the 'Highway 61 Revisited' and 'Blonde On Blonde' LPs. It makes clear that the words on these albums do relate to what is normally agreed to be his folk song repertoire. It also gets us a lot further than most alternative accounts. It avoids (and exposes the emptiness of) the easy judgement of

* 'English Tradition and Idiom', Volume II, *Scrutiny* magazine, 1933; reprinted in *Selections From Scrutiny* No. 2, Cambridge University Press, 1968.

Paris, 1966. This was on the tour where each concert had a solo acoustic-guitared set and then a set with the group that became The Band (but had a different drummer). This part of the event was booed everywhere except Australia.

'obscurity' – the judgement so often levelled at Dylan's mid-60s work. It's ironic that while this 'obscurity' is so properly explained by attention to the creative impulse which makes for folk idiom, it should have been the folk purists who most vociferously condemned this section of Dylan's output.

There is another aspect of this general inquiry, which up to now has merely been stumbled against from time to time. That is: what has followed the 'positive culture' that Leavis says has disappeared? What has been the aftermath, for folk culture, of the twentieth-century acceleration in industrial technology? Are there any 'folk' left? What has happened to the countryman's life, daily and communal, now that the traditionally agricultural society is all but extinct in England and is in America locked in incongruous partnership with a mechanical hierarchy of insecticide-spray aircraft, pylon totem-poles, giant TV screens and the linguistic tricks of Madison Avenue?

Bell's essay deals with a part of this theme, though with fewer of the changes that have occurred this century, simply because he was writing in the early 1930s. Nevertheless, his observations are interesting. He traces the decline of the 'uneducated' countryman in England, and writes of the young men:

> The first taste of education and standard English has had the effect of making them acutely self-conscious. They realize (and agricultural depression helps this) not that they stand supreme in a fundamental way of life but that they are the last left on a sinking ship. No one decries civilization who has not experienced it ad nauseam. Modernity offers dim but infinite possibilities to the young countryman if only he can rid his boots of this impeding clay. Pylons, petrol pumps and other 'defacements' are to him symbols of a noble power. The motor-bus, motor-bicycle, wireless, are that power's beckonings. But he is late, he is held hapless in a ruining countryside, everyone else is laughing at him, he feels. . . . The old men had their defence. They knew what they were. But he can't stay where they are. The contentment of it is gone . . .

And so Bell comes to argue that we

> must go to America for a modern counterpart of the old idiomatic vigour of common speech. American slang may be ugly and unpleasant, but it has the fascination of abounding vitality, hectic and spurious though that may be. It presupposes knowledge of a thousand sophistications, of intimacy with the life of a modern city, just as the traditional idiom presupposed a familiarity with nature and the processes of agriculture.

Bell underestimates the staying-power of the old life, in England and America. In England, many of the 'young countrymen' of 1933 held on in their agricultural villages and are still there today – in 'uneducated' old age – with, despite their TV sets, their inventive idiom by no means extinct. It is under pressure but it is not yet ruined. In America, agricultural living has hung on also, so that there is still no coast-to-coast city idiom of the kind Bell plainly envisaged.

Yet Scott Fitzgerald was able, as early as 1925, to write to his publisher (from Paris, mind you) that

> . . . the American peasant as 'real' material scarcely exists. He is scarcely 10 % of the population, isn't bound to the soil at all . . . and, if [he] has any sensitivity whatever (except a most sentimental conception of himself,

which our writers persistently shut their eyes to), he is in the towns before he's twenty.

That too is oversimplified; but in Guthrie's dazzling autobiography, *Bound For Glory*, and in the story of the blues – which is the story of an exodus from down-home to Chicago – we have the more complex truth: and it does not basically contradict Fitzgerald's view.

Dylan himself touches on this migration process in his beautiful *To Ramona*:

> I can see you are torn between staying and returning
> Back to the South . . .

and in effect again, on *Slow Train Coming*:

> I had a woman, down in Alabama
> She was a backwoods girl
> But she sure was realistic . . .

As Thomas Wolfe said, you can't go home again.

What remains, as much in England as in America, is an incredible hotch-potch of environmental influence. If it were otherwise, there would be no 'purist' folk movement, except in the museums, and no problem in defining what today's folk music can be.

The hotch-potch echoes in the environment of countryman and city kid alike. McLuhan is right in the simple observation that you can't shut out sounds, ideas or other people once they are globally broadcast. Not even the Southern Appalachian valley-dweller can today have an insulated, self-expanding culture. Among the 1980s Okies, the language of even the oldest men and women must now be intruded upon by the language of *Time* magazine and the tubespeak of American television.

Everywhere in the West, minority cultures are being tossed together and mixed with, on the one hand, lumpen uniformity and on the other, what passes as the *haute culture* of our age, so that whatever our class and whatever our geographic centre, we have – and the process accelerates all the time – more in common with one another, more shared experience, than the men and women of any generation since the heyday of the Elizabethan Age in England. Full circle. And this wheel's on fire – we are caught up in a kind of vulgar, neurotic renaissance. Hail the return, as McLuhan insists, to oral primacy.

Small wonder that Dylan should select – or rather, find himself at home in – an artistic medium not merely literary but involving a return to a medieval interdependence of words and music.

The viability of media other than books was obvious enough from such a statistic as Aidan Chambers offered, in his survey *The Reluctant Reader* in 1960. He maintained that 60 per cent of the children leaving school in Britain in 1969 would never pick up a book again: 60 per cent. 'Popular songs,' said Dylan, in 1965, 'are the only art form that describes the temper of the times . . . That's where the people hang out. It's not in books; it's not on the stage; it's not in the galleries.'

In the meantime, the uprooting confusion is in spate. The artist who doesn't try for 'originality' as something in limbo, but who uses re-creatively the heritage imbibed with his native air, must find himself, today, not with a clearly-defined ethnic background, but with a totally kaleidoscopic one ('collidescopic' is McLuhan's word).

Dylan's position inside the kaleidoscope is clear. A middle-class trader's son, and Jewish, from small mid-western towns – Duluth and Hibbing – and then from the University of Minnesota, he had a perfectly natural exposure to innumerable winds

Hibbing High School graduation photo, 1959.

of culture. The Mississippi River flows down from Minnesota, through Iowa, Missouri, Arkansas and Louisiana – flows 1,700 miles to the Gulf of Mexico. For Dylan, Highway 61 leads to the dust-bowled '30s, Kerouac and Kant, Chuck Berry's neon-California and Eliot's wasteland simultaneously.

Present-day confusion is less reductive than future uniformity. Increasing centralization is well advanced, moving as rapidly as Stalin moved his workers to the industrializing cities of the USSR: and the inevitable consequences are obvious. John Steinbeck set out, at the beginning of the '60s, to search for America. His conclusions are set down in *Travels With Charley*, and they include the following observations:

> . . . regional speech is in the process of disappearing, not gone but going. Forty years of radio and twenty years of television must have this impact. Communication must destroy localness . . . speech becomes standardized, perhaps better English than we have ever used. Just as our bread, mixed and baked, packaged and sold without benefit of accident or human frailty, is uniformly good and uniformly tasteless, so will our speech become one speech . . . no region can hold out for long against the highway, the high-tension line, and the national television.

Plenty of people can be optimistic about this. Some things, at the moment, look not bad. Dylan told *Rolling Stone* magazine that 'people are making music. That's a good sign. There are certainly more people around making music than there was when I was growing up, I know that.'

A movie-star like Rod Steiger can be optimistic, too, about the passing of regional, rural living – though from rather a different perspective. He told the *Guardian*:

> Transportation is bringing us more together than thousands of idealists ever have. . . . We're all citizens of the world, brothers and sisters under the skin, not because of idealism, but because the jumbo-jets are going to take us all over by the thousand.

The myth of all of us, millionaires, farm-workers and unemployed, tripping round together up in the sky, is interesting – and was, in effect, exploded long ago by Matthew Arnold, eminent Victorian. What is the good, asked Arnold, of those trains whizzing from Islington to Camberwell with letters three times a day, if all they can tell the inhabitants of dismal, illiberal Camberwell is that it's dismal and illiberal in Islington as well?

But you can take a wide view without showing, as Steiger does, such callous disregard for economic realities and the quality of life. Steinbeck manages it, again in *Travels With Charley*, and provides a suitable comment with which to finish accounting for the importance of folk heritage in Dylan's work:

> What are roots and how long have we had them? If our species has existed for a couple of million years, what is its history? Our remote ancestors followed the game, moved with the food supply, and fled from evil weather ... Only when agriculture came into practice – and that's not very long ago in terms of the whole history – did a place achieve meaning and value and permanence. But land is a tangible, and tangibles have a way of getting into a few hands. ... Roots were in ownership of land, in tangible and immovable possessions. In this view we are a restless species with a very short history of roots, and those not widely distributed. Perhaps we have overrated roots as a psychic need.

If Dylan has grown in part from folk roots – psychically needed or not – and created art of universal greatness, so too the culture he has added to has had its effect on his contribution. The English literary tradition, as well as the American is continued in Dylan's work (continued in both senses), and its influence in that work is wide-ranging.

PART TWO

I can't remember anyone ever asking Dylan about his reading habits, so I must do things the proper way round and judge his literary background from the evidence not of the man but of his work. That work seems to me to contain many recollections of major English poets. I have mentioned D. H. Lawrence already, if insufficiently; I have not yet dealt with all the others – with Donne or Blake or Browning or Eliot. (Eliot, of course, is American, not English, but I include him here because, like Henry James, he gave himself to Old World high culture, rather than, like Hemingway, shying away from it.)

Dylan's work sometimes calls John Donne to mind, I think.

Donne's modernity stems partly from a directness of statement so well represented in his famous opening lines: 'For Godsake hold your tongue, and let me love'; 'Now thou hast lov'd me one whole day'; 'Oh do not die, for I shall hate/All women so when thou art gone'; and one of Dylan's contributions has been to reintroduce such directness to white popular music. (Black music, even in its pop-orientated forms, has always had a *double-entendre* device so crude as to become directness, effectively, as '50s records like the Penguins' *Baby Let Me Bang Your Box* illustrate, though that quality of directness is hardly Metaphysical.)

That Donne immediacy – directness balanced by intelligent discretion – is at work here:

> Go 'way from my window
> Leave at your own chosen speed

(the song is *It Ain't Me Babe*). And here:

> You got a lot o' nerve, to say you are my friend

(*Positively 4th Street*). And here:

> I hate myself for loving you

(the opening line of *Dirge*, from 'Planet Waves').

These and others share with Donne more than plain directness – more than the conversational tone. More, even, than the measuredness both writers communicate, which takes its power from the sense that intellect is engaged in the communicating. Common to both is the bond between the passion and the rhythm.

It was another poet, Coleridge, who pointed this out in Donne's case. He wrote: 'To read Dryden, Pope, etc, you need only count syllables; but to read Donne you must measure Time, and discover the time of each word by the sense of Passion.'

That must go down as an equally useful approach to Dylan's metre. Coleridge's point is proved by songs like *The Lonesome Death of Hattie Carroll* – or, come to that, *Like A Rolling Stone*. The vibrant and intricate changes of rhythm in each occur through the investment of different words with differing degrees of feeling. In *Hattie Carroll* the guitar-work enforces this relationship. It acts as a musical graph of Dylan's heartbeats. The drumming on *Like A Rolling Stone* does the same. (A much earlier example is the drumming on Presley's *Hound Dog*.)

Another point in relation to Donne is this. Donne's tricksiness appeals to our habit of expending the intellect on trivia – and Dylan is not exempt from this, as songs from *I Shall Be Free No. 10* through to *Million Dollar Bash* transparently show.

Donne in this sense suits our times very well. It takes a serious man to be funny; it takes a sizeable mind to write satisfying minor love-songs. Donne would have made a great pop song-writer for this reason. He couldn't have written pure teenybop stuff, any more than Dylan would choose to. He couldn't have done *Sugar Sugar* or *Mull of Kintyre* or *My Fair Lady*, which is music for teenybop senility. But he could have done excellent tricksy little things for people like, say, Elvis Costello.

A line from Donne's *The Good-Morrow*, for instance, would, adapted slightly, make a perfect Carole King title: 'You Make One Little Room An Everywhere'. And the famous pop line 'catch a falling star' originates with Donne, not Perry Como.

In particular, the openings of two Donne poems are perfectly fitted to the best of pop. One is from *Song* and runs:

> Sweetest love, I do not goe
> For weariness of thee,
> Nor in hope the world can show
> A fitter Love for mee . . .

which would do very nicely for Dylan – or the Band, or Mick Jagger.

The other John Donne opening which would make intelligent, delicate, strong, tricksy pop is from his poem *The Triple Foole*:

> I am two fooles, I know,
> For loving, and for saying so
> In whining poetry . . .

That shows perfectly the kind of conscious flirtation with ideas and nonsense that Dylan has exploited so well. It's in the same class as *Peggy Day*, with its

> Love to spend the night with Peggy Day

or as *Open The Door Richard*:*

> . . . one must always flush out his house
> If he don't expect to be housing flushes

Perhaps the Dylan song most involved in this kind of tricksiness is *4th Time Around*,

---

* The sheet-music gives the title as *Open The Door Homer* which, although the name Homer gets no mention in the song, is just as likely a title: indeed just the sort of disparity Dylan enjoys creating.

from 'Blonde On Blonde', with its incredible stretched-out metaphors of sexual innuendo culminating in the rebounding pun on 'crutch' (dealt with in detail in chapter 5), which Donne would have appreciated.

Finally, it is striking that Dylan finds it hard, just as Donne found it, to subjugate his intensity and passion into an appropriate devotional stance in the later religious work. Both artists exhibit a constant difficulty with the war of the Flesh and the Spirit. Donne's secular love poetry gets to pointing towards Christ (notably in *The Canonization* where orgasm is likened to the death of Christ and the Resurrection) just as Dylan's does, on 'Street Legal' and 'Blood On the Tracks' in particular; and in the religious work of both the passion they'd applied to lovers is no less lustily transferred to the Lord. At the same time, the religious work of both lacks general appeal, so that both artists end up with a substantial body of very popular secular work and a largely unheeded religious output.

Going on to William Blake, I turn first (taking the ridiculous before the sublime) to A. J. Weberman. Weberman called himself the world's only living Dylanologist, presided over a kind of Dylan museum of unreleased tape-recordings, posters, magazine-articles and, I imagine, Bobby Dylan T-shirts, and gave up college to do so. He was sitting there in college and suddenly it came to him. 'Well fuck this shit, man,' he claims to have said to himself. 'Interpreting Dylan is a hundred times more interesting than going to school so I dropped out of school and became a Dylanologist full time. . . . I really pushed my brain and I began to get some insight into Dylan.'

Weberman played detective. He sniffed through files, kept an ear to the ground for useful rumours and combed Dylan's output for coded messages. Example: when Dylan uses the word 'lady' he means 'oligarchy'. So pushing our brains and letting insight dawn, we have 'Lay, Oligarchy, Lay', 'Sad-Eyed Oligarchy of the Lowlands' and so on.

I bring this in here because there is an excellent reply to Weberman's position in an article by Greil Marcus and because the reply Marcus offers brings in, and usefully, William Blake. The article, called 'Let The Record Play Itself' appeared in the San Francisco *Express-Times* (no date).

Marcus explains the existence of Webermanesque interpretations by saying that people apparently have a need to know

> if Dylan is a transvestite or on heroin or stubbed his toe buying beer; and they want to convince themselves that Dylan is . . . wonderfully obscure and ambiguous, so that they won't have to feel insecure about listening to someone who did, after all, play all that really loud music that got in the way of the words. The game is still going on . . .*As I Went Out One Morning*, a song in which Tom Paine guest stars, is about a dinner Dylan attended years ago, at which he was presented with the Tom Paine Award by the Emergency Civil Liberties Committee. Dylan, during his acceptance speech, said something about how he might understand how Lee Harvey Oswald felt, and the audience booed. This interpretation makes Dylan a real interesting guy. He waits for years to get a chance to get back at an unfriendly audience, and all Tom Paine means to him is the bad memory of an award dinner. Poor Tom Paine. The fellow who came up with this job [Weberman] has said: 'I consider Bob Dylan America's greatest poet.' Well, naturally; why should such a mind waste his time on a lesser figure? It's not just that such terms are pointless . . . but is this sort of thing – the Tom Paine Award Dinner Revenge – is this what makes a great poet?

Poetry, music, songs, stories, are all part of that realm of creation that deepens our lives and can endow our lives with a special kind of grace, tension, perhaps with beauty and splendor. Meaning has many levels – one might meet the artist himself on one of those levels, find friends on another, reach a fine solitude in the light of another man's creation on yet another level. That kind of power in art might be scary – it might be sure enough to survive interpretation and the enforcement of the particular . . . Take these lines from *London* by William Blake:

> 'But most thro' midnight streets I hear
> How the youthful Harlot's curse
> Blasts the newborn infant's tear
> And blights with plagues the Marriage hearse.'*

Now what that 'means', it was once explained to me, is that a prostitute got syphilis, gave birth to a deformed child, the father of which also died of the disease . . . That can all be confirmed by balancing and referring the images in the verse – but is it necessary to grasp that . . . in order to feel the weight and power of Blake's vision of London? Blake's words transcend the situation about which he's writing.

Likewise, says Marcus, with Dylan:

> One will never 'understand' *Just Like A Woman* by proving, logically, that it is about transvestites or Britain (Queen Mary and the fog) even if, by some chance, the song 'really is about' such things.

Dylan himself argues this case graphically at the end of *Gates of Eden* where he commends his lover for valuing her dreams 'with no attempts to shovel the glimpse into the ditch of what each one means'. He won't like the last chapter of this book, I'm afraid, which *is* expositional.

It isn't surprising that Marcus invokes Blake when alluding to the meaning of 'meaning' in poetry. This is partly because Blake's words are his own much more emphatically than with other poets one can readily call to mind.

Blake fought off the vagueness and tiredness of meaning that common social usage imposes on words, by simply refusing to recognize that vagueness. His own thought didn't succumb to it, so his writing disregards it. He concentrated his thought. A great deal of intellect is telescoped (and is used in the process of telescoping) into very few lines in his poetry.

And yet, if Blake's words are in this way his own, don't his poems belong actually to the reader?

> And did those feet in ancient time
> Walk upon England's mountains green?
> And was the holy Lamb of God
> On England's pleasant pastures seen?
>
> And did the Countenance Divine
> Shine forth upon our clouded hills?
> And was Jerusalem builded here
> Among these dark Satanic Mills?

---

* And compare those lines of Blake's on London with these of Dylan on New York; Blake's stark visionary influence is clear:

> I went out on Lower Broadway/And I felt that place within
> That hollow place where martyrs weep/And angels play with sin

Bring me my Bow of burning gold:
Bring me my Arrows of desire:
Bring me my Spear: O clouds unfold!
Bring me my Chariot of fire.

I will not cease from Mental Fight,
Nor shall my Sword sleep in my hand
Till we have built Jerusalem
In England's green and pleasant Land.

That is a hymn, in England. The scholarship of F.W. Bateson, on the other hand, emerged in 1950 with an interpretation so different as to be ironic. Blake wrote it, Bateson established, as an anti-ecclesiastical manifesto. The altars of Anglican churches were the 'dark Satanic Mills' that clouded men's vision of spiritual reality and polluted the sanctity of man's desires.*

But what about the hymn? What about the meaning almost everyone except Bateson and Blake himself has given that poem?

We have had D.H. Lawrence's answer: never trust the artist, trust the tale.

The Blakeian influence on Dylan is apparent first as a question of 'thought': that is, in a labour of thought which achieves an economy of language, by its concentration, and a tone almost of disinterestedness about what is actually experienced with intense emotion by the writer. In Blake we see this, for instance, in *The Sick Rose*. In Dylan we see it in the make-up of the 'John Wesley Harding' album (especially on *I Dreamed I Saw St Augustine*) and in other individual songs throughout his repertoire. It is there, for example, in a song already looked at, *Love Minus Zero/No Limit*. That song, in fact, refers to the same theme as *The Sick Rose*: the theme of possessiveness destroying love.

Blake's short poem comes from the *Songs of Experience* and runs as follows:

O Rose, thou art sick!
The invisible worm
That flies in the night,
In the howling storm,
Has found out thy bed
Of crimson joy:
And his dark secret love
Does thy life destroy.

* You don't need the scholarship, actually. You don't have to go far through even the best-known work of Blake to get at a clearer statement of his views on the debilitating effects of institutionalized religion. *The Garden of Love* is representative:

I went to the Garden of Love/And saw what I never had seen:
A Chapel was built in the midst,/Where I used to play on
  the green.
And the gates of this Chapel were shut,/And 'Thou Shalt Not'
  writ over the door;
So I turn'd to the Garden of Love/That so many sweet flowers
  bore;
And I saw it was filled with graves,/And tomb-stones where
  flowers should be;
And Priests in black gowns were walking their rounds
And binding with briars my joys and desires.

Dylan deals with this same theme by positing an antithetical consciousness – an awareness of what a love that is not like a sick rose needs for survival:

> My love she speaks like silence
> Without ideals or violence
> She doesn't have to say she's faithful
> Yet she's true like ice, like fire

The awareness I mention is conveyed by Dylan confronting the listener with a series of contrasts: the contrast between 'without ideals' and '(without) violence' – both of which colour that 'silence'; and the contrast, noted in an earlier context, between the tired, socially dulled 'faithful' and 'true' and the qualifying, regenerative 'like ice, like fire'.

As if thrown at these quick-firing contrasts, the listener is himself thrown into thought: he must flex his mental limbs or drown; and so, with the effort of swimming, he becomes conscious of the values Dylan conveys in the song, and aware that they are the values of health in love. Blakeian values, put across with Blakeian economy.

The last stanza of the song invokes the 'tyger' of Blake's most famous poem. The tyger (like ice, like fire) is elemental; naked life. And Dylan's tyger is a raven:

> The wind howls like a hammer
> The night blows raining
> My love she's like some raven
> At my window with a broken wing.

The ultimate and immediate effect of the first two lines there is to invigorate. In the first, this is achieved by juxtaposing the wind's sound and sheer physical force – a feat of concentrated language that rivals anything in English poetry. In the second, the sense of a corresponding release of energy comes, in the words, from telescoping the wind's activity with the rain's; and is enforced in the music by a half-staccato rhythm:

which is strengthened, paradoxically, by the redressing *softness* (and openness) in Dylan's voice.

The energy of that line carries over – beyond the pause created by its own cadence – to invest the 'raven' image with an associated litheness. And so we are carried to the potent centre of the song. On the surface, the woman in the song is admired and respected, and the voice plays a part in emphasizing this; but the fundamental thing is why she is so highly valued, what wins this respect and admiration – and 'she's like some raven' confirms the answer that has been implicit throughout the song.

If the 'raven' corresponds to Blake's tyger, it corresponds also to D.H. Lawrence's *Snake* and Coleridge's albatross. It represents the spiritually noble, ensymbolled in physical perfection. (So in the Dylan song, the 'raven' is a symbol within a symbol.)

Coleridge's albatross is violated by the base thoughtlessness of human approach; Lawrence's snake suffers at the bidding of similar instincts (and Lawrence, whose fault as a poet is also a strength sometimes, an over-explicitness, even puts in the line 'And I thought of the Albatross'). But Blake keeps a respectful, awe-filled distance from his tyger; and Dylan's technique is similar: he likewise knows his place. The awe felt for his 'raven's' nobility is indicated, lightly and subtly enough, by that word 'some': 'like some raven' suggests the half-bewildered sense of privilege experienced, as no apparently exchangeable word could do.

But the 'raven' has a broken wing, has been brought down, so that, though it might seem to him unbelievable (and this impression is enforced by the temporary nature of 'a broken wing': it will heal) the mortal artist can pay his tributes from a position of equality, can walk appreciatively among his gods. The 'raven' is at his window. Each can give strength to the other, if human possessiveness does not intrude, nor the urge to destroy. And the artist's fine awareness of this, as it makes itself felt, gives the song its tension, its underlying concrete power.

Very much like Blake's *Sick Rose*, the brevity of *Love Minus Zero/No Limit* belies its importance. It is light, delicate, poised; yet it handles intensely-felt emotional experience, experience distilled by thought, so that what we are offered has neither an obtrusive atmosphere of intense feeling – none, as Leavis said of Blake, 'of the Shelleyan "I feel, I suffer, I yearn"' – nor an obtrusive suggestion of how much intellect has gone into its making.

One might apply that contrast of Blake and Shelley to one of the essential differences between Dylan and another poet-singer, Leonard Cohen. Cohen in any case often paddles in the maudlin, but an associated weakness in his work is exactly that Shelleyan quality of saying, as it were, 'Look at me: God! I'm sensitive!' A fundamental strength of Dylan's sensitivity is to avoid calling attention to itself.

Dylan's work is faithful to Blakeian characteristics too in the eruption of the occasional written gestures of mockery, aimed at a hostile public.

T. S. Eliot wrote that Blake had nothing to distract him from, or corrupt, his interests; one thinks, in contrast, of the pressures on Dylan – the films 'Don't Look Back', 'Eat The Document' and (even) 'Renaldo & Clara', exposed their enormity – and yet how little he has allowed them to interfere with his pre-occupations. 'I'm not interested in myself as a performer,' said Dylan in 1966. 'Performers are people who perform for other people. Unlike actors, I know what I'm saying. It's very simple in my mind. It doesn't matter what kind of audience reaction this whole thing gets. What happens on stage is straight. It doesn't expect any reward or fines from any kind of outside agitators ... [It] would exist whether anybody was looking or not.' And when Eliot tells us that Blake approached everything with a mind unclouded by current opinions, we can profitably reflect on how little of Dylan's variegated achievement has been shadowed by the clouds of other people's ideas. Dylan has had to reject other people's ideas of what singing should be, what songwriting formulae dictate, what the pseudo-ethnic togetherness of his early Greenwich Village patrons demanded, and more besides. There is the additional testimony of his determined move over to what others labelled Folk-Rock, then Acid-Rock; his adroit retreat from all outside affairs from late '66 until nearly two years later; his (infuriating to others) residence in New York State while an acid-rock/psychedelic scene he had played an unwitting part in founding played on and on into hopeless narcissistic decadence in California; and all his more recent pushes against the tide of the times.

Dylan and Blake share also the desire to fight off accusations of abnormality. Blake found it astonishing and perplexing that people should have considered him and his work deliberately puzzling and peculiar; Dylan told *Playboy*, in their mammoth interview with him in 1966: '. . . people actually have the gall to think that I have some kind of fantastic imagination. It gets very lonesome.'

This commonly-felt sense of isolation provokes stunningly similar face-pulling defiance in Blake and Dylan. Blake produced *Island In The Moon* and Dylan wrote waspish liner-notes on the 'Highway 61 Revisited' album. They share striking convergences of tone and technique. The following is from *Island In The Moon*:

> . . . in a great hurry, Inflammable Gass the Wind-finder enter'd. They seem'd to rise & salute each other. Etruscan Column & Inflammable Gass fix'd their eyes on each other; their tongues went in question and answer, but their thoughts were otherwise employ'd. 'I don't like his eyes,' said Etruscan Column. 'He's a foolish puppy,' said Inflammable Gass, smiling on him. The 3 Philosophers – the Cynic smiling, the Epicurean seeming studying the flame of the candle, & the Pythagorean playing with the cat – listen'd with open mouths . . . Then Quid call'd upon Obtuse Angle for a song, & he, wiping his face & looking on the corner of the ceiling, sang: To be or not to be/Of great capacity/Like Sir Isaac Newton,/Or Locke, or Doctor South . . .

And from the sleeve of Dylan's 'Highway 61 Revisited':

> Savage Rose & Openly are bravely blowing kisses to the Jade Hexagram-Carnaby Street & To all of the mysterious juveniles & the Cream Judge is writing a book on the true meaning of a pear – last year, he wrote one on famous dogs of the Civil War & now he has false teeth and no children . . . when the Cream met Savage Rose & Openly, he was introduced to them by none other than Lifelessness – Lifelessness is the Great Enemy & always wears a hipguard – he is very hipguard . . . Lifelessness said when introducing everybody 'go save the world' & 'involvement! that's the issue' & things like that & Savage Rose winked at Openly & the Cream went off with his arm in a sling singing 'so much for yesterday' . . . the clown appears – puts a gag over Autumn's mouth & says 'there are two kinds of people – simple people & normal people' this usually gets a big laugh from the sandpit & White Heap sneezes – passes out & wakes up & rips open Autumn's gag & says 'What do you mean you're Autumn and without you there'd be no Spring! you fool! without Spring, there'd be no you! what do you think of that???.' then Savage Rose & Openly come by & kick him in the brains & colour him pink for being a phony philosopher – then the clown comes by . . . & some college kid who's read all about Nietzsche comes by & says 'Nietzsche never wore an umpire's suit' & Paul says 'You wanna buy some clothes' & then Rose & John come out of the bar & they're going up to Harlem . . .

When you consider in relation to Blake what *is* a difficult and central work of Dylan's, you come inevitably to *The Gates of Eden*. The purposive force of what is palpably Blakeian impinges in every verse. It is the major Dylan song that is most like Blake, and like the most characteristic Blake at that. It begins with this:

> Of war and peace the truth just twists
> Its curfew gull it glides
> Upon four-legged forest clouds
> The cowboy angel rides

> With his candle lit into the sun
> Though its glow is waxed in black
> All except when 'neath the trees of Eden.

And after seven others comes this concluding verse:

> At dawn my lover comes to me
> And tells me of her dreams
> With no attempts to shovel the glimpse
> Into the ditch of what each one means;
> At times I think there are no words but these
> To tell what's true
> And there are no truths outside the gates of Eden.

In the whole, we have what Eliot, talking of Blake, calls naked vision.

The general themes of *Gates of Eden* could not be more Blakeian; and nor could their treatment. Dylan is treating of balances of opposites – of material wealth and spiritual; of earthly reality and the imaginatively real; of the body and soul; of false gods and true vision; of self-gratification and salvation; of mortal ambitions and the celestial city; of sins and forgiveness; of evil and good.

Not only are these Blake's themes, but they receive directly comparable handling. Both artists address themselves 'not to common sense, but to individual sense.' For Blake, as Max Plowman phrased it, 'all things existed in Eternity . . . All things had external existence, and their manifestation in Time was a subjective sensory impression . . . and what he desired to do was to restore to the minds of men the continuous consciousness of infinity which he believed rationalism – or the tyranny of the reasoning over the poetic faculty – had largely obliterated . . . He spoke of "seeing the Eternal which is always present to the wise"; and said that "if the doors of perception were cleansed, everything would appear to man as it is, infinite!"' (*An Introduction To The Study of Blake*, Max Plowman, Frank Cass, 2nd edition, 1967).

Gates of Eden is certainly an attempt to focus attention on that 'continuous consciousness of infinity', an attempt to point through the doors of perception; and Dylan's vision takes in our world, a world which largely fails to see 'the Eternal which is always present to the wise'.

Dylan tries to harmonize with (it is the Blakeian use of the phrase, meaning to come level with) songs the lonesome sparrow sings: the sparrow flying, humbly enough, between the earth and the heavens, passing between and observing equally, the time-trapped foolish and the real, the infinite. The vision evokes this balance of flight, this tracking between opposites.

(Perhaps I'm appropriating the sparrow to an extent here. In the context, it must shoulder – if sparrows have shoulders – its Biblical responsibilities. Not a bird valued or admired by society, it is thereby more easily possible for its sense of proportion to remain intact. Its salvation need not involve the difficulties of the proverbial camel negotiating the needle.)

This evocation of balance is very neatly enforced by the contrasts completed in every verse of the song:

> . . . he weeps to wicked birds of prey
> Who pick up on his breadcrumb sins.
> There are no sins inside the gates of Eden.

and:

> men wholly totally free
> To do anything they wish to do but die

and:

> ... the princess and the prince discuss
> What's real and what is not

and many more. Friends and other strangers, the glimpse and the ditch, a savage soldier who merely complains, the candle cradled into the sun.

This elaborate establishing of opposite poles has its corollary in the frequent internal rhymes, which lend weight to the underlying duality of everything presented. Waxed and black; all in all can only fall; Aladdin and his lamp; relationships of ownership; the foreign sun it squints upon; wholly totally free; no attempts to shovel the glimpse.

Not only do the contrasts referred to enforce a sense of the ever-present balance the song establishes: they also clarify its nature. The glimpse and the ditch focus the gulf between the perceptions of reason and of the poetic faculty; the incongruity of prince and princess discussing 'reality' calls to mind the same dichotomy.

I can't claim it's all crystal-clear. There is plenty that seems, to me at least, irrevocably obscure. The third verse, for instance, certainly evades me. It isn't that nothing of it impinges. There is a great deal of power in its last three lines: a power that has to do with the visual imagery at that point, with the dream-picture:

> Upon the beach where hound-dogs bay
> At ships with tattooed sails,
> Heading for the gates of Eden.

That word 'sails' impersonates the verb more than the noun, producing the movement of a huge black fleet sailing. Somehow there is a powerful accompanying sense of silence, and finally a pure dramatic force given by the combination of that silence with the purposive, inevitable momentum of 'Heading, for, the gates, of Eden.' This dramatic impact is electrified by the interplay of words and tune. With stunning sureness of touch, that 'Heading for', introduced with a switch to a more economic rhythm, stays on the same musical note as 'sails' and so darkens the sense of purposiveness already noted.

Yet the rest of the verse fails to elicit much response, beyond a sneaking desire to ask the kind of questions that Weberman – remember Weberman? – might ask. Who is the deafened, shoeless hunter? Is it an event, or normality, for hounds to sit on beaches baying out to sea? Are the hounds coyotes and the sea therefore really a desert? Is the soldier Buffy St Marie's Universal Soldier, whose ostrich-act is to say, well, I'm just doing my job, and who is answerable to the politicians – shoeless hunters in that they do their fighting vicariously? And if so, could the baying hounds be the callous American franchise – the Great Silent Majority baying for the blood of those who frighten them, those with vision: pirates, ships with tattooed sails.

And it's no good if you want to ask that sort of question: it's obscure because it only holds your interest on the surface. Its power is infirmly argumentative, not poetic, and so it doesn't convince. The poetic force lies in that part of the song which doesn't encourage questions but gives the imagination and the emotions palpable answers, yielding insights of poetic reality whether they remain as dream-pictures or not.

More than enough of *Gates of Eden* does that, but one should not say too little about its flaws. They seem to me large ones, but wholly of the kind cited above: that is to say, there are parts of the song which try to sustain themselves merely by argument – they lack poetic power.

Yet this is niggardly reservation in the face of the total achievement. The song as a whole accommodates infinite replaying. It is effectively reminiscent of Blake; but it ranks as a major achievement, and gets its Blakeian stature, on its own merits. It has every distinction of great poetry, flawed but indestructible.

Gates of Eden crops up again – to the extent that its form is the Dramatic Monologue – when we come down a little nearer to earth to consider Bob Dylan and Robert Browning together.

Notes Towards A Definition: the dramatic monologue differs from the soliloquy, to which it superficially approximates, in starting with an already established perspective, instead of searching for one as it runs its course. It looks outwards, so that self-revelation appears incidental. It takes the form of a one-sided conversation – half of a dialogue in which the imagined other participant gets only an implicit hearing. It is an open-ended excerpt from the mind of the speaker: it has, in Robert Langbaum's words, '. . . no necessary beginning and end but only arbitrary limits, limits which do not cut the action off from the events that precede and follow, but shade into those events, suggesting as much as possible of the speaker's whole life and experience'.

The unity of the form is its singleness of viewpoint: there is none of the inward search for such a viewpoint that characterizes the soliloquy and gives that form its very different purpose and possibilities.

Browning mastered, as no one before him, this form, the dramatic monologue. Dylan has used it as no one else since.

Not that the similarity ends there. This is Browning (from *Up At A Villa – Down In The City*):

> Look, two and two go the priests, then the monks with
>   cowls and sandals
> And the penitents dressed in white shirts, a-holding
>   the yellow candles
> One, he carries a flag up straight, and another a cross
>   with handles,
> And the Duke's guard brings up the rear, for the better
>   prevention of scandals.

This is Dylan (from *Subterranean Homesick Blues*):

> Better jump down a manhole
> Light y'self a candle,
> Don't wear sandals,
> Try to avoid the scandals
> Don't wanna be a bum
> Y' better chew gum
> The pump don't work
> 'Cause the vandals
> Took the handles.

When Browning uses such rhyme-schemes, G. K. Chesterton dismisses them as 'only mathematical triumphs, not triumphs of any kind of assonance'. When Dylan writes like that, Ewen McColl pulls a face. Both 'critics' miss the point. The Browning piece works because the rhyme's preposterousness is consciously embraced as part of the irony. Dylan's works similarly. You can't make the effort of rhyming 'manhole' with 'candle' and then pile up sandals, scandals, vandals and handles in such proximity without being deliberate about it. In Dylan's music this purposiveness is complemented by the clipped concentration on four neighbouring notes – a

concentrated musical 'monotony' that very neatly associates itself with the lyric idea of gum-chewing, so that the deadpan element of delivery is double-barrelled.

There is, anyhow, more in the comparison of those two passages than the startling coincidence in rhyming words. If you read out the Browning verse in Bob Dylan's 'Blonde On Blonde' voice (relishing Dylanesque words like 'penitent') you find them perfectly compatible. The brand of irony exhibited is common to both of them.

Elsewhere, this shows up in equally dramatic similarities of technique. Part of Browning's *Bishop Blougram's Apology* runs as follows:

> You Cigadibs, who, thirty years of age
> Write stately for *Blackwood's Magazine*
> Believe you see two points in Hamlet's soul
> Unseized by the Germans yet . . .

In *Ballad of a Thin Man* Dylan sings:

> You've been with the professors and they've all liked your looks
> With great lawyers you have discussed lepers and crooks
> You've bin through all of F. Scott Fitzgerald's books
> You're very well read, it's well known;
> But something is happening here and you don't know what it is,
> Do you, Mr Jones?

These two examples of mockery, adopting almost the same tone of voice – the difference being merely that the Bishop has to sound middle-aged and the Dylan persona sounds younger – become identical in tone when addressing their silent interlocutors. You, Cigadibs. Do you, Mr Jones?

Not only do the techniques resemble each other – and strongly enough to add to the impression that Dylan has looked acquisitively at Robert Browning's work. They are put to comparable uses. Both attack the complacency which makes men use their intellects as blindfolds. Norman Mailer says that people smoke cigarettes to distance themselves from experience; Browning and Dylan maintain that burning up with the theoretical has the same effect. Bishop Blougram reproves Cigadibs for not being alive to the real world; Dylan posits the artificial safeness of vicarious living.

And the same song extends his attack:

> You have many contacts
> Among the lumberjacks
> To get you facts
> When someone attacks
> Your imagination

(*Mathematical* rhymes again, too!)

The same theme is echoed in Dylan's *Tombstone Blues*:

> Now I wish I could write you a melody so plain
> That could hold you, dear lady, from going insane
> That could ease you, and cool you, and cease the pain
> Of your useless and pointless knowledge

and perhaps also in *Temporary Like Achilles*:

> I'm trying to read your poetry
> But I'm helpless like a rich man's child . . .

and again, with a different focus, in *Desolation Row*:

> Her profession's her religion,
> Her sin is her lifelessness

When the irony of Browning, as well as of Dylan, turns to this theme of life versus nullity of experience, the results are comparable more than once. Here is Browning again:

> Lord so-and-so — his coat bedropped with wax
> All Peter's chains about his waist, his back
> Brave with the needlework of Noodledom —
> Believes!

Here is Dylan (again from *Desolation Row*):

> And Ezra Pound and T. S. Eliot
> Fighting in the Captain's tower,
> While calypso singers laugh at them
> And fishermen hold flowers
> Between the windows of the sea
> Where lovely mermaids flow
> And nobody has to think too much
> About Desolation Row

and Browning again:

> you know physics, something of geology,
> Mathematics are your pastime; souls shall rise in their
> degree;
> Butterflies may dread extinction, — you'll not die, it
> cannot be!

In Dylan's *Desolation Row* we have a classic utilization of the dramatic monologue form, with its exposition of how one mind sees the world around it, so that to listen to the song is like watching a film shot entirely from one camera-angle, an angle that would not be our own. But what may consequently appear fantastic is real. Implicitly throughout the song, and explicitly here at the end, Dylan argues the sanity of his 'perverse' perspective:

> Right now I can't read too good
> Don't send me no more letters, no:
> Not unless you mail them from
> Desolation Row.

In this, Dylan's use of the dramatic conforms to Browning's use of it. The differences are in the scope of the form in the hands of the two artists.

Browning usually identifies the narrator and his environment explicitly; Dylan often fills in these details only implicitly – frequently using a belated introduction of his persona's position to achieve a particular effect. Thus in *Desolation Row* it is only in the final verse that the persona dwells on his own position at all, and it is sprung on the listener that the whole song has been communicating on a person-to-person, and intensely personal, level:

> When you asked me how I was doing
> Was that some kind of joke?

And as we come upon this deliberately held-back switch from an apparently generally polemical dream to the personal pressing involvement of 'you', 'me' and 'I', the urgency and power of the vision Dylan offers is effectively magnified.

In *Gates of Eden* the technique is the same. The last stanza so fixes the perspective that the rest of the song is thrown back upon us, with a demand for an immediate re-assessment. The end of the song gives us the narrator's reflection that

> At times I think there are no words
> But these to tell what's true
> And there are no truths outside the gates of Eden.

and, quoting Steve MacDonogh's comments,

> we are brought back to the starting-point of the monologue, where

> > 'The truth just twists
> > Its curfew gull just glides.'

> ... [and we] are made to examine what has gone before, the mention of
> the speaker's lover – providing the dramatic location of the song –
> bringing us back to a more concrete ... level of understanding.

Another difference in the use to which Browning and Dylan put the dramatic monologue is that whereas Browning projects varied fictional characters, Dylan, like other modern poets, projects himself. This is one reason why – as, in fact, with F. Scott Fitzgerald, whose fictional heroes were largely himself from the unfortunate Anthony Patch to the unfortunate Mr Hobby – it is exceptionally difficult, and not necessarily worth trying for, to distinguish the work from the man.

There is a consequent further divergence between Browning's conventions and Dylan's. With Browning, the silent interlocutor is not merely silent but actually unnecessary. A mere tip of the hat to Victorian expectations. In contrast, Dylan's 'silent' interlocutor is not merely eloquent in helping to draw out the narrator's mood and predicament, but in many cases has a felt presence the exploration of which is central to the song's purpose.

In his songs to women, where they are the 'silent' ones, the portrayal of their characters is a main ingredient. On 'Blonde On Blonde', for example, the image of a particular woman is deliberately established by the one-sided dialogue in *Most Likely You Go Your Way And I'll Go Mine*:

> You say my kisses are not like his
> But this time I'm not gonna tell you why that is
> I'm just gonna let you pass
> Yes and I'll go last

By attributing to the woman the clichéd thought exposed in that first line, this 'exchange' shows itself as much concerned to colour in the woman as the narrator himself.

The same emphasis of purpose is apparent in many other songs – in *4th Time Around*, where two women are portrayed in this extraordinarily implying way; in *One Of Us Must Know (Sooner Or Later)*; *Leopard-Skin Pill-Box Hat*; *I'll Be Your Baby Tonight* to some extent; and perhaps most of all in *Positively 4th Street*:

> You see me on the street,
> You always act surprised;
> You say How Are You – Good Luck!
> But you don't mean it
> When you know as well as me
> You'd rather see me paralysed:
> Why don't you just come out once and scream it?

The effect, in this passage, hardly depends at all on the 'How are you?' and the 'Good Luck!' that the woman is permitted to actually *say*: the force of his portrayal comes from that masterfully irregular last line. Its length and pent-up cadence half-echo, half-mimic the scream she won't reveal: effectively, we see it in her eyes, hear it in her head, and we can see her standing there.

In all these songs, we see the women's faces, as we never do with Browning's Cigadibs.

Abandoning the dramatic monologue at this suitable juncture, it has to be said that there are two other notable corridors between Dylan's work and Robert Browning's. The first is their equal relish for the blatantly grotesque.

Chesterton, thinking of Behemoth in the book of Job, wrote that '. . . the notion of the hippopotamus as a household pet is curiously in the spirit of the humour of Browning.' It has the appeal of incongruity, and this scatters itself throughout Browning's work, in rhymes, names, ludicrous alliteration (that 'needlework of Noodledom') and in a Puckish garlanding together of temperamental incompatibles, as in *The Cardinal and the Dog*. In this short poem, the Cardinal lies on his death-bed at Verona and cries out aloud to try to stop 'a black Dog of vast bigness, eyes flaming' from jumping all over the sheets.

It is an area of humour Dylan enjoys as fully. His sense of the grotesque continually invades his visions both of carefree living ('Saddle me up a big white goose/Tie me on her and turn her loose') and of Apocalypse.

There is the common circus imagery – camels, clowns, freaks, masked faces, organ-grinders, dwarfs and 'the phantom of the opera': plus physically normal people with their trousers down, from the President of the United States to Dylan himself: 'They asked me for some collateral an' I pulled down my pants.'

There is also a celebration of the incongruous in Dylan's work that echoes

Browning as much as anyone. *Leopard-Skin Pill-Box Hat* devotes itself to this mood. It isn't only the panache of, say, 'You know it balances on your head just like a mattress balances on a bottle of wine' sung with appropriate top-heaviness (Chaplin on a tightrope) as just one line within a formal 3-line, 12-bar framework. It's also the obvious pleasure taken in Dylan – prophet, visionary, seer – singing a whole song about someone's ridiculous hat.

This same mood, Dylan as Puck, also figures beguilingly in songs like *Million Dollar Bash* – where a Browning-like alliterative lunacy is much in evidence. The needlework of Noodledom lives!:

> Well that big dumb blonde
> With her wheel gorged
> And Turtle, that friend of theirs
> With his cheques all forged
> And his cheeks in a chunk
> With his cheese in the cash
> They're all gonna meet
> At that Million Dollar Bash

Serenading the ludicrous is, with more restraint and subtlety, a major ingredient in the brilliant *The Drifter's Escape*, from 'John Wesley Harding'. It is both here, in the idea of the attendant and the nurse crying out in chorus and in the inanity of that chorus itself:

> 'Oh stop that cursèd jury,'
> Cried the attendant and the nurse
> 'The trial was bad enou-u-u-ugh
> But this is ten times worse!'

(which captures perfectly the vagary of Browning) and at the end, where the 'explanation' of the drifter's escape is absurdly fortuitous in the same way as Shakespeare's famous device for getting a character in *A Winter's Tale* off the stage – 'Exit pursued by a bear':

> Just then a bolt of lightning
> Struck the courthouse out of shape
> And while everybody knelt to pray
> The drifter did escape.

There is, finally, a more serious feature of most of Dylan's work that reaches back to Browning – to Browning the archetypal Victorian in experiencing (like Dorothea Brooke in George Eliot's *Middlemarch*) 'aspiration without an object'. Experiencing, that is, religious ardour without being able to focus it on traditional Christianity. Unable to worship God, George Eliot consecrated duty. Faced with the same predicament, Browning idealized love. So did Dylan.

As Houghton explains it in his fine re-assessing book, *The Victorian Frame of Mind*:

> In an age of transition in which crucial problems, both practical and
> theoretical, exercised the thinking mind at the expense of the sensibility,
> and in which baffled thought so often issued in a feeling of impotence
> and a mood of despair, the thinker could find in love a resolution of
> psychological tensions, and a religion . . . to take the place of
> Christianity.

The first hint of this process at work in Dylan comes at the end of the 'John Wesley

Harding' album, where the agonized search for a more noble America ends in 'Close your eyes, close the door'.

Browning substitutes for Christianity a conception of fulfilment which demands that intellect and feeling be fused and interdependent – and this conception the pre-Born Again Dylan shares. In *Men And Women* Browning writes: 'Where the heart is, let the brain lie also' – which could well be a Dylan aphorism. In Browning's *Paracelsus* the hero embodies knowledge and Aprile embodies love. Paracelsus tells Aprile:

> . . . We must never part.
> Are we not halves of one dissevered world
> Whom this strange chance unites once more?
>   Part? never!
> Till thou the lover, knows; and I, the knower
> Love – until both are saved.

The same idea of partnership colours all of Dylan's love songs. He addresses his lovers intelligently, demanding the engagement of their intellects, and the strength of his feeling, in such addresses, can be gauged by his openness in doing so.

This is plain from a song like the unreleased *I'll Keep It With Mine* (1964):

> I can't help it if you might think I'm odd
> If I say I'm loving you not for what you are
> But for what you're not

from *Wedding Song* a decade later, from *Oh Sister* (1976), and from *You're A Big Girl Now* (1975):

> Love is so simple
> (To quote a phrase)
> You've known it all the time
> I'm learning it these days

and, with a distinctive demanding intensity, from the final urging stanza of *Changing Of The Guards* (1978):

> Peace will come with tranquillity and splendour
> On the wheels of fire
> But will offer no reward when the false idols fall
> And cruel death surrenders
> With its pale ghost retreating
> Between the king and queen of swords.

The mutual exploration of Bishop Blougram and Cigadibs mixes thought and emotion just as Paracelsus mixes with Aprile; and there we have the same characteristic mixture in Dylan's appraisals and 'dialogues': his addresses to women deal in a combined judgement on emotional and intellectual worth ('You just want to be on the side that's winning') – partly because honesty in emotion is dependent on a lack of dishonesty in thought. When Dylan admires, he admires both intellect and feeling; when he denigrates, both are scorned. The scorn is made graphically clear in *Positively 4th Street*, *Dirge* and *Idiot Wind*.

In the context of this elevation of love, Houghton's account is enlightening in terms of the whole tone of the 'Nashville Skyline' album. Add to that account the upshot of that quotation from Paracelsus – he ends his speech on the word 'saved' – and lines like these become clear:

> One more night,
> I will wait for the light.

'Nashville Skyline' admits the failure of 'John Wesley Harding's' attempt to find psychic salvation in the myths of a bygone America, back in that continent's uncorrupted past. That quest has failed and the Dylan of 'Nashville Skyline' has re-directed his search towards fulfilment through love. As with the Victorians, that way lies salvation. 'Love is all there is'.

Correspondingly, when Dylan comes, at the end of the 1970s, to seek his salvation through Christ after all, he recognizes that what remains constant is the aspiration, and that it is only the object of it that changes. This is stressed on *Saving Grace*, from the 'Saved' album (1980).

> But to search for love – that ain't no more than vanity
> As I look around this world all that I'm finding
> Is the saving grace that's over me.

[The poets of nineteenth-century England share something else with Dylan and his contemporaries: the use of drugs. I don't know whether Browning used opium (or, like the eminently respectable Sherlock Holmes, cocaine), but his wife, at least, took both morphine and opium on regular prescription, and it is well enough known that the earlier Romantics got stoned a good deal: and this does provide an obvious theme for comparison with an artist like Dylan today. The fieldwork on the Romantics in this respect has been done by Alethea Hayter's book *Opium And The Romantic Imagination* (Faber) and more than one commentator has provided some speculative comparing of that era with our own in a drugs context, including Kenneth Allsop in a piece in *Encounter* magazine called 'The Technicolour Wasteland'.]

There is another Victorian whom Dylan's work occasionally recalls – namely, Lewis Carroll.

If, for instance, a substantial portion of Dylan's *The Drifter's Escape* seems to remind one vaguely of the pack-of-cards trial scene in 'Alice', this is principally because it echoes the knowingly preposterous tone (and the metre) of many of the Lewis Carroll verses. The Dylan lines begin with this:

> Well the judge he cast his robe aside
> A tear came to his eye
> 'You'd fail to understand,' he said
> 'Why must you even try?'

and *The Lobster Quadrille* includes this:

> 'What matters it how far we go?' his scaly friend replied.
> 'There is another shore, you know, upon the other side . . .'

where the Dylan tune fits as if purpose-built – as indeed it does the verses read as 'evidence' in the card-pack trial; and it's easy to imagine Dylan singing this one:

> He sent them word I had not gone
> (We know it to be true):
> If she should push the matter on
> What would become of you?

Resemblance extends also through much of the *Walrus And The Carpenter* poem; and finally, while the song about Tweedledum and Tweedledee ends with these lines:

> Just then flew down a monstrous crow
> As black as a tar-barrel
> Which frightened both the heroes so
> They quite forgot their quarrel

the Dylan song ends like this:

> Just then a bolt of lightning
> Struck the courthouse out of shape
> And while everybody knelt to pray
> The drifter did escape.

As, now, for affiliations with Eliot, well, the finely chiselled language of Dylan owes something emphatic to the tutoring of Eliot's early poetry; but the first thing to be said is this: Folk-rock was Dylan's *Prufrock*.

With it, Dylan – like Eliot in 1917 – was alone in answering the demands of the times for a new poetry.

Prufrock threw away 'the canons of the poetical' and made nonsense of the distinction between 'seriousness' and 'levity' in art. It broke the rules laid down by tradition as to what the language of poetry should be. Folk-rock broke the rules again, and with similar results (even to the early hostility of academics to Eliot being echoed in the initial response to 'the electric Dylan').

It used 'pop' as opposed to 'serious' music, and married it to fresh language, including much slang and entailing a full use of the double-meanings and double-imagery of cult terms – especially drug terms. (For example, 'railroad' used also to mean the vein into which heroin, etc, is injected.) The result was 'poetry that freely expresses a modern sensibility, the . . . modes of experience of one fully alive in his own age.' That description was written nearly fifty years ago, to cover Eliot's early

work. It is every bit as accurate a comment on 'Highway 61 Revisited' and 'Blonde On Blonde'.

The other affiliations between Dylan and Eliot stem from this. There is the attempt to turn formlessness into form itself. *The Waste Land* tries it openly; Dylan's attempts are usually checked by his allegiance to regular verses – a musical check on his lyrics. But though they may be regular, the verses of a song like *Subterranean Homesick Blues* are hardly conventional – and the departure from convention reflects the attempt to interpret the formlessness of the age. 'I accept chaos,' Dylan wrote on the album cover of 'Bringing It All Back Home': 'I am not sure whether it accepts me.'

Allied with the formlessness is the uprooting, urbanizing process dealt with earlier in this chapter – and so Dylan shares with Eliot the use of urban imagery and the expression of urban dissillusion.

Eliot first developed this in poems like *Preludes* (from the 'Prufrock' collection):

> The morning comes to consciousness
> Of faint stale smells of beer
> From the sawdust-trampled street
> With all its muddy feet that press
> To early coffee-stands

Dylan begins his *Visions Of Johanna* with:

> Ain't it just like the night
> To play tricks when you're tryin' to be so quiet
> We sit here stranded
> We're all doin' our best to deny it . . .
> In this room the heat-pipes just cough
> The country music station plays soft
> But there's nothing
> Really nothing to turn off

Yet only occasionally do you catch, in Eliot, the feeling of warmness towards language that is a Dylan trademark and which, in the context of urban disillusion, gives an added complexity and force to Dylan's work.

Not surprisingly, it is only in his early work that you come across a passage of Eliot's that Dylan might have written. An instance can be found in an early poem *Rhapsody on a Windy Night*. Dylan could have written some of this:

> Along the reaches of the street . . .
> Every street lamp that I pass
> Beats like a fatalistic drum,
> And through the spaces of the dark
> Midnight shakes the memory
> As a madman shakes a dead geranium.
>
> . . . The street-lamp said, 'Regard that woman
> Who hesitates toward you in the light of the door
> Which opens on her like a grin.
> You see the border of her dress
> Is torn and stained with sand . . .'

That leaves no doubt about the influence of Eliot on Dylan. It's plainly a source of direct strength, carrying the tutor's message: chisel your language. And Dylan has certainly done it:

Idiot wind
Blowin' like a circle around my skull
From the Grand Coulee Dam to the Capitol . . .

Down the road to ecstasy
I followed you beneath the stars
Hounded by your memory
And all your ragin' glory
. . . I kiss goodbye the howling beast
On the borderline
That separated you from me
(*Idiot Wind*).

Again:

He sits in your room, his tomb
With a fist full of tacks
Preoccupied with his vengeance
Cursing the dead that can't answer him back
You know that he has no intentions
Of looking your way
Unless it's to say that he needs you
To test his inventions
(*Can You Please Crawl Out Your Window*).

Or again — and here bringing in Eliot's use of allusion:

Yonder stands your orphan with his gun,
Crying like a fire in the sun.
Look out, the saints are coming through
And it's all over now, Baby Blue.

The highway is for gamblers, better use your sense.
Take what you have gathered from coincidence.
The vagabond who's rapping at your door
Is standing in the clothes that you once wore:
Strike another match, go.
Start anew;
And it's all over now, Baby Blue.

That this influence has been direct is in any case confirmed by Dylan's allusions to
Eliot's phrases. That oddly-presented 'geranium' crops up again in *Sad-Eyed Lady of
the Lowlands*; in *Visions of Johanna*, there are echoes of *The Waste Land*'s handful of
dust: Marie holds a handful of rain.

In the room the women come and go
Talking of Michaelangelo

writes Eliot: Dylan's *All Along The Watchtower* changes the tense:

While all the women came and went.

This kind of obtuse allusion-making is, of course, a game that Eliot himself perfected.
In the third section of *The Waste Land*, for instance, he writes:

To Carthage then I came
Burning burning burning burning

which, subtly enough for most of us, quotes from St Augustine's *Confessions*:

> To Carthage then I came, where a cauldron of
> unholy loves sang all about mine ears . . .

while in Dylan's *The Wicked Messenger*, the hero comes from Eli—like the boy Samuel to the Israelites at Shiloh—with a note which reads: 'The soles of my feet, I swear they're burning'. It is no coincidence that Dylan's song *I Dreamed I Saw St Augustine* is so faithful to the spirit of the Augustine Eliot evocation.

The clearest of Dylan's cross-references occurs in the penultimate verse of *Desolation Row* (a title, of course, not unlike *The Waste Land*)—the verse that does more than simply mention Eliot specifically:

> And Ezra Pound and T.S. Eliot
> Fighting in the captain's tower . . .
> Between the windows of the sea
> Where lovely mermaids flow
> And nobody has to think too much about
> Desolation Row.

This parallels the ending of *The Love Song of J. Alfred Prufrock*:

> We have lingered in the chambers of the sea
> By sea-girls wreathed with seaweed red and brown
> Till human voices wake us, and we drown.

Same imagery, same contrast, same argument.

As for what Dylan has taken from the mainstream of *American* literature—well what a strange thing that is. So little of it before the twentieth century and such a vast amount of it in the last eighty years. To deal with modern American poetry alone would take a whole book (so that what follows can only hope to provide some kind of eccentric, personalized outline), while there has also been a formidable amount of the kind of quick, urban prose that one side of Bob Dylan enjoys so much and has taken some strengths from—Guthrie's own autobiography (already dealt with elsewhere in this study); Steinbeck; Nathanael West (to whom Dylan made acknowledgement by calling one of his 'New Morning' songs *Day Of The Locusts*); Chandler; Kerouac; Damon Runyan; Dos Passos; Fitzgerald; Mailer; Miller; Burroughs; and so on and so on right through to Hunter S. Thompson.

My outline restricts itself therefore to some elements of American poetry and their impingement on Dylan's songwriting scope.

There are two difficulties with this, in terms of pre-twentieth century US poetry.

The first is that so much of it echoes *English* literature anyway. Edward Taylor, often regarded as America's first great poet, was born in England. Emerson didn't begin writing poetry until after he had travelled abroad, touring Italy and meeting Coleridge, Carlyle and Wordsworth in England. Longfellow was a professor of modern languages and literature, spent a lot of time in foreign travel and pursuing an absorption with European literature, and as a poet offers obvious resemblances to Tennyson. Edgar Allan Poe went to school in England and worked outside the sphere of the reigning Boston-New York literati of his day. It was among British poets and critics that Whitman found his first admirers, and after the long period of disfavour into which his work fell after his death, it was in response to D.H. Lawrence's marvellous book *Studies In Classic American Literature* that Whitman was readmitted to the American poetic pantheon of greats.

After Whitman, it is true, there is a large amount of truly American poetry, but then come Pound and Eliot and the Lost Generation, all trying to be unAmerican in Europe.

The other difficulty we come across, in measuring the influence on Bob Dylan's work of pre-twentieth century American poetry, is that the balladry of that poetry is so close to the traditions of folk-song as to make it impossible to say where Dylan derives from the one or from the other.

A poem like Vachel Lindsay's *Simon Legree – A Negro Sermon*, for instance, finds an echo in early Dylan material such as *Black Cross*, but the echo can as well be traced back to the folk-songs which Dylan absorbed.

So let's begin where the echo is clearer – with Emerson. As an Englishman, I automatically link the pantheism of Dylan's *Lay Down Your Weary Tune* with Wordsworth; but looking at the equivalent nineteenth-century poetry written by Americans and today learnt by American middle-class children in schools, it is the pantheism of Ralph Waldo Emerson that shines out just as brightly – revealing at once a source of inspiration and tradition for that excellent Dylan song.

> I inhaled the violet's breath,
> Around me stood the oaks and firs;
> Pine cones and acorns lay on the ground;
> Over me soared the eternal sky,
> Full of light and deity;
> Again I say, again I heard,
> The rolling river, the morning bird; –
> Beauty through my senses stole;
> I yielded myself to the perfect whole.

(*Each And All*, Emerson.)

> I stood unwound beneath the skies
> And clouds unbound by laws. . .
> I gazed into the river's mirror
> And watched its winding strum. . .
> The last of leaves fell from the trees
> And clung to a new love's breast

(*Lay Down Your Weary Tune*, Dylan.)

Another correspondence occurs, between Emerson's *Goodbye*:

> Goodbye to Flattery's fawning face. . .
> To crowded halls, to court and street
> To frozen hearts and hasting feet

and Dylan's *Wedding Song*:

> I've said goodbye to haunted rooms
> And faces in the street
> To the courtyards of the Jester. . .

And then of course there is Longfellow, and his reputation's millstone, *Hiawatha*, which jingles in the memory as rhythm – the rhythm that is the basis of so much American song.

It is a rhythm that suggests the music-and-words art; it does not stubbornly insist on its words-on-the-page lineage.

No only *Hiawatha*. Poems like *Hymn To The Night*, *The Day Is Done*, *My Lost Youth*, *The Fire Of Driftwood*, *The Bells Of San Blas*, *The Arrow And The Song*, *The*

Ropewalk — all have their primacy in jingling rhythms that wield assured, consistent drum-beats.

And drummed into the memory from schooldays, this tradition of words as parts of song — of words as music — acts as a momentum of inspiration, however unconscious it may be, for Dylan. Longfellow's is the literary voice that murmurs underneath, just as, from the oral tradition, the old folk-song patterns do.

It isn't odd, therefore, that specific snatches of Longfellow can be read in Dylan's artist-voice, nor that it is less a matter of conscious technique that matches than a matter of *ease of tone* (derived from the rhythmic familiarity) and *ease of vocabulary* (derived from the familiarity of the voice that Longfellow gave to American writing).

Here is such a snatch, from Longfellow's *The Day Is Done*:

> I see the lights of the village
> Gleam through the rain and the mist
> And a feeling of sadness comes o'er me
> That my soul cannot resist.

The ease of tone and of vocabulary there correspond so completely to the exhibition of the same qualities in Dylan's writing that no one would be surprised if Dylan had himself written exactly those lines anywhere on a 1970s album such as 'New Morning' or 'Planet Waves' or even 'Blood On The Tracks'.

And it is the same milieu entirely — the same operation of ease of tone and vocabulary upon the *careful* straightforwardness of what is being said — that Dylan gives us in the better parts of *Sara*, on 'Desire':

> Now the beach is deserted except for some kelp
> And the wreck of an old ship that lies on the shore
> You always responded when I needed your help
> You gave me a map and a key to your door.

The rhythmic melody of that song, moreover, is itself an exact echo of Longfellow's *Curfew*:

> No voice in the chambers
> No sound in the hall!
> Sleep and oblivion
> Reign over all!
> The book is completed
> And closed, like the day
> And the hand that has written it
> Lays it away.

As for the mood and vocabulary of *that*, well what could be more quintessentially Dylanesque?

What of Walt Whitman? Only this: that it is Whitman's insistence on the interminable-list-as-poetry that made possible Dylan's *A Hard Rain's Gonna Fall* and *Chimes of Freedom* and the whole idea of the 12-minute rock song, which seems suddenly to arise out of nowhere (or out of the longer old folk-ballads) from a context of 2½-minute pop songs. *Leaves Of Grass* compared with a conventional poem parallels *Desolation Row* compared with a normal pop song. Plus, of course, it is Whitman's egocentricity displayed as length which makes possible also Allen Ginsberg's *Howl*, itself a major influence on Dylan's mid-60s work (as I suggest in more detail shortly).

But it is the echo of Edgar Allan Poe that hangs emphatically over Dylan's later work, for good and ill.

Poe's short poem *To Helen*, of which everyone knows two lines, usually without knowing where or whom they come from, is the simple key – removing the puzzle of them – to all those embarrassingly florid pseudo-classical phrases of Dylan's that sit so uneasily in the choruses of *Sara*.

Where Helen is addressed in terms of

> Thy hyacinth hair, thy classic face
> Thy Naiad airs . . .

which Poe says have brought him home

> To the glory that was Greece
> And the grandeur that was Rome

(the lines everyone knows, of course) and adds:

> How statue-like I see thee stand. . .
> Ah, Psyche, from the regions which
> Are Holy Land!

so Sara is bombarded with:

> Sweet Virgin Angel. . .
> Radiant jewel, mystical wife

and

> Scorpio Sphinx in a calico dress

and

> Glamorous nymph with an arrow and bow.

Poe's influence has also been to the good – and very strong and direct it is too. It is the heart of Poe's stunning, direct confidence with rhymes, and particularly internal rhymes, that Dylan so positively inherits.

The tour-de-force example of Dylan's *No Time To Think* (1978):

> I've seen all these decoys through a set of deep turquoise
> Eyes and I feel so depressed. . .

> The bridge that you travel on goes to the Babylon
> Girl with the rose in her hair. . .

> Stripped of all virtue as you crawl through the dirt you
> Can give but you cannot receive. . .

is precursed by that of Poe's scintillating *The Raven*:

> And the silken sad uncertain rustling of each purple curtain
> Thrilled me – filled me with fantastic terrors never felt before
> So that now, to still the beating of my heart, I stood repeating
> 'Tis some visitor entreating entrance at my chamber door—'

After Poe, there is a dramatic gap, except for one or two minor items which touch a little on Dylan's art. Them aside, the gap seems to me to last through all of the American poetry that came between Poe's death in 1849 and Kenneth Patchen's emergence in the mid-1930s.

The minor items? Well, first Vachel Lindsay, already mentioned. Second, Mr Edwin Arlington Robinson – not a name bandied about much these days, but, like Poe and Whitman, a self-taught poet (and a Pulitzer prize-winning one at that), the bulk of whose work was achieved between 1910 and 1935, after an earlier career on the New York subways.

His poems forge the way either directly or via his influence on older ballads for something in Dylan's early song-writing. Robinson's short, sharp, quirky poems like *Richard Cory*, *Reuben Bright*, *Charles Carville's Eyes* – these contain those little detonations of observation which Dylan echoes in the better flashes of his hobo-hero, old-friend-hero songs.

(This is from *Richard Cory*:

> And he was always quietly arrayed
> And he was always human when he talked;
> But still he fluttered pulses when he said
> 'Good morning', and he glittered when he walked.)

The echo of Robinson is perhaps not a point to insist upon. It is more in the nature of a hunch, a suggestion of a link there somehow, and offering it is simply to go along with F.R. Leavis' definition of the critic's task – that of saying/asking: 'This is so, isn't it?'

The other minor correspondence I'd offer is that between e.e. cummings and Dylan. There's the superficial correspondence of cummings' long obtuse titles (*If Up's The Word*; *And A World Grows Greener*) and Dylan's (*It Takes A Lot To Laugh, It Takes A Train To Cry*) but when it comes down to it, cummings' are in each case titles that are the opening line of the poem in question; with Dylan, such titles are wilfully cryptic summaries of the mood contained in the song concerned.

But beyond that, I think it is a tone of pushy assertiveness that cummings often resorts to:

> his flesh was flesh his blood was blood;
> no hungry man but wished him food;
> no cripple wouldn't creep one mile
> uphill to only see him smile

(from *My Father Moved Through Dooms Of Love*)

that Dylan debases further into those sentimentalized portraits of hobo-saints and friends in early songs like *Only A Hobo* and *He Was A Friend Of Mine* and which he returns to, for instance, in *Hurricane* and *Joey* on the 'Desire' album in 1976.

We come next to Kenneth Patchen, and in doing so we move, even more so than in alighting on e.e. cummings, from the kind of American poetry that is taught in schools, and comes from what can be called the academic mainstream, to the kind of poetry that you find for yourself after you've left school. Patchen's work was done in the 1930s-50s and beyond, and he was, if such a thing is possible, typical of the jazz-influenced, jazz-culture-influenced generation of writers who ended up being called the Beat Generation.

It is my very unremarkable thesis that Patchen, Kerouac and Allen Ginsberg between them constructed an artistic milieu which Dylan, twenty-odd years later, seemed so avant-garde in launching upon a mass market and a new generation. The Dylan of 1965-66 swims in a milieu taken from these three men and their contemporaries. In a way all Dylan did with it was to put it up on stage with a guitar. His greatness lies in the way he did that, the cohesive, individual voice with which he re-presented it and the brilliance of his timing in doing so.

In Patchen's case, his influence on Dylan, whether direct or not, is first of all evident throughout Dylan's novel *Tarantula*. This, for example, would fit well anywhere inside that excellent book:

I knew the General only by name of course.
I said Wartface what have you done with her?
I said You Dirtylouse tell me where is she now?
His duck-eyes shifted to the guard. All right, Sam.
. . .Who is that fat turd I said – he hit me with his jewelled fist.
While his man held me he put a lighted cigarette on my eyelid.
I smelt the burning flesh through his excellent perfume.
On the wall it said 'Democracy must be saved at all costs.'
The floor was littered with letters of endorsement from liberals.

(and of course there's that direct cigarette-eyelid connection, that Dylan resuscitates in *Memphis Blues Again* – just as a phrase of Patchen's, which opens his poem *Beautiful You Are*: 'Cathedral evening', is used unaltered in Dylan's *Chimes Of Freedom*).

This, too, would pass for Dylan's work in *Tarantula*:

When they fitted the black cap over his head
He knew that he'd never have another chance to be president.

(It is from Patchen's *All The Bright Foam Of Talk*.)

Dylan inherits ideas from Patchen too, I think – or again, perhaps just from the milieu that Patchen was a creative part of. The poem *The Rites Of Darkness* encompasses a lot of Dylan's Gemini-schizoid feelings about the glamour of urban wickedness and decadence and at the same time the ever-visible presence of God, and about the nature of truth and beauty.

But no one sees the giant horse
That climbs the steps which stretch forth
Between the calling lights and that hill
Straight up to the throne of God

offers a notion that Dylan restated in the terrific *Three Angels*:

The angels play on their horns all day. . .
But does anyone hear the music they play?

while this, from Patchen's poem:

We can't believe in anything
Because nothing is pure enough.
Because nothing will ever happen
To make us good in our own sight.

encapsulates succinctly attitudes Dylan has touched on many times, from the poem about Joan Baez through to *Dirge* and *Shelter From The Storm* where

Beauty walks a razor's edge
Some day I'll make it mine
If I could only turn back the clock. . .

I think, then, though I've never come across anyone who has said so, except Gaye Goodchild in an essay on *Tarantula*, that Dylan has inherited something of both style and content from Patchen, and from that tradition of American poetry in which you let the poem write itself, as it were.

And as it says on the dust-jacket of my copy of *The Selected Poems Of Kenneth Patchen*, his work focuses on 'his direct and passionate concern with the most essential elements in the tragic, comic, blundering and at rare moments glorious

world around us. He wrote about the things we can feel with our whole being – the senselessness of war, the need for love among men on earth, the presence of God in man, the love for a beloved woman, social injustice, and the continual resurgence of the beautiful in life.' Which is precisely what can reasonably be said (though one might not choose to express it quite like that) about the recurrent concerns in Dylan's work.

Ginsberg too, more than Corso or Ferlinghetti, and as much as Patchen or Kerouac, opens for Dylan, and for his whole generation, the window on the bright, babbling, surreal, self-indulgent, sleazy, intensely alert world that no predecessor had pointed to. *Howl* (1956) might not have been possible without Whitman, but Dylan's debt to *Howl* is far greater than Ginsberg's to *Leaves Of Grass*.

The world that opened up here:

> . . .who jumped in limousines with the Chinaman of Oklahoma on the
> impulse of winter midnight streetlight smalltown rain,
> . . .who went out whoring through Colorado in myriad stolen nightcars. . .
> . . .who faded out in vast sordid movies, were shifted in dreams, woke on a
> sudden Manhattan, and picked themselves up out of basements hungover
> with heartless Tokay and horrors of Third Avenue iron dreams. . .

– there is not one line from this huge sprawling poem that cannot claim to be the deranged inspired midwife of the Dylan of the mid-1960s, the Dylan of 'the motorcycle black madonna two-wheel gypsy queen', and all the rest.

Dylan's achievement, subsequently, of course, has included the remarkable fact of his being able to turn right round and become a major influence on Allen Ginsberg, as Ginsberg's liner-notes to Dylan's 'Desire' album testify. And it is precious rarely in American literature (or any other literature for that matter) that that sort of generational turn-around happens.

With Robbie Robertson of The Hawks (later The Crackers, later The Band), Michael McClure and Allen Ginsburg; in San Francisco, 1965.

Chapter 4
Dylan and Rock Music

'You might make it on your own but you don't make
it with this band: you're fired,' said Bobby Vee
to Bob Dylan, who had, till that moment, been his
pianist for a while. Or so the story goes.

IT WAS ROCK-A-DAY JOHNNY SINGIN' TELL YOUR MA, TELL YOUR PA,
OUR LOVE'S A-GONNA GROW WAH WAH...

Pop history isn't about a social phenomenon. Who cares whether Nik Cohn's
ancestors ripped up cinema seats for Bill Haley, or whether that was storming
bastilles of post-war tedium? The sociological approach gets you nowhere: the music
is what matters.

So Bill Haley is utterly unimportant. His influence was nil because his musical
value was nil. He failed to make it because his music was boring and his voice was
about as riveting as a dishcloth. When rock took off, it wasn't thanks to Bill Haley.

Rock happened as a strange appealing mixture of 'race' and country music. Mix
Fats Domino with Hank Williams and you get the beginning of rock 'n' roll. (In fact,
that very combination occurred. The song *Jambalaya* uses creole language but was
written by Hank Williams; Fats Domino's version is a true classic.)

But rock took off *en masse* for whites because of Elvis Presley. Without Presley,
Bill Haley's thing would have been a nine-day blunder, like the Twist, and just as
false; without Haley, Elvis would still have been a massive original talent. It simply
wasn't Haley in 1955 that mattered, it was Presley in 1956 – and even the *Billboard*
charts bear this out.

Rock Around The Clock topped the US Hot 100 in '55 only to be followed for the
rest of that year by appalling Mitch Miller, the Four Aces, the saccharine piano of
Roger Williams and the saccharine gravel of Tennessee Ernie Ford. Nineteen fifty-six
began just as comfortably, with Dean Martin. Then – the false craze exposed – Kay
Starr climbed up there with her peekaboo *Rock 'n' Roll Waltz*, just as Frank Sinatra
and Ella Fitzgerald were to yawn in on the Twist craze in 1962, crooning in the
coffin-nails. After Kay Starr, it was naturally back to dinner-suits with the Nelson
Riddle Orchestra and Les Baxter.

And that would have been that, but for *Heartbreak Hotel*, Presley's second single
but his first nation-wide release. It owed as much to Bill Haley as Dylan owes to
Ringo Starr, and on its own, it transformed the US charts and more besides. (The
Number Ones that succeeded it that year were *Hound Dog* and *Don't Be Cruel*, both
by Presley, the Platters' *My Prayer* and back to Elvis for *Love Me Tender*.) Popular
music was forced to notice that the Second World War had come and gone. The give-
me-the-moonlight regime was vanquished.

Presley became the prototype: rock 'n' roll was made in his image.

In England, to begin with, Tommy Steele was supposed to be an Elvis: and in his
attempts he focused on one of the changes that happened when popular music went
pop. Before, you had to enunciate – every word had to be heard, though why that
should have been the case is difficult to imagine, not only because the words so
carefully delivered weren't generally worth any attention. It's quite impossible,
after all, to distinguish words sung in opera, so that it hardly matters whether an

opera is performed in English, Italian or Urdu. With pop, language regained its operatic function. The meaning of words, as a general rule, mattered less than their sounds, and the voice became an instrument. The grown-ups who laughed at Presley's 'mumbling' didn't understand. It was actually nice to have part of the record where you didn't know what you were singing when you sang along with it. I still can't make out all the words on lots of '50s records that I know, as records, very well. For instance, in *Let's Jump The Broomstick*, by Brenda Lee, there is what sounds to me like this:

> Gonna Alabama
> Getcha-catcha-kamma

Who needs to translate? – it's perfectly satisfying left like that.

(This revised usage of words was another Presley innovation: on Bill Haley's records, you can hear every word, from 'one o'clock' right through to 'twelve o'clock rock'.)

So there was Tommy Steele, back in England in 1957, trying to be Elvis Presley and therefore very consciously slurring the words. Only Tommy Steele did it, of course, like any Cockney novice would, by leaving out all the consonants. It sounded, on his smash hit *Singing The Blues*, like this:

> Weeeeeeeeeeeeeeeeeeeeelllllll –
> I never felt more like a-singin' the blues
> CoIe'uroraIe'uoozz
> Your love, dear

And this showed up the whole gigantic difference between American and British pop. The best of the American stars had music that grew out of their own local roots. They picked up genuine skills and techniques unselfconsciously. Their English equivalents always had to imitate. Tommy Steele was hardly from the same world as Elvis Presley: he was the archetypal Cockney, from a decent British slum, whose musical heritage was *Knays Ap Muvvah Braan*, and who sang with a guitar strictly for laughs (at first) when on leave from the Merchant Navy.

Steele was superseded in Britain principally by Cliff Richard, as '6.5 Special' was superseded by Jack Good's 'Oh Boy!'. (It's fashionable to hail Jack Good as a visionary, a pop genius from way back when, but really the only way his show stood out powerfully from the BBC's diffident '6.5 Special' was that Jack Good's studio was dark and trained a spotlight on the performer. Apart from that it was a copy. Lord Rockingham's XI, with their infuriating *Hoots Mon*, equalled asthmatic old Don Lang and his so-called Frantic Five.)

Cliff Richard was like Brigitte Bardot – or rather, like Bardot pretending to be Presley. He had a baby-doll face and pouted a lot. His hair was black, which made him sexier than Tommy Steele straight away, and he had long sideburns (or 'sideboards', as they were often called in England). He wore black shirts and white ties, which gave a little bit of teddy-boy toughness to his image. He wasn't very good at the songs, and his early rock records are hopeless (though this was partly the Shadows' fault). In fact Cliff was so bad that he has consistently improved. All the other big names of the pop '50s have declined in power and artistry; Cliff Richard has grown better and better at timing and phrasing and control. He enjoys the advantage of having had no skill to start with, no basic exciting ingredient to get stale and tired over the years.

The other male solo stars, or would-be stars, who emerged in Britain tended not only to imitate Presley but also to take on names designed to suggest his attributes: Marty Wilde, Billy Fury, Duffy Power, Vince Eager; and later, Robb Storme and, with more subtlety, Lance Fortune and Johnny Gentle.

Yet no matter how hard they copied, they never learnt. As Nik Cohn said, the gulf between America and Britain showed at its widest when Elvis Presley became God and Tommy Steele made it to the London Palladium instead.

In America, Ricky Nelson was pushed as a replacement Presley when Elvis went into the army. Gene Vincent tried it too; so did the very underrated Conway Twitty. Twitty must have been very badly managed, because after his first hit, the million-selling *It's Only Make-Believe*, he went into a rapid decline in popularity until his resuscitation in the US country market of the 1970s – and yet he cut many, many good records, from *Is A Bluebird Blue?* through a great *C'est Si Bon* to the masterly *I Hope I Think I Wish*.

So Presley was not a suffocating influence in America – he got a lot of people started on things that weren't just copies. Duane Eddy said that 'none of us would have got anywhere without Elvis', and Duane Eddy didn't sound at all like Elvis Presley.

The Americans not only had other things to offer; they were also very much smarter than the British, and a lot more independent-minded. (Hard to credit, today, I know.)

Partly, this was because they had vital popular music to draw on, and partly it was because pop in America was never handled through one monopolistic institution.

In America, local radio-stations shaped the pop environment; in Britain, everything was obstructed, diluted, mishandled and misdispensed by BBC Radio, which had no idea what pop music was, didn't know how long it would last, didn't like or approve of it – and so hardly bothered to adapt to its demands. Radio Luxembourg, the only alternative life-line, was little better. Reception was terrible, it was evenings only, and the DJs were mostly the same old men: Jack Jackson, Sam Costa, Pete Murray, plus younger, greasier people who tried to convert you to mainstream jazz. David Gell – a suitable name – had a show where either the title or the slogan was 'Music For Sophisticats'. Imagine what that was like.

In one way Luxembourg really was better than the BBC: it wasn't at the mercy of the infamous Musicians' Union. The BBC was its hapless lackey, and fell in with its insistence that teenagers couldn't hear pop on the radio without listening at the same time to elderly orchestras and 'combos' which were politely said to perform 'live'.

In any case, you have to single out the BBC, because of its hold over Britain's air-waves, as the worst uniformity-machine of all in pop. And all this worked against the individual, the genuinely new, the imaginative and the delicate.

American radio, as compared to the BBC, was very like the American telephone system as compared to telecom, though nowadays most US radio is pretty dreadful – over-formularized through sheer greed. Which goes to show that 'free enterprise' can stifle anything at least as fully as a nationalized industry if it tries. (A good British example is/was the British motorcycle industry, whose death was cheerfully presided over by its management in the teeth of impressive engineering and design teams which were unconsulted and eventually abandoned.)

Variety was also inbuilt for US pop and effectively excluded from its British equivalent because of the record-company situation. In America, there were myriad small companies attuned to local communities and able to breathe because of local radio. By 1961, there were over 6,000 independent labels in America, and consequently hundreds of pop artists got auditioned, recorded, played and popularized who, regardless of their talent, would not have stood a chance in Britain. There, records were in the hands of The Big Four – Decca, EMI, Pye and Philips. It

From the photo session used for an ad for Fender instruments: the only commercial Dylan has ever done. (And then to my knowledge the only time he's ever played bass-guitar. . .).

would be hard to say which was the most blinkered, slow-moving and un-imaginative. They watched each other slavishly, and so exacerbated the imitation process. To imitate was always safer than to innovate, and playing things safe was all they knew. Their reactions to The Beatles showed this well. Decca rejected them because they didn't sound quite like anyone else around at the time. Eventually EMI risked them because hell, what can you lose when you don't have to pay an orchestra for the session? Then bless my soul, people were buying their records! – maybe Eden Kane and Helen Shapiro aren't the right sounds any more! So all the recording managers rushed up to Liverpool – funny place, Liverpool: in the provinces, y'know – to sign up groups like The Beatles. And since they didn't really understand what The Beatles were like, they had to sign up more or less everybody.

Today, an even worse uniformity has crept across America too – but in the '50s and early '60s, American pop was quite a contrast. Even at its most imitative, it had far more variety than British. After Presley, teenage artists sprang up from all over the States, ready and able to revamp almost every form of previous popular music. Not just rockers trying for Presley's toughness and energy but also a good many truly individual voices who saw their chance and took it.

The best, are already legends: Little Richard, Chuck Berry and Jerry Lee Lewis. The many others included Buddy Knox, Lloyd Price and Ricky Nelson.

Nashville country music produced the great Everly Brothers, who first made it big back in 1957 and who still sound good today.

Country pop also provided Don Gibson, John D. Loudermilk, Chet Atkins, Floyd Cramer, Patsy Cline and Skeeter Davis – as well as Johnny Cash and Marty Robbins.

Also from the '50s in America came Neil Sedaka, ex-classical pianist. He had the best, most exciting teenybop sound there was. He moved from *Ring-A-Rockin'* and

1969 Johnny Cash TV Show, with Dylan exhibiting an extraordinary talent for visual mimicry.

92

the amazing *I Go Ape* through to *Calendar Girl* and *Breaking Up Is Hard To Do*.
Brenda Lee was great too. She began recording very young and very raw, producing
Let's Jump The Broomstick and then the great *Sweet Nuthins* (which was, to add a
little fact to all this value-judgement, the last record issued on 78 rpm wax in
England, except for gimmick-issues years afterwards). Then she moved through
exquisite ballads which were still essentially pop.

Late-50s America also promoted a number of groups which found sounds of their
own and which developed these well and independently. The Platters were first.
Later came The Crickets, Fleetwoods, Coasters, Teddy Bears, Danny & The Juniors,
Dion & The Belmonts, and The Drifters. And finally, there were the odd individual
voices – with talents as original in their own ways as Presley's talent was. Sam Cooke,
who was very popular but never popular enough, especially in Britain; Ritchie
Valens, who died; Chuck Berry, who was immensely clever; Duane Eddy, who
couldn't last but who made hits that still sound good; and the very great Buddy
Holly.

Holly's voice, iridescing through *It Doesn't Matter Any More*, lingered all through
the summer of '59. It was the record that pinned down the year, just as 'Blonde On
Blonde' was to pin down 1966–67. And alongside it that autumn clustered the
variegated sounds and images of the pop America which had flowered in the
aftermath of Elvis' earlier impact.

By 24 March 1960, when Sgt Presley was discharged from the US Army, there
really was a whole scene going, and a scene of mixed-up confusion at that.

At this point, enter Bob Dylan. Some time the previous year he'd been playing
harmonica in a Central City, Colorado strip-joint, and by this time he must have
reached New York City, guitar at the ready and still listening to everything. By this
time too he must have soaked up all the cumulative residue of skills – in lyric-writing
as well as in the music – of Presley, Chuck Berry and Domino.

The myth has been created that 1960 was an all-time low in pop, which would
suggest that there was nothing much for Dylan to gather from it; would suggest that
he'd have had to go back to the early rock giants for his pop education. But the myth
is a lie. Nineteen-sixty wasn't the best year ever, that's for sure, but it introduced
some beautiful sounds – a situation that held all through '61 and '62 as well. The only
thing missing was a genuine trend. All the good things were disconnected; separate
end-products of the earlier rock years. This very disconnectedness made for
unprecedented variety: so not only had Dylan grown up through the early years but
he also had, at the start of his own career, a great deal happening in pop worth
picking up on.

What were the things that invalidate the myth of pre-Beatles infertility?

The first thing to say (and which Nik Cohn conveniently forgot about) is that
'60–61 was actually a time when some rock came back. Gene Vincent with *Pistol
Packin' Mama*; Eddie Cochran with *Cut Across Shorty*; and Brenda Lee with *Sweet
Nuthins*. Connie Francis tried it on *Robot Man*; Ricky Nelson tried it, with blaring
saxes, on *I Got My Eyes On You (And I Like What I See)*. The Piltdown Men arrived;
US Bonds came along with *New Orleans* and *Quarter To Three*; and Freddie Cannon
did *The Urge*. The Everly Brothers did *Lucille*; Jerry Lee Lewis came back with a
classic version of *What'd I Say*; Presley himself did *Little Sister*, *A Mess of Blues* and *I
Feel So Bad*. Del Shannon made a gallant attempt on his hit *Hats Off to Larry*, and they
issued a great but doctored Buddy Holly rocker, *Baby I Don't Care*.

Apart from this unchristened rock revival, on came a super-abundance of sounds
that were newer, maybe cleverer, and which certainly stick in the mind.

Blues singer Bobby Bland made it with *Let The Little Girl Dance*. Floyd Cramer
started something with *On The Rebound* – something that came to final fruition on

Dylan's 'Nashville Skyline' track, *Tell Me That It Isn't True*. The Ventures did *Perfidia* and Johnny & The Hurricanes did their *Rockin' Goose*. Duane Eddy went from *Shazam* through to *Dance With The Guitar Man*. Troy Shondell cut *This Time*. Clarence Frogman Henry was around, and making truly delightful concert appearances as well as the records *But I Do, You Always Hurt The One You Love, Ain't Got No Home, Lonely Street* and a great, great flop called *A Little Too Much* (not the Ricky Nelson song). Roy Orbison arrived, with grace and elegance and a voice that could not fail – the prototype voice from Dylan's *Wild Mountain Thyme, I Forgot More* and part at least of *Lay Lady Lay*. Ray Charles balanced nicely between soul and a bowl of slop. The Marcels did *Blue Moon* and Ernie K. Doe did *Mother-In-Law*. Dion found his *Runaround Sue* sound and Neil Sedaka found *Breakin' Up Is Hard To Do*. The Everly Brothers were better than ever, with *Cathy's Clown, Nashville Blues* and *Stick With Me Baby/Temptation*.

Tamla-Motown was young enough to be refreshing, as on *Please Mr Postman* by The Marvelettes and Mary Wells' *My Guy*. Phil Spector came along like Armageddon with The Crystals, Bob B. Soxx & The Blue Jeans and later The Ronettes. The Tokens did *The Lion Sleeps Tonight*, and *B'Wa Nina* – both so bad they were good. Little Eva emerged, and so did Bruce Chanel. Presley made his beautiful *Surrender*, and Sam Cooke sang *Nothing Can Change This Love*. There was *Monster Mash* by Bobby Boris Pickett & The Crypt-Kickers.

Add to all that the arrival of the Four Seasons, Jay & The Americans, the Shirelles' *Will You Love Me Tomorrow* – a minor breakthrough – and *Tell Him* by The Exciters. Then add *I Sold My Heart To The Junkman* by the Blue-Belles, and *I'm Blue* by the Ikettes. *Letter Full Of Tears* by Gladys Knight & The Pips. *Snap Your Fingers* by (the American) Joe Henderson. The Contours' *Do You Love Me* and the Isleys' *Twist And Shout*. Ketty Lester's *Love Letters* and Claude King's wonderful *Wolverton Mountain*. The devastating *What's A Matter Baby?* by a satanic Timi Yuro; and perhaps the very greatest of the lot, one minute twenty-eight seconds' worth of *Stay*, by Maurice Williams & The Zodiacs.

Far from being bad years, plainly, 1960–62 were very rich, and very diversified. The dominant influence, if there was one, was the search for a new duo-racial RnB-type music. Lots of the vocal groups were looking for that, and in England at least it was accepted that these Americans had found it. So Billy Fury moved on to phase three: not Presley, not Eddie Cochran, but by covering *Letter Full Of Tears* he became a mixture of processed cheese and Gladys Knight & The Pips. A complex sound, and to go with it, rumours that he wrote strange and secret poetry no one was allowed to read. Decca were obviously quite proud of the new sound they'd given him – so Lyn Cornell, an ex-back-up singer from Jack Good's 'Oh! Boy' TV show, covered *I Sold My Heart To The Junkman*, and Liverpool's Beryl Marsden covered Barbara George's *I Know*.

Underscoring developments at the time of this RnB quest there was, as usual, a corresponding country strength. It was there behind most of the rock revival records; it was there for Floyd Cramer; Ray Charles mixed it with his soul-singing. *Blue Moon* and *You Always Hurt The One You Love* are sort of country songs. The Everlys were from Country country and relied heavily on the songs of the Bryants – which included their *Nashville Blues*. And Roy Orbison emerged, like Presley and Johnny Cash before him, after a less successful start on the Memphis label, Sun. Long after *Only The Lonely* and the move to Monument Records, he was still singing country songs on albums, including the much-recorded *All I Have To Do Is Dream*.

So altogether there was plenty happening for Dylan to notice, react to, pick up on: his pop education didn't need to have finished – couldn't have finished – in the '50s.

London, 1963. Dylan was flown in by an uncharacteristically adventurous BBC-TV producer and given a bit-part in a television play. He sat on a staircase, muffed his one line, and sang Blowin' In The Wind *and the never-heard-since* Swan On The River. *The BBC has wiped this, because of 'lack of storage space.'*

EVERYTHING'S BIN RETURNED WHICH WAS OWED
PART I

What Dylan did gain from the years up to '59 were lessons learnt from Fats Domino and Chuck Berry, Elvis Presley and Buddy Holly: relatively specific things from highly distinctive artists.

Fats Domino taught white pop fans about idiosyncratic flexibility in lyrics – particularly in rhymes – through odd emphasis (a Dylan trick) and odd pronunciation. In Domino's *Good Hearted Man* he manages, by his accent and his disregard for consonants, to make the word 'man' rhyme with 'ashamed' – no mean feat. He put out a record called *Rockin' Bicycle* but he sang it 'Rockin' Bi-sic-l', and the words of that song are interesting too, in a simple but individualistic way.

There's plenty of evidence in Dylan's work of Domino's oddities of emphasis. For instance, in *Absolutely Sweet Marie*:

> Well I waited for you when I was *half*-sick
> Yes I waited for you when you hated me
> Well I wai-ee-ted for you inside of the frozen *tra*-ffic
> When ya knew I had some other place to be:

Domino also comes up, maybe accidentally, with the pathetic use of bathos, which again is something that Dylan has used. I can't remember the title but there is a Domino song which includes this amazing couplet:

> Her hands were soft as cotton
> Her face could never be forgotten.

95

From Chuck Berry, Dylan learnt a lot more. Berry was ahead of his time.

Berry offered an urban slang-sophistication slicker than any city blues man before him. He offered a bold and captivating use of cars, planes, highways, refrigerators and skyscrapers, and also the accompanying details: seat-belts, bus-conductors, ginger ale and terminal-gates. And he brought all this into his love songs. He put love in an everyday metropolis, fast and cluttered, as no one had done before him. In Chuck Berry's cities, real people – individuals – struggled and fretted and gave vent to ironic perceptions. And it was all so controlled, so admirably neat. This is the first verse of his great song *Nadine*:

> As I got on a city bus and found a vacant seat
> I thought I saw my future bride walking up the street
> I shouted to the driver 'Hey Conductor! – you must
> Slow down! I think I see her, please let me off this bus.

In *Maybellene* he manages to cram three car-names in as many lines:

> As I was motivatin' over the hill
> I saw Maybellene in a Coup de Ville
> A Cadillac a-rollin' on the open road
> Nothin' will outrun my V8 Ford

and in *You Never Can Tell* every couplet has a special kind of wit and economy:

> They bought a souped-up Jidney, 'was a cherry red '53,
> They drove it down to New Orleans to celebrate their anniversary ...

Chuck Berry also specialized in place-names, as no one before him or since has done. He releases the power of romance in each one, and thereby flies with relish through a part of the American dream. Place-names are scattered around like syllables in songs like *Back In The USA*, *Sweet Little Sixteen* and *The Promised Land*.

The last of these is the story of the poor-boy from Virginia who makes it to success-land, California – although we never discover what he really finds there. The song mentions lots and lots of place-names in passing, or rather, while the poor-boy's passing through, and a corresponding number of methods of transport. 'And that hound broke down an' left us all stranded in down-town Birmingham.' It ends up like this:

> ... come down easy,
> Taxi to the terminal-zone;
> Cut your engines an' cool your wings
> An' let me make it to the telephone:
> 'Los Angeles, give me Norfolk, Virginia,
> Try Waterford 1009,
> Tell the folks back home this is the promised land calling
> An' the poor-boy's on the line!'

Who else could take up two lines of a song in giving the operator the number?

He humanizes the operator as well, of course, by explaining his message to her. Dylan is probably conscious of turning this on its head when he uses the telephone to emphasize isolation in *Talkin' World War III Blues*:

> So I called up the operator of time
> Just to hear a voice of some kind
> 'When you hear the beep it will be three o'clock.'
> She said that for over an hour
> And I hung up.

The urban slickness, precision and irony are there in many Dylan songs, including *On The Road Again* – which could almost be *You Never Can Tell* turning sour, with its wild domestic detail. And Dylan uses the same Berry qualities on *From A Buick Six*, *Highway 61 Revisited, Memphis Blues Again, Bob Dylan's 115th Dream, Visions of Johanna* and so on.

The corresponding musical influence is even more wide-spread. Chuck Berry's distinctive, driving cameos, tight-knit and self-sufficient, inspired most of the rock side of Dylan's 'Bringing It All Back Home' and much of 'Highway 61' and many other unreleased cuts, including, in slow-motion, *Barbed Wire Fence*.

Dylan also took over Berry's manipulation of objects and the details and adman phrases that surround them. There are plenty of equivalents of that 'souped-up . . . cherry-red '53' in Dylan's rock songs: and, for example, in *4th Time Around* and *It's Alright Ma, I'm Only Bleeding.*

Dylan doesn't go in for the massed place-names which Berry parades so generously, although there is one song – less characteristic than just interesting – which crams in all the following names (it's an unreleased song called *Wanted Man*): California, Buffalo, Kansas City, Ohio, Mississippi, Cheyenne, Colorado, 'Georgia by the sea' (!), El Paso, Juarez (used again later at the beginning of *Just Like Tom Thumb's Blues*), Shreveport, Abeline, Albuquerque, Syracuse, Tallahassee and Baton Rouge.

It's also true that Dylan could never have written a song like *Tombstone Blues* without Chuck Berry; and nor could *Subterranean Homesick Blues* have come into being without him, either in its musical format or its words. It needed Berry's *Too Much Monkey Business* first.

The Berry song's technique is to pile up disconnected ideas, building up – like a list – the pressures that are on the story's narrator, and suggesting their unreasonableness by their phrased sharpness and their multiplicity. This is done fairly straightforwardly, but the simplicity adds to the effect. It's by no means artless. The last verse runs:

> Workin' in the fillin' station
> Too many tasks
> Wipe the windows
> Check the tyres
> Check the oil
> Dollar gas?!

Dylan, taking this up, makes it serve in a far more complex capacity. He widens the context and the predicament of the man under pressure. Chuck Berry might have a nasty job but Dylan has to fight off the whole of society:

> Ah, get born, keep warm,
> Short pants, romance, learn to dance,
> Get dressed, get blessed,
> Try to be a success,
> Please her, please him, buy gifts,
> Don't steal, don't lift,
> Twenty years of schoolin' an' they put you on the day shift
> Look out kid . . .

Lastly, Chuck Berry – like Little Richard – indulged a sort of consciously-laughing and highly effective quirk which made for line-endings on little words that prose would never emphasize. They don't just work as fill-ins: they help define the mood and add to the individuality of the songs. There's a totally characteristic example, which could have come from either Little Richard or Chuck Berry, in the Credence Clearwater tribute-song *Travellin' Band* where the rhyming line after 'hotel' is 'oh well'. Dylan picks up on this too. He doesn't use it in quite the same way, ever, and the most interesting examples are where he modifies its function most, in two of his narrative funny-songs, *Motorpsycho Nitemare* and *The Ballad of Frankie Lee and Judas Priest*:

> He said he's gonna kill (*pause*)
> Me if I don't get out the door in ten seconds flat

and

> For sixteen nights and days he raved
> But on the seventeenth he burst (*pause!*)
> Into the arms of Judas Priest

But it's important to recall, I think, that Berry was pioneering all this at a time when most people were either saying 'Rock, baby, rock', or 'I love you when you do the —'.

If Dylan learnt a lot from Chuck Berry, who stood out in splendid contrast to the sickly inanities of the worst of '60s pop he learnt a lot also from Elvis Presley.

As everyone must know, Presley came from Tupelo, Mississippi, where he was born poor in the 1930s and moved to Memphis with his mother and unemployed father when he was thirteen; later he got a job driving a truck. (There's a very nice Dylan allusion to this, delivered in a tough, Presley voice, on the unreleased tape cut with The Band between 'Blonde On Blonde' and 'John Wesley Harding': 'Goin' down t' Tennessee! get me a truck or somethin' '.)

Very much a Southerner, Presley said Yes Ma'am, No Sir to hostile press reporters, was inward with a simple gospelly religion (via The First Assembly Church of God) and was in love with the voice of Mahalia Jackson.

Presley had the formula for rock 'n' roll within him: a natural upbringing on blues and country music in its living environment. His first record, issued by Sun for distribution only in the Memphis area, was Arthur Big Boy Crudup's blues *That's All Right Mama*, sung with a kind of subdued freneticism that sounds hillbilly, amateurish and absolutely genuine. The change to *Heartbreak Hotel* is a large but a logical one.

From '56 to '60, his music was fine. The poor southern white made good, the prophet of rock, the sexual threat to bourgeois virginity, the pop equivalent of Brando in 'The Wild One', the untouchable and inaccessible prototype superstar: all this was maintained by the records, not the reporters. And when he had gone plastic and The Beatles were screamed at instead, the failure, correspondingly, was in Presley's music, not in his image. Had his output 1962–64 been up to his pre-army standard, then the Beatles might have got no further than those wonderful 1961 American groups like Maurice Williams and the Zodiacs, Cathy Jean and the Room-Mates, Nino and the Ebb-Tides. The gap was open for Beatlemania not because of Presley's age or because kids were tired of solo stars but because something drastic had happened to his music.

What was it that had gone out of Presley's work? All the sex; all that curious amalgam of insinuation and bluntness which Presley had introduced to pop and which Jagger was picking up on; all the pregnant charisma that had, from the very beginning, more than compensated for the false posturing of everything in the pre-Dylan years; all the therapeutic, role-distancing humour; an impeccable control in a strong voice that understood (rare thing then) nuance; and an avowing, ever-present nobility.

When he started, the two most important things in his music were lack of inhibition, and sex. Lack of inhibition is very important. Adolescents admired him because he could be socially unacceptable and get away with it, on stage and on record and in the mind, even if not more than once on the Ed Sullivan TV show. Sullivan was right, by his own lights, to take Presley's hips out of camera-range: they were being rude. And certainly a lot of teen-singers who came after him were to discover that getting up on stage and yelling WAAAAAAAAHHHHHH!!! is like exposing yourself in public without being stigmatized.

Sexually, Presley offered a new world, at any rate to whites, and offered it with a blunt statement of interests. There was none of the sycophantic 'dating' appeal that was the context of the most of the '50s stars' recorded love-affairs. *At The Hop*, *Teenager In Love*, *Lonely Boy*: these were the typical titles of the time – but not for Elvis. His titles suited the black labels that announced them (just as in England Cliff Richard suited the flat green of the old Columbia label).

Trouble, *I Got Stung*, *Jailhouse Rock*, *Paralysed*, *King Creole* – these all fitted the various significant elements that made Presley a unique, thrusting and ominous force. He embodied an untapped violence – consider that prophetic, pre-Townsend line, 'He don't stop playin' till his guitar breaks' – that a song like *Trouble* made explicit and the kind of hard bravado that *Jailhouse Rock* merged with ecstasy. *Jailhouse Rock* is a direct descendant of *Hound Dog*, where the voice seems to rage like King Kong in chains.

Of course, lots of rock stars tried to be aggressive and masculine. Lots, too, made love to the stage microphone – Gene Vincent most endearingly: but only Elvis Presley projected himself so well that he seemed often to be bearing down sexually on the listener.

This comes across best in the love songs. Here, he offered the constant implication of prior sexual experience and a corresponding cynicism which others could never bring off.

> Hey babe – I ain't askin' much o' you
> No n-no n-no n-no no baby – ain't askin' much o' you:
> Just a big-uh big-uh big-uh hunk of love will do

That, for example, came across in 1959 as freshly candid, its message the forerunner of that line from Dylan's *If You Gotta Go, Go Now*: 'It's not that I'm askin' for anything you never gave before'. The two extracts share the same ambiguity, the same ostensible politeness. Obviously, the mindless virginity-assumptions of others were as far away from late-50s Elvis as from mid-60s Dylan.

It was a unique stance at the time – unique, at least, in reaching the mass of white middle-class adolescents. Black pop naturally insinuated also, but more as a series of in-jokes than as a manifesto for white libido.

Even the likes of Chuck Berry, a black star with broad duo-racial appeal, cut innumerable maudlin slow-shuffles where all the words seemed to say, roughly:

> Can I carry your books home from school, darlin'
> Cos gee – you're lookin' good.

And think of the other white heart-throbs. Take Rick (then Ricky) Nelson's forte:

> I hate to face y'r dad
> Too bad
> I know he's gonna be mad
> It's late . . .
> Hope this won't be our last date;

or take the mournful, sexless world of Eddie Cochran (though admittedly these lines are classics, encapsulating most of pre-Dylan pop America):

> Six hot-dogs oughta be just right
> After such a wonderful night . . .

Presley, in contrast, got down to the eternal verities of passion underlying the middle-class Saturday night:

> If you wanna be loved, baby you gotta love me too
> Cos I ain't for no one-sided love affair:

> Well a fair exchange ain't no robbery
> An' the whole world knows that it's true . . .

And Presley's cynicism had such pungency – it provided, over the years, a sharp, concerted attack on the two-faced conventions which were imposed on the children of the '50s.

> Why make me plead
> For something you need?

His delivery gave a stylishness and authority to these open, soliciting songs which was utterly lacking in the other rock artists. Not just by sneers but by his pent-up tremble in the bass notes, the sudden full-throated rasps and the almost confessional, mellow country moans. Presley was saying 'let's fuck' a full six years before John and Paul were wanting to hold your hand. Millions of eager seventeen-year-olds, weary of the Fabian-style pudge-next-door who only did want to hold their hands, could respond a good deal more honestly when Elvis sang *Stuck On You*, *Treat Me Nice* and *Baby Lets Play House*.

Not surprisingly, considering the time-span of Presley's ascendance, there were other songs which, if quoted carefully, could give an opposite picture – a picture of Presley as effete and, like all the Bobby Vees and Vintons, sycophantic. *Girl Of My Best Friend* is a good example:

> What if she got real mad and told him so?:
> I could never face either one again . . .

But first, the delivery was never remotely effete, and even at his most melodic (which he was never afraid to be anyway and which he always carried off without false delicacy) there was a saving power. And second, such examples were simply untypical of what Presley stood for. In the same way, the sensitive unisex aura of Buddy Holly – who avoided plasticity in an opposite way to Presley – was sometimes absent from his work yet remained its distinctive feature. *Annie's Bin A-Workin' On The Midnight Shift* is an exception in the Holly repertoire, not an archetype.

A final point on Presley's sexuality. It is true that the pre-rock chart-toppers and radio-favourites, the night-club stars whose idea of perfection was a Cole Porter song and the Nelson Riddle Orchestra, dealt with sex too – but never, never with passion. Physical contact, desire, sexual aspiration always come across from Sinatra, Torme, Fitzgerald, Tony Bennett and the rest as a kind of world-weary joke that goes with old age. The standard it's-one-in-the-morning-and-we're-pretty-smooth treatments of *I've Got You Under My Skin*, *Night and Day*, etc, could easily be addressed to a can of flat beer.

Against this lifeless background, Presley's initial impact coast-to-coast in America and in Britain also, was holocaustic. Yet lack of inhibition, sex and the voice to carry it was not all that he offered. He also gave out a fair share of the vital humour which goes with the best hard-line rock and which Fats Domino, Chuck Berry and Little Richard used very well.

This kind of humour shows itself aware of outside values and of the inextricable mixture of the important and the trivial, the real and the stylized in the pop medium. And if you go back now to the original Presley recordings, the pungency and freshness of this humour still hits home. Think of the self-awareness of Elvis, polite Southern boy with grafted-on rebel image, pounding out this:

> Ah sure would be delighted with your com-pan-y:
> Come on an' do the Jailhouse Rock with me . . .

Or less subtle flashes such as this:

> If you can't find a partner use a wooden chair
> And let's rock

or:

> She wore a clingin' dress that fit so tight
> She couldn't sit down so we danced all night

or:

> Well there ain't nothin' wrong with the long-haired music
> Like Brahms, Beethoven and Bach,
> But I was raised with a guitar in ma hand
> An' I was born to rock. Well. . . .

or finally:

> Samson tol' Delilah – Delilah say Yeah? –
> Keep yo' cotton-pickin' fingers out ma curly hair
> Oh yeah, ever since the world began
> Hard-Headed Woman bin the thorn in the side of man.

And yes, the deliberate yet essentially unselfconscious 'negro' reference in that last example indicates how inward, how fundamental a strength, is Presley's understanding of the blues. Its idiom comes in naturally enough.

Mess of Blues; *One Night*; *That's All Right Mama*; *Reconsider Baby* (a Lowell Fulson song); *Blueberry Hill*; *Anyplace Is Paradise*; *Lawdy Miss Clawdy*; *It Feels So Right*; *Heartbreak Hotel*; listen to any of these today and the claim that Presley is a great white blues singer (albeit a commercial one) is hard to deny. And that he brought all this before a vast, non-specialist white audience in the drab Eisenhower era was a really explosive achievement.

Some of these tracks still sound undiminished in quality. *Heartbreak Hotel* still sounds strangely ahead of its time, even now. And *Lawdy Miss Clawdy* remains a vital, exciting classic, sufficiently accurate and unadulterated to make the best of Tamla-Motown-Stax sound like the Black & White Minstrel Show.

Presley's voice had nobility – a clear, charismatic rarity to which a generation rallied and felt uplifted in hoping to protect: just as another generation intensely desired to protect the man whose voice lit up *I Threw It All Away*.

There are many other links between the two. In the first place, Dylan would have heard at least part of his old blues material second-hand through Presley. Elvis' *Milkcow Blues Boogie* (which Dylan has adapted from in *It Takes A Lot To Laugh, It Takes A Train To Cry*) is an old song by Kokomo Arnold – not a well-known name, I'd guess, up in Minnesota – who was born in Lovejoy, Georgia, in 1901.

Also, Dylan's lyric and tune on *One More Night* are heavily reminiscent of Elvis' record of *Blue Moon Of Kentucky*. *That's All Right, Mama*, Presley's first record, is down there in the Bob Dylan songbook. The piano-work on Dylan's *Mixed-Up Confusion* owes a lot to the spirit of that on *Lawdy Miss Clawdy*; and the clear allusion to Floyd Cramer's piano-style on the end of *Tell Me That It Isn't True* is an allusion to a style much associated with Elvis and his RCA Victor studios at Nashville.

The opening lines of *Lay Lady Lay* are doing what Presley has stood for all along. Dylan may be sexier (and his sexuality somehow brings in his intelligence) and therefore better at it, but its the same kind of ennobled overture that comes across in a hundred Elvis songs:

> Lay, lady, lay —
> Lay across ma big brass be-ed

and altogether the immaculate soulfulness of *I Threw It All Away* is like Presley's great *Is It So Strange?*.

A smaller but none the less indicative parallel can be found between an Elvis record mentioned, *Milkcow Blues Boogie*, and *Dylan's 115th Dream*. Both cuts begin and then stop and start again; Elvis says 'Hold it fellas!' and Dylan replaces this with 'Hey, wait a minute fellas!' And that is not the only Dylan amendment of a Presley line. In the much later Elvis song *Cotton Candy Land* there is this pre-packed glycerine line: 'We'll ride upon a big white swan'; and Dylan revisits it with suitable irreverence — in his knowingly gauche *Country Pie* — to 'Saddle me up a big white goose!' (Bathos, no less).

There are many take-offs of Elvis slipped into Dylan's work — but it's significant of the considerable value of Presley's influence that they are never so much take-offs as tributes. Presley is melodramatic, and Dylan mocks that, mocks the exaggeration, but always he does it with a smile that confesses he can't help falling for Presley, that he notices the good things just as keenly. These take-offs/tributes include the end, musically, of *Peggy Day*:

> *ting, ting, ta-ba-ba* Love to, *ba ba-ba-ba ba*,
> Spend the night *ba-ba-ba-ba-ba-ba-bam*,
> With Peggy Da-ay — *ba-am, ba-am, ba-am, ba-am-ba-ba-am*!

Elvis' songs often really do end like this, right from his very early *I Got A Woman* through to *Beach Boy Blues, Steppin' Out Of Line* and *Rock-a-Hula Baby*.

Dylan doesn't stop there. On the 'Basement Tapes' version of *The Mighty Quinn*, which is very different from the 'Self Portrait' one, the Dylan voice is deliberately near to the Presley voice of *Trouble*. And there are two versions of *Nothing Was Delivered* from those sessions which evoke the Presley world. The one with the heavy piano-backing is a finely measured acknowledgement of Elvis' handling of Domino's *Blueberry Hill*; the version with Dylan's monologue is a wide-open laugh at Presley's monologue posturing on *That's When Your Heartaches Begin, I'm Yours, Are You Lonesome Tonight* and, again, *Trouble*. On the last of these especially, Elvis 'talks tough', like a kind of upstart Lee Marvin:

> I don' look f' trouble but I
> Never ran
> I don' take no orders from
> No kinda man

and Dylan simply makes the hollowness transparent by using the same bravado on weaker lines. Elvis stands there as if all-powerful, delivering the goods; Dylan comes on like a swindled consumer to talk from positions of weakness:

Now you must, you must provide some answers
For what you sell has not bin received
And the sooner you come up with those answers
You know the sooner you can leave.

I had written that phrase about Presley's toughness – 'like a kind of upstart Lee Marvin' – long before Dylan made 'Pat Garrett & Billy The Kid' with Marvin-surrogate James Coburn: but for the soundtrack album of that film, Dylan does three versions of a song called *Billy*, the last of which – *Billy 7* – is actually a beautiful imitation of how Coburn would sound if *he* were singing it. And the effect of this is, of course, to give us a Dylan parodying exactly the kind of toughness which belongs to Presley. He parallels the ethic of those lines just quoted from *Trouble* unerringly and sings with an astonishingly deep voice set against sleazy, smoky guitar-lines and even sound-effects of ominous thunder:

They say that Pat Garrett's got your number
Sleep with one eye open when you slumber
Every little sound just might be thunder
Thunder from the barrel of his gun

Dylan has also come clean, in the 1970s, in acknowledging the special place Elvis Presley occupies in his canon of influences. The 'New Morning' song, *Went To See*

In the film 'Pat Garrett & Billy The Kid', 1973. It was after this film that Dylan, a New Yorker throughout his career, settled in California. He returned to the East Coast in 1974 for the 'Blood On The Tracks' sessions and some unannounced club guest-spots in 1975.

The Gypsy seems to be about going to see Presley, and Dylan makes known his idolization of Elvis not just by lines like

> He can move you from the rear
> Drive you from your beer
> Bring you through the mirror
> He did it in Las Vegas and he can do it here

but also by capturing the inevitable awkwardness of their meeting in these humorous lines:

> I went to see the gypsy
> Staying in a big hotel
> He smiled when he saw me coming
> And he said 'Well, well, well!'
> His room was dark and crowded
> Lights were low and dim
> 'How are you?' he said to me
> I said it back to him! . . .

And when his record-company issued their ragbag album of warm-ups and reject tracks – 'Dylan' (1973) – it contained Bob Dylan versions of two songs that were Presley hits. Just as Elvis did versions of Dylan's *Don't Think Twice, It's All Right* and *Tomorrow Is A Long Time*, so Dylan had done Elvis' *A Fool Such As I* (which sounds, from the music, to have been a warm-up for the 'Nashville Skyline' sessions) and an amazing version of *Can't Help Falling In Love* (a warm-up, I'd guess, from the 'New Morning' recordings).

Years ago, when Dylan was held to be the absolute opposite, the antithesis, of Presley, it would have been, if not actually heretical, at least controversial to argue that Dylan could owe Elvis anything. Now, despite the lack of commentary published on his recordings, recognition is growing for what Presley has achieved. I have grown up with his records, I have always believed in him – so it's hard for me to judge whether somebody largely unfamiliar with his output could, on going through it attentively now, understand its greatness enough to get a glow like I get from it. It's probably too late for that – the clichés and artifice that are a discountable part of it to me must almost certainly be too obtrusive for new listeners to cope with except on a few classic tracks. If that is the case it's a major barrier to appreciating what Dylan has got from Presley – because there's more to that appreciation than I have managed to convey. But it's there in the music.

For different reasons it's even harder to write anything useful about Buddy Holly. He had more personal talent, more charisma and more potential than anyone except Presley. Even on his very early recordings, where the studio sound, the arrangements and the type of song featured all drew heavily on Presley's earliest Sun cuts, you could not but be aware of a very different talent feeling its way and testing its strengths. By the time he was having hits, he not only had a distinctive sound but also an integrity and an inquiring interest in country music and city blues. The famous Holly sound is on songs like *That'll Be The Day* (Version 2: and it's instructive to compare it to the earlier, unstable version); *Peggy Sue*; *Heartbeat*; *Every Day*; *Listen To Me*; *Tell Me How* and so on. Maybe his later ones are the best, with their slightly mellower sound – in particular, *Peggy Sue Got Married*; *That's What They Say*; *What To Do*; and the truly immortal record that was his latest release at the time of his death, Paul Anka's composition *It Doesn't Matter Any More* coupled with *Raining In My Heart*.

Holly's voice transcends the limits set by the words of his songs. *What To Do*, transcribed on to the printed page, may be fatuous and trite:

> The record-hops and all the
> Happy times we had;
> The soda-shops, the walks to school
> Now make me sad, oh!
>
> What to do
> I know my heartache's showin'
> Still not knowin'
> What to do

but on record, Holly's voice moulds it, lights it up, so that it becomes a good deal more than trite – more even than acceptable sentimentality. Artistically, Holly hasn't died, and never will. His voice at its best was the first artistic permanence, the first universal statement ever made by pop music.

Holly died, if anyone doesn't know it, with Ritchie Valens in 1959, in a chartered single-engined plane which crashed in the snow in the early hours of February 3rd, on its way to North Dakota. The last things studio-recorded before his death were in some ways a little odd. Titles were *True Love Ways* and *Moondreams*, and they were very mellow indeed. (One of them even used an aspidistra saxophone sound.) But if there's a hint that he might have been already slacking off into popular balladland, the evidence of his musical interests belies it. He cut the only white commercial blues that could even touch Presley's best, *Lawdy Miss Clawdy*: the song was called *Mailman, Bring Me No More Blues*. He could handle Bo Diddley and Chuck Berry too, not just competently but adding something of his own in a way that showed rare understanding. *Bo Diddley* and *Brown-Eyed Handsome Man* make the point with a kind of raw panache.

As for the music on his own songs, it's riddled with the clichés of the time, but he handled these clichés with intelligence enough to show that had he lived he would have readily discarded them. People talk automatically about the Claptons of this world as 'the great guitarists'; I think there's a sense in which Holly was a great guitarist, boxed in by the restrictions of convention in his time. If he had lived . . . Greil Marcus said that Buddy Holly would have joined Dylan for a duet on, say, *I Don't Believe You*. That sounds true to me, and true in part because of the similarities that exist in any case between the two singers.

They were both small, delicate-looking people, yet they both gave out a big sound – which gives them a certain resemblance in image. To call it little-boy-lost is too simple, but on stage there was a suggestion that both of them were lost in their own worlds of loudness – except that that implies wrongly that they weren't in control of the sound. Little-boy-uncorrupted seems a slightly less clumsy tag.

Control is the second point of resemblance. It's a thing that was missing altogether from rock when the British beat-group boom got going in 1964. One of the main things that marked out such groups from the solo stars they replaced was that a loose, ramshackle sound was considered good enough and a rather erratic vocal technique came into vogue. Suddenly, singers weren't sure where they were throwing their voices and didn't care which notes, if any, they were going to catch. Many of the solo stars had known exactly what their voices were doing – even when they were ripping it up. Little Richard was wild, but he was always in control. Presley always had this same sort of precision. So did the Everlys and Jackie Wilson – especially on his classic *Reet Petite* (1956).

Buddy Holly had it too. Control in Holly was a special thing, tantamount to integrity – a precision demanded by artistic considerations, which was one of the things that made for his greatness. Dylan learnt a lot about such considerations, I would say, directly from Buddy Holly. There are times when both of them appear not to have this control, times when bits of phrasing sound at first hearing like bad mistakes, but they never are. The wild swoop-up/hiccup at the end of the title-phrase in Holly's *Tell Me How* is an example; Dylan provides others in *The Times They Are A-Changin'* and, among others, *Drifter's Escape*. The oddities are not mistakes, they're far more right than the expected alternative bits that don't appear. A few more playings and they both prove their points. The control and precision were perfect after all, and when that realization dawns, both artists have taught you something.

You can trace the effects of this teaching, as Holly gave it to Dylan, right down to similarities of timing, phrasing, emphasis, pronunciation. Greil Marcus, as usual, has dealt very well with this. 'Dylan and Holly', he wrote in *Rolling Stone* (28 June, 1969), 'share a clipped staccato delivery that communicates a sly sense of cool, almost teenage masculinity,' and he cites Buddy Holly's performance on *Annie's Bin A-Workin' On The Midnight Shift*. There, says Marcus, 'the phrasing is simply what we know as pure Dylan' –

> If she tells you she wants to use the caahhh!
> Never explains what she wants it faaahhh!

Marcus goes on from there to make another but a connected point, in discussing some of the home-tape-recordings of Holly's voice which were released, after his death, with backing-tracks added:

> Sometimes, these ancient cuts provide a real sense of what rock 'n' roll might have become had Holly lived. The same shock of recognition that knocked out the audiences at the Fillmore West when The Band . . . lit into Little Richard, takes place, with the same song, when the ghost of Buddy Holly is joined by the Fireballs for *Slippin' And Slidin'* . . . An agile, humorous vocal is carried by a band that knows all the tricks. They break it open with the Everly Brothers' own seductive intro, constantly switching, musically, from song to song, while Holly ties it together. The guitarist actually sounds like Robbie Robertson, throwing in bright little patterns around the constant whoosh of the cymbals . . . it's certainly one of the best things Buddy Holly ever did.

The same 'shock of recognition' is there when Marcus first suggests the Holly-Dylan duet that would have happened if Holly had lived.

There must be a good deal of similarity that is perhaps too intangible to document in order for that idea to strike home so sharply. Obviously, the *Annie's Bin A-Workin'* resemblance is tangible enough – and we have it on innumerable Dylan tracks from *I Want You* to *On The Road Again* and from *Absolutely Sweet Marie* back to *When The Ship Comes In*. The last of these may seem a strange choice, but Buddy Holly could have sung *When The Ship Comes In*. It has all the right tensions, all the polarities of high and low notes, rushes and lapses, that Holly alone among the pre-Dylan stars could easily control.

That brings home another fusion of delivery: an intangible additive in the voices. Both Dylan and Holly suggest a level of emotion at work below the words, way out beyond the scope of the lyric. Holly shows it incredibly well on, for example, *True Love Ways*, and Dylan uses it everywhere.

In the end, perhaps the best way to encompass what Dylan has done via Holly is to say that Dylan, really, has replaced him.

On-stage in San Francisco, November 1965, with Robbie Robertson (and The Hawks). These were the prototype rock-concerts following on from the Newport Folk Festival in July, which preceded the controversial 1966 world tour.

You could say, without undue exaggeration, that Dylan has replaced Nashville too. He has put all it stands for into a handful of songs – it is all there at the end of 'John Wesley Harding' and on 'Nashville Skyline'.

I've been considering the major influences on Dylan's pop/rock music, and it's tempting to carry on through his countrified output, the material just mentioned, from exactly the same perspective. When you hear a song like his *I'll Be Your Baby Tonight* (from 'John Wesley Harding'), it is easy to say, ah yes, Hank Williams – yet switch straight from the Dylan song to any Hank Williams album and the strong and derivative resemblance you imagined just vanishes. *I'll Be Your Baby Tonight* isn't really like Hank Williams at all.

The answer is that the perspective is all wrong. Dylan owes a lot, not to Hank Williams (or anyone else) in particular, but simply to Nashville; it isn't 'influences' so much as stimulus. Dylan hears Don Gibson bring something close to perfection, in its own small way, with *Sea Of Heartbreak*; Dylan hears Jerry Lee Lewis break into extraordinary lyrical piano-work on beautifully poised performances of songs like *Cold Cold Heart*, *Your Cheating Heart*, *Together Again* and *How's My Ex Treating You*; Dylan hears and befriends Johnny Cash (whose self-penned number, *Understand Your Man*, forms the basis of the tune for *Don't Think Twice, It's All Right*); Dylan hears Flatt & Scruggs, Patsy Cline, Jack Scott, Marty Robbins and a hundred others, with and without international 'names' – all exploring different paths but from the same prolific headquarters. So with 'Nashville Skyline' Dylan decides to commit himself to a country music album and the result is stunning because he sees through to basics in whatever he tackles – that's why he's brilliant at whatever he tries. He turns out an album unrivalled in country music, an album so precisely right, so

107

faithfully lifelike and yet so alive, that it almost makes the rest of Nashville redundant.*

In its own right, that's a major achievement – yet in the full context of what Dylan, as an artist, has done, it is only of minor importance. Country music just isn't that valuable. A one-man Nashville has so much less to offer than the Dylan of 'Highway 61' to 'John Wesley Harding', or of 'Blood On The Tracks'.

But all the influences, including Nashville, have helped Dylan produce great work; and in turn Dylan has made it possible for a revolution to take place in rock music. And there is another aspect of Dylan worth dealing with in the context of the old pop as much as the new rock: that is, not Dylan the artist but Dylan the star.

WHO'S GONNA THROW THAT MINSTREL BOY A COIN?

Dylan is the greatest rock 'n' roll star in the world. Partly, of course, this is because he's the best rock writer and singer and performer there has ever been; but

---

* One country album that seems to justify the 'influences' approach to Dylan's country output is the smooth and gentle 'Nashville Airplane' (!) by the reunited Flatt & Scruggs. The back-up musicians are the same on 'Airplane' and 'Skyline'; several of the tracks of the former are Dylan songs – but not, in the main, his country songs: songs instead like *Rainy Day Women Nos 12 & 35* sung country; and one track, by Flatt & Scruggs, *Freida Florentine*, is very much a dress rehearsal for Dylan's *Nashville Skyline Rag*. But then again, Dylan's own *Cough Song*, recorded years earlier, is also very like *Nashville Skyline Rag*.

THE PICNIC AT BLACKBUSHE AERODROME

BOB DYLAN
SPECIAL GUEST
ERIC CLAPTON
and his band

**THE BOB DYLAN PICNIC
AT BLACKBUSHE AIRFIELD
SATURDAY, 15 JULY 1978
Travel to FLEET station (Southern Region)
where special buses will run to and from
the concert site**

TRAINS

Waterloo depart:
06 12 — 06 54+ — 07 12 — 07 24+ — 07 42 — 07 54+ — 08 12 —
08 34+ — 08 42 — 08 54+ — 09 12 — 09 24+ — 09 42 — 09 54+ —
10 12 — 10 34+ — 10 42 — 11 05+ — 11 12 — 11 34+ — 11 42 —
11 53+ — 12 05+ — 12 12 — 12 24+ — 12 42
+ also calling Clapham Junction and Wimbledon

Fleet depart:
22 43 — 23 08 — 23 18 — 23 30 — 23 39 — 23 48 — 23 57 —
00 06 — 00 15 — 00 25 — 00 40 — 00 55 — 01 10 — 01 30 —
01 47 — 02 02 — 02 17 — 02 32 — 02 47 — 03 02

The 22 43 and 23 18 trains will call at Woking, Surbiton and
Waterloo only.

The remaining return trains will call at Woking, Surbiton,
Wimbledon, Clapham Junction and Waterloo.

All train times shown are subject to alteration.

The combined rail/bus fare from WATERLOO, CLAPHAM
JUNCTION and WIMBLEDON will be £3 (half fare for children
under 14 years). These tickets will be valid from 19 00 Friday,
14 July through to 12 00 Sunday, 16 July, one journey in each
direction only.

Anyone returning from Fleet by train after 12 00 on the Sunday
will have to buy an ordinary single ticket to their destination, and
no refunds on the combined rail/bus ticket will be paid.

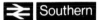 **Southern**

Published by British Rail Southern AD1632/A20/6778

It is an odd sort of superstardom Dylan uniquely exhibits being much less famous among the general public than, say, John Cleese, yet able to enjoy the sort of pulling power as recently as 1978 that involved shifting a quarter of a million people to Blackbushe Aerodrome, with queues on the motorway.

partly – and the two aren't by any means totally distinguishable – it's because he's become an idol, a superstar. In the summer of 1978 – a full twelve years later than his '60s cult zenith of popularity, and at a time when punk was at its height – Bob Dylan pulled a quarter of a million people to Blackbushe for one concert. Special trains, RAC routes, the lot.

There are certain strategies which dictate impressively whether 'star material' makes it to legend status. One such successful strategy is to build up your rarity value. You reach a point when it is fatal to appear too often, when the occasional rumour is more effective than frequent hard news, when it's better to only release one record a year than attempt a three-monthly assault on the charts, when it's best not to talk at all to the outside world, when it's necessary to shun the company of other celebrities, wise to turn down huge money offers, and above all essential to avoid the TV medium.

This starts out as a simple show-biz rule – 'always leave the public shouting for more' – but it ends up vastly more complex and all-embracing in a pop world attended to by teeny-boppers and students, business executives and lefties – a world split between singles and albums, TV shows and weekend festivals, stage concerts, dance-halls, discotheques and films, and under the constant if idle scrutiny of 'quality' newspapers, tabloids, weary Fleet Street music-papers, and trendy paperbacks. You have to learn to dodge them all. Otherwise they burn you out before you're half-way there.

The star not only has that to deal with, but has to dodge, every day, a hundred other reductive approaches. In the early '60s in England, there was a programme on

BBC Radio (the Light Programme) called 'Saturday Club'. This was a two-hour mixture of records and live appearances partly by pop artists and partly by played-out old dance bands/combos/foot-tappin' guitarists. Plainly, a programme to avoid. No true star would have touched it with the wrong end of his chromium-plated microphone. Yet plenty of famous pop names agreed to perform on it not just as newcomers but long after they had become established. Bad strategy, bad management.

The man with the best manager was Presley. Once established, Presley withdrew from all these lowly aspects of the pop scene, built up a reputation for declining huge appearance-fees, stopped talking to newsmen, avoided television like the plague – and consequently emerged as the best-selling, highest-paid, most god-like and untouchable dream since Greta Garbo.

Presley never came to Britain – turning down, among other things, an offer of $100,000 for one performance inside a magnifying bubble in the centre of a vast sports stadium. He couldn't, it was explained, afford to make the trip for 'that sort of figure'. It was 'not quite what we had in mind'.

In contrast, Paul Anka performances were, in many parts of the world, two a penny. Result: Paul Anka became eminently touchable, the boy next door, one of myriad second-class stars. When you saw his name mentioned, momentary interest was engaged: you read the item. If he was coming to your home-town, well, maybe you'd go and see his show if the supporting acts weren't too awful and if the price was right. But when you read the name Elvis Presley, lights flashed – and you knew you'd go anywhere, pay any price, to see him.

His TV spectacular in 1968 (1969 in England: thanks again, BBC) was his first television appearance for over eight years. And that's the way to do it.

That's how Dylan does it too. You wouldn't catch Dylan on 'Top Of The Pops', or in bed for peace, or on the 'Parkinson Show'. His scarcity-value is enormous. Rumours about what he's doing are whispered around now and then; he limits himself, effectively, to albums, and never brings out more than one a year. When California was bursting with supposedly-incredible rock groups and was crowded out with every pace-setting Beautiful Person in the world, Dylan remained pointedly 3,000 miles away, in splendid isolation in New York State. 'Involvement is death,' he once wrote.

It sounds easy – refuse to appear for £50 and eventually someone will offer you £500. Do that once, throwing in a little controversy while you're at it – and then start refusing again. Easy or not, most people don't manage it: most people don't appear to even understand. They're delighted with any rush of publicity, they pose for fifty photographers and comply with every tasteless idea these men come up with, they commit themselves to films which, if they're lucky, will never get a general release – and a year or two later they're astonished to find themselves rated about as exciting as Ray Connif.

It's true that much of Dylan's uncooperativeness with the media is in response to their intrusions, their attempts to raise a man who is a great and a serious artist to their own level of vulgarity (on the journalistic Peter Principle); but it also comes from Dylan's shrewdness as an image-builder, a Garbo in rock music.

He plays with reporters brilliantly, showing up their bumbling, uncomprehending platitudes, keeping his distance, controlling them. A few examples. He allowed a film to be made, a semi-montage of parts of his 1965 tour of England. The reviews were a triumph for Dylan. The Cleveland *Plain Dealer* spluttered out this:

> Should be buried.... This is a cheap, in part, a dirty movie, if it is a movie at all.... It is certainly not for moviegoers who bathe and/or shave. It is

'underground' and should be buried at once. Burn a rag, as was once said of filth. Phew!

It wouldn't have been very satisfactory if the Cleveland *Plain Dealer* had liked the film. Bad for the image. As for *Newsweek*, it really had to grovel – and in a way that must have amused Dylan greatly:

> 'Don't Look Back' [said Newsweek] is really about fame and how it menaces art, about the press and how it categorizes, bowdlerizes, sterilizes, universalizes or conventionalizes an original like Dylan into something it can dimly understand.

Dimly understand was right. The *New Yorker* informed its readership that parts of the film 'catch some moving essence of being young now'.

Back in England four years later, for his one-hour appearance at the Isle of Wight, Dylan held a press conference. Not a convenient one, in London, on his arrival at the airport, but one instead on the Isle of Wight itself. They all flew out there to ask him their questions, of course, and the questions were what you'd expect:

REPORTER: A lot of the young people who admire you seem to be mixed-up in a lot of drug-taking and so forth. Do you agree with this? What are your views on this problem?

DYLAN: (assuming thick country accent): Oh I don't have any of them views; I sure wish I did – I sure would like to share them with y'all.

It isn't just funny answers, it's an ability to manipulate completely, to counteract instantaneously the amorality of the media – and that seems to me a gigantic achievement. In our mass society, it is revolutionary warfare. Norman Mailer must be proud of him; no one else in the western world has learnt to fight like this. The goat comes along, asks its questions, tries to have its customary shit – and Dylan, instead of evading like a politician, by mouthing other goat-like platitudes, cuts through it all and so manages to speak directly to the people who are still 'out there' and who don't rely on the *Reader's Digest* to give them their world-view.

This triumph does more in the way of keeping Dylan a star than just maintaining his scarcity-value. It also allows him to feed secrets to his fans, which in pop is very important. There you are at home reading a rumour in *Melody Maker*, August '69. The rumour says that when Dylan comes to the Isle of Wight at the end of the month for his first appearance in Britain for over three years, he might finish his performance with a jam-session, with George Harrison, John Lennon, a couple of Rolling Stones, Eric Clapton and Ginger Baker, Humble Pie and the Bee Gees joining him on stage! And it's highly pleasurable to be in on a secret, to cut through this rubbish and know the mind of this incredible man – because you know all the while that he's let the rumour grow by simply not denying it, that he's watched in amusement as the snowball machine rolls it out: and you know perfectly well that it won't happen. He'll no more appear on stage with those people than he'll enter the Eurovision Song Contest.

There are lots more peripheral pleasures involved in the star-fan system in pop, and Dylan doesn't miss a trick. He's not just ten steps ahead of the media: he's three steps ahead of you too – which enhances the fun of sharing secrets. It's fun hanging on to the reins of his unfailing unpredictability.

You see him in concert in Liverpool in 1966. The board outside the theatre (which is really a huge, depressing cinema) says

2.45: THE SOUND OF MUSIC.   7 P.M. BOB DYLAN

The launch of the electric Dylan: on-stage with the Paul Butterfield band, July 1965: Mike Bloomfield (guitar); Sam Lay (drums); Jerome (bass); Dylan and Al Kooper (keyboards).

— and that's a joke the newsmen (and the cinema management too) wouldn't even notice. Anyway, you go in, you wait, and Dylan comes on for the solo half of his performance. He tunes up carefully before every number, he hardly glances at the audience, he wears a shabby, crumpled grey suit – and he doesn't speak. No 'Hi! It's wonderful to be here!', no 'Thank you very much, thank you', no 'I'd like to do a song now called . . .'. The first time he speaks is in the second half, when the folk morons are booing and heckling. Somebody shouts out, uncomprehendingly, 'Where's the poet gone?' and Dylan smiles, comes up to the microphone with a gentle corrective reproach: 'Not where's the poet, where's the saint gone.' And at the very end, no encore. Dylan almost runs off the stage at the end and is out of the theatre and away – with the audience still hoping against hope that he's still there really, that really he's just behind the curtain.

Great – the press don't understand it at all, but you do. You're in on the secrets and you've witnessed the agile rejection of all the showbiz charades.

And then you see him at the Isle of Wight and he twists it all around. 'Thank you, thank you – great to be here,' he says, in the little shy voice of a moderate man, as if he's ever so surprised to find all those thousands of people turning up just to hear him. And he's dressed immaculately in white, just for the flashbulbs and spotlights. Fifty-five minutes later, he says 'We're gonna do one last song for ya now. It was a big hit for, I believe, Manfred Mann. Great group, great group.' He sings *The Mighty Quinn* and walks off. The hoping against all hope begins – and back he comes, happy to please all the folks out there applauding. But the song he sings is yet another lampoon:

Who's gonna throw that minstrel boy a coin?
Who's gonna let it roll?

So where does that leave you, except still applauding twenty minutes after he has gone away? You stand there clapping not only the artist, but the idol as well.

EVERYTHING'S BIN RETURNED WHICH WAS OWED
PART II

Despite the influences of Holly, Presley, Berry and the rest, Dylan's work is far more original than derivative. *He* has been the big influence: he created the re-birth in rock.

Dylan goes beyond other people – with every new album there's a progression; and this has happened so fast that in one sense Dylan has always been an outsider in pop – has always been ahead of his time.

The first time a lot of pop fans noticed him was when the *The Times They Are A-Changin'* came out as a single in 1964. To pop-trained ears, it was a laughable record. The singer had a voice that made Johnny Duncan and The Blue Grass Boys sound in the same league as Mario Lanza – and plainly, the man hadn't even the most elementary sense of timing. He brought in the second syllable of that titleword 'Changing' far too soon – at a quite ridiculous point. What was the record-company playing at? Just because Bob Dylan was the writer of an interesting song called *Blowing In The Wind* didn't mean he could expect to start singing all his other songs himself.

With that behind him Dylan invented a new form, folk-rock. 'Another Side of Bob Dylan' his fourth album, is essentially rock music. The sound on the album is a rock sound, despite the fact that the backing is 'really' just Dylan with solo guitar and

In the 1950s it had been Colonel Tom Parker and Elvis Presley. In the mid-60s, it was Albert Grossman and Bob Dylan. Dylan phased Grossman out by the end of the decade.

harmonica – despite the fact that 'really' it is his last solo album. The rock sound is evident everywhere on it, and Dylan doesn't achieve this by going mad on his guitar/harmonica/piano. He achieves it by implication.

Motorpsycho Nitemare is very much the same sort of song as *Bob Dylan's 115th Dream*, on the rock side of the fifth album; but 'Nitemare' doesn't differ from 'Dream' in being solo-work rather than rock – it differs in having a better and a heavier implicit rock sound behind it. And the whole of the fourth album has exactly that same superiority to the fifth. The explicit backings on the latter are often thin and clickety but the music the fourth album puts into your head – perhaps especially on *Spanish Harlem Incident*, *I Don't Believe You* and *Chimes Of Freedom* – is dazzling: strong and rich. It has the sort of richness Dylan achieved in concert in 1966 (not just in the rock half of the concerts either, but on the solo *Mr Tambourine Man* of that time too) and on tracks like *One Of Us Must Know* in the 'Blonde On Blonde' collection.

With 'Another Side Of Bob Dylan', and more so with 'Bringing It All Back Home', many of the folk fans flinched away, and the pop world didn't really catch on either till it was spoon-fed with the singles of *Subterranean Homesick Blues* and *Like A Rolling Stone*. Even with these, Bob Dylan was still clearly an outsider not just because such records were different, but also because they were peculiar. They lasted longer than two-and-a-half minutes: very odd.

But they made an impact: and again Dylan's originality as a rock artist was very clear. The folk fans who carried on listening called his new music 'folk rock' because, well, he was a folksinger and yet there he was using electric guitars and things; and from the other side, the pop fans who began to listen also called it 'folk rock' because, well, it was certainly rock and yet it was strange, it demanded intelligent attention.

Both groups of people were right. This was a new music, an original music. Dylan had made a profound connection between folk's articulacy and rock's virility. Here was rock music, part of the pop world, yet with it Bob Dylan was pumping out something of infinitely more dimensions than any one else had ever thought of in pop before. Pop had its isolationism torn away from it and was made to contemplate part of the real world too.

Perhaps it was just because Dylan was fully conscious of this achievement that he demanded such high standards from his rock musicians.

Even for his first appearance in rock music, at the Newport Folk Festival in 1965 (a slice of which is included in the film 'Festival'), he only enlisted the best – they were, then, from the Paul Butterfield Blues Band. And as the words on Dylan's electric albums got more and more impressionistic, less and less specific, the music got ever more precisely 'right'. (And this is why by the time of 'Nashville Skyline' the musicianship clinches Dylan's country stuff as both more commercial and more ethnic than other people's.)

If the oddness of Dylan as a pop figure, with all his perplexing innovations, suggested that intelligence was assaulting the pop scene, that didn't mean that no clever people besides Bob Dylan had ever made their mark in pop. It isn't true that success depends on stupidity, as outsiders tend to assume.

Being a bit dumb can help, of course: could Neil Diamond vulgarize everything so gladly if he was sensitive enough to puke up after every show? How could Diana Ross carry on if she could see herself as others see her? How could she even smile like that? And it's well known that in England pop as a business is kept going by cliques of sharp but brainless cockneys.

But you don't need to be thick. Phil Spector, Mick Jagger, John Lennon, Joan Armatrading, Elvis Costello, David Bowie – all intelligent artists. Yet they haven't accomplished any fundamental changes as Dylan has. They've come into rock music

Conflicting styles – with the late Phil Ochs at the Newport Folk Festival, 1964.   © JIM MARSHALL 1981

accepting it more or less as they've found it: all they've done is find themselves a corner each to sit in.

In contrast, Dylan has used his artistic intelligence to recreate the rock milieu. Far from accepting what he found and settling down in some lucrative little niche, he has burst the whole pop world wide open and built a new one (and with much more than the bricks of the old).

Before him, you could have said that pop was like football. Millions of people liked it – millions of people like fish and chips – but it didn't matter. Dylan made it matter. He showed that a rock song could provide an appropriate form for universal statements. So the pop world split in two. Half was music that has rattled on   115 regardless of change – regardless of Dylan. The other music, labelled 'progressive' when it began in the mid-1960s, couldn't have happened without Dylan.

You can't blame The Beatles for the 'improvements' in bubblegum, and you can't blame Dylan for all the cheap and nasty developments which his work inspired before serious musicianship and artistry in rock music found itself.

First, predictably, in Dylan's wake, came the Great Pop Protest Craze. It was, as Richard Mabey wrote:*

> not a very long-lived fad, nor in statistical terms a very successful one. But it aroused a spirited controversy and left a faint but seemingly permanent impression . . . It had, in theory, every element that a truly popular form should have, and suffered, in practice, every injury that can befall such a form as it is shunted through our mass communications network . . .

The 'seemingly permanent impression' the protest craze left was, nevertheless, that people in pop felt obliged or permitted to engage with the outside world: to be seen to have outside interests, to think, to produce material that was less mass-minded. Dylan had already said it – the protest free-for-all just tarnished the Dylan legacy.

Some of what happened afterwards *was* pretty tarnished too. In England, Maureen Cleave could legitimately include the following in a glance back over 1966:†

> . . . pop singers in interviews said they were reading the works of Huxley, Sartre and Dr Timothy Leary. One even claimed to be reading *Ulysses* . . . But there were compensatory laughs . . . Andrew Oldham said Scott Engel of the Walker Brothers was the Joan Crawford of pop music, and Scott Walker said no he wasn't – he was the Greta Garbo . . . The *Sunday Telegraph* described Andrew Oldham as the Rolling Stones' 'creative manager' . . .
>
> Any pop singer, at a loss for something to say, said he was thinking of opening a boutique. (As Clement Freud so rightly pointed out, one feels such a fool without a boutique nowadays.) . . . Mick Jagger took to producing: 'Jagger', said an admirer, 'who brought Nureyev to rock 'n' roll is now the Zeffirelli of pop.' We saw the story of Donovan's life on television: 'My job,' he said, 'is writing beautiful things about beauty. You see, my life is beautiful.' . . .
>
> Nervous exhaustion was all the rage. Scott Engel was exhausted nervously; so was a Kink, a Yardbird and a Cream. Mick Jagger was reported to be nervously exhausted after buying furniture for his new flat . . . in the last few months even nervous exhaustion was on the decline.
>
> It was replaced by the conviction that everything was beautiful, groovy and gentle. Pop singers floated around loving people in a patronizing manner that was even more infuriating than their protest songs. 'When you are aware,' Donovan said, 'there are no such things as hate and envy: there is only love.'
>
> 'This industry of human happiness,' said Andrew Oldham crossly. Oh yes, there were laughs in plenty; but . . . it was the end of an era . . .
>
> The pop singers themselves have grown old; their faces on television look old, world-weary; bored faces that have seen it all. The future is bleak

---

* *The Pop Process* by Richard Mabey, Hutchinson Educational Limited, 1969.
† I take this from the Maureen Cleave article as quoted in full in the Mabey book.

The white-face make-up used on the Rolling Thunder Revues of 1976 and 1977
and captured vividly in the 'Renaldo and Clara' film of 1977.

Above: *With Susie Rotolo in New York, from the session used on the 'Freewheelin' Bob Dylan' album cover.*

Below: *January 1968: Dylan's first public appearance since the motorcycle accident that pulled him out of an insanely heavy world-tour schedule in July 1966. With Pete Seeger, Judy Collins and Arlo Guthrie at the Woody Guthrie Memorial Concert, New York City.*

> . . . but the present, while they sort themselves out, is pretty sordid.
> Nineteen sixty-six is the year the whole thing turned sour. Many found
> they hadn't made the money they ought to have made. The shock reduced
> them to complete inactivity . . . What, one wonders, will happen to them?
> They can't all be absorbed by boutiques.

And yes, suddenly it was go to San Francisco with a flower in your hair, and after that Frank Zappa told the lefties at LSE that 'revolution is this year's flower power'.

You can't blame Dylan. He'd finished recording his 'protests' in 1963, and on his last solo album (the one with the rock sound) had issued his dismissive evaluation, *My Back Pages*. By the time the protest craze was happening, it was one too many mornings and a thousand miles behind its founder.

With *Mr Tambourine Man*, Dylan had started something else: the pop exploration of drugs. He carried it through – based, we all assume, on heavy personal use – and in the year that Maureen Cleave was characterizing as 'sour', Dylan issued 'Blonde On Blonde': acid-rock. It may not have been apparent at the time, but this was the great regenerative force. In terms of pop history, it was the single most important recording since Presley's *Heartbreak Hotel*.

It was less the drugs than what Dylan had done with druggy music that caused the 'underground' explosion that followed 'Blonde On Blonde' – and explosion of groups with (at first) strange names and genuine exploratory work. Dylan was father to all these groups – to Moby Grape, Big Brother & The Holding Company, The Doors, The Velvet Underground, Sopwith Camel, Country Joe & The Fish, Jefferson Airplane, The Byrds, Iron Butterfly, Dr John The Night-Tripper, Procul Harum, etc, etc, etc. They were all descendants of Dylan: and so was *Sgt Pepper's Lonely Hearts' Club Band*.

As his protest music had popularized and part-unified the anti-Establishment focus, so too his acid-rock/surrealist music made possible an alternative to that Establishment outside of tiny avant-garde minorities: he was catalyst in the mass adoption of the 'underground' that became what we now look back on as being representative 1960s culture. If the protest craze had shown that serious expression in pop music would have to steer clear, in future, of the Hit Parade and the leeches down Tin Pan Alley, then Dylan had shown that a viable alternative really was possible, given a certain singleness of purpose and a thing pop had never recognized before – integrity. Dylan's protest songs survived the craze, on the whole; Dylan carried on exploring without regard for trends, never a slave to pop's unwritten rules. And in this, to a greater or lesser extent, the underground groups were his offspring.

Not only that. The attempt to learn from drugs, the attempt to recreate drug experiences, the rejection of common-sense logic and the acceptance of mystery – Dylan accelerated the awakening to all this. His was the giant silhouette hovering above the crowds at the Rock Music Festivals that characterized the era. And if such festivals confirmed that pop had changed and that the new music was 'concerned more with incantation than with communication' then Wilfred Mellers was justified in introducing that phrase in the context of reviewing 'Blonde On Blonde'.

Dylan himself, characteristically, always denied responsibility. No sooner had the Beautiful People scene, the-all-you-need-is-love-and-a-rock-band scene, reached breakneck speed in San Francisco than Dylan was, well, breaking his neck, or claiming so, and staying away.

After a two-year silence, he issued 'John Wesley Harding', which was a rejection of the new music, the love generation, drugs, revolution and almost every other focus of solidarity set up and encouraged by his earlier work. As Jon Landau wrote in *Crawdaddy*, May '68 (many years before he became that 'new Dylan' Bruce Springsteen's producer):

> 'John Wesley Harding' is a profoundly egotistical album. For an album of this kind to be released amidst *Sgt Pepper*, *Their Satanic Majesties Request*, *Strange Days* and *After Bathing at Baxter's*, somebody must have had a lot of confidence in what he was doing . . . Dylan seems to feel no need to respond to the predominate trends in pop music at all. And he is the only major pop artist about whom this can be said. The Dylan of 'John Wesley Harding' is a truly independent artist who doesn't feel responsible to anyone else, whether they be fans or his contemporaries.

It wasn't really a rock album at all; it certainly hadn't got a rock sound, except for the country-rock of the last two tracks – and they were less integral parts of the whole than signposts to yet another future. *Down Along The Cove* and *I'll Be Your Baby Tonight* foreshadowed 'Nashville Skyline'.

'John Wesley Harding' was out of even the new pop world (which was by then different enough from the old for the word 'pop' to seem embarrassing and inappropriate and the word 'rock' just had to replace it). But the new world rolled on, from the opportunity-blueprints of 'Blonde On Blonde', using the medium as an art form and producing, at its best, an abundance of creative, self-made music.

Even where the sources were musically/lyrically very different, it was still Dylan who had opened the door. Frank Zappa for instance, didn't need 'Blonde On Blonde' (or 'Highway 61 Revisited') musically but he needed Dylan to establish that 'pop' artists could claim and merit serious attention. And, like all the rest, he needed the example of Dylan's successfully ruthless focus on established values. Without him, the Mothers really would have been a freak show, largely unheeded and soon forgotten.

Bob Dylan, single-handed, had created the sheer possibility of the situation Paul Williams was able to describe in the issue of *Crawdaddy* that was quoted above:

> Rock groups who take themselves seriously [wrote Williams] are not always eager to cater to what they believe is the public taste – and of course their direct contact is not with the public but with the record companies and the radio stations, who have their own ideas as to what the public taste might be . . . The performer, then, is in a difficult position. Should he try to please the public, the record company or himself?

Before Dylan, that question would never have got asked. Before Dylan, everyone put the public first. They all bowed to what they imagined were the common denominators of public taste. Dylan not only showed them all, or their successors, that you didn't have to go along with this: he also showed that when you didn't go along with it but offered honestly some personally satisfying alternative, you could release an undiscovered openness in the public. Bob Dylan unchained public taste. He did more than anybody else to develop in a mass audience the kind of receptiveness to things imaginative and non-trivial that was, before, the sole prerogative of elite minorities. His art has had that concrete an impact.

That's a sizeable claim, but it's well worth standing by. Dylan himself, of course, wouldn't dream of standing by it. The interview he granted *Rolling Stone* (December 13, 1969) served to emphasize this:

RS: Many people . . . all felt tremendously affected by your music and
　　　what you're saying in the lyrics.

BD: Did they?

RS: Sure. They felt it had a particular relevance to their lives . . . I mean, you must be aware of the way that people come on to you.

BD: Not entirely. Why don't you explain it to me.

RS: I guess if you reduce it to its simplest terms, the expectation of your audience – the portion of your audience that I'm familiar with – feels that you have the answer.

BD: What answer?

RS: Like from the film 'Don't Look Back' – people asking you 'Why? What is it? Where is it?' . . . Do you feel responsible to those people?

BD: I don't want to make anybody worry about it . . . if I could ease somebody's mind, I'd be the first to do it. I want to lighten every load. Straighten out every burden. I don't want anybody to be hung-up . . . (laughs) especially over me, or anything I do. That's not the point at all.

RS: Let me put it another way – what I'm getting at is that you're an extremely important figure in music and an extremely important figure in the experience of growing up today. Whether you put yourself in that position or not, you're in that position. And you must have thought about it – and I'm curious to know what you think about that.

BD: What would I think about it? What can I do?

RS: You wonder if you're really that person.

BD: What person?

RS: A great 'youth leader' . . .

BD: . . . there must be people trained to do this type of work. And I'm just one person doing what I do. Trying to get along – staying out of people's hair, that's all.

RS: You've been a tremendous influence on a lot of musicians and writers.* They're very obviously affected by your style, the way you do things –

BD: Who?

The answer to that question, in the late 1960s, of course, was everyone. In the 1970s, as a result, Dylan's influence has been disseminated broadly. Yet that influence is also plain as a source of inspiration for many specific artists who have themselves had impact in the last ten years.

Bruce Springsteen is one brand of Dylan with added ingredient Boyish Enthusiasm; John Prine is another, with a more determined backwoods grittiness. Tom Petty takes his fey styling angst from Dylan, while Bob Seger turns Dylan's husky-voiced romance-of-the-American-road into full-blown operetta.

The Pretenders' abrasive lyrics, and those of the New Wave generally, owe more than a little to Dylan's precedent-setting in that area. John Cooper Clarke even looks as much like Dylan '66 as possible. Mick Jones of The Clash keeps his admiration secret, but went to at least two of Dylan's 1978 British concerts.

*Not least on writers like those who put *Rolling Stone* together. A small but eloquent testimony to this effect is provided merely by the headlines in 'the alternative press'. Dylan phrases, as if they were the Western World's Mao's Thoughts, are littered continuously throughout the underground's literature. It is one of Dylan's most minor achievements (though it hints of greater ones) that his songs have answered a thousand sub-editors' prayers, right through to the 1980s, in which London's affluently trendy, lefter-than-thou magazine *Time Out* has a political cartoon series called 'Maggie's Farm'.

Bowie has always owed his idea of the enigmatic superstar to Dylan, just as Joni Mitchell owes a similar debt as regards her notion of the singer-songwriter.

Television and Talking Heads represent re-applications of the mid-60s Dylan style of ascetic, minimalist weirdness; and Patti Smith has borrowed wholesale from Dylan her conception of spiky decadence and of being a successor to the Beat Poets, and her irrational need to mention Rimbaud or Baudelaire in almost every public sentence.

Joe Ely has founded his compulsive visions of the new Tex-Mex music on Dylan's old ones. Dire Straits owe Dylan the voice they use – right down to the timing and italicized phrasing. And Elvis Costello inherits from Bob Dylan that penchant for extremely clever rhymes, that general irreverent briskness, that anti-romantic romanticism, and that blending of re-worked old pop-song melodies with new complicated lyrics. Indeed, just as Dylan re-worked Chuck Berry's *Too Much Monkey Business* into his own *Subterranean Homesick Blues*, so Costello re-worked that into his own *Pump It Up*: same tune, same lyric-as-list, same jerky monotone delivery.

Dylan himself would rather dodge all this responsibility. Later in that same Rolling Stone interview I was quoting – with the interviewer still trying for an answer of acceptance somewhere – there is this final refusal to accept:

> RS: Do you think that you've played any role in the change of
>   popular music in the last few years?
> BD: I hope not. (laughs)

Anyone who handles an interview like that – teaching the journalist something about the incisive use of language while he's at it – has to deserve applause – but no one else besides Dylan should concur with his denials of responsibility.

Chapter 5

Dylan's Use of Language
Towards Complexity

Pourin' off of every page
Like it was written in my soul
From me to you
Tangled up in blue
(from Dylan's *Tangled Up In Blue*)

Dylan's work through the 1960s shows a vivid growth in the complexity of his use of language. At the end of that decade, with few later exceptions, he begins to pare down and to opt for a new simplicity in his writing. This chapter and the next chart these two opposite progressions of his artistry.

Let's not make difficulties over defining 'imagery' and so on. As if to underline a disregard for unnecessary quibbles, I begin with part of a David Horowitz article which refers happily to Dylan's 'symbolic language' without saying what *that* means. Horowitz's term covers what, in dealing with the same song, I would mean by 'imagery'. The song is the early one *A Hard Rain's A-Gonna Fall*, and Horowitz writes:

> The artistic problems involved in treating such a subject (the threat of nuclear wipe-out – raised at the time of the song's composition by the 1962 Cuba Crisis) seriously (Dylan has given it a splendid satiric treatment in *Talking World War III Blues*) are seemingly insurmountable; but Dylan has done so in the only way possible: by employing an approach that is symbolic. Only a symbolic language could bear the strain of an event as absolute and apocalyptic as the total destruction of life on earth. Dylan's instinctive awareness of the capacities of symbolism is, in this song, turned to brilliant use. In *Hard Rain*, Dylan has adapted the melody and refrain of the traditional English song, *Lord Randall*, and by this very fact has set his own 'story' in a frame of concreteness;
>
> > 'O where have you been, my blue-eyed son,
> > And where have you been, my darlin' young one?'
>
> But the actual tale which is told in answer to the traditional question takes place on an altogether different plane of reality from that of its source:
>
> > 'I've stumbled on the side of twelve misty mountains
> > I've walked an' I've crawled on six crooked highways
> > I've stepped in the middle of seven sad forests
> > I've bin out in front of a dozen dead oceans
> > I've bin ten thousand miles in the mouth of a graveyard
> > An' it's a hard, it's a hard, it's a hard, an' it's a hard,
> > It's a hard rain's a-gonna fall.'

The cumulative effect of these images, an effect which is reinforced by the repeated rhythmic figure of the guitar accompaniment, is little short of overwhelming. We are besieged with images of dead and dying life, a kind of dynamic stasis, a perfect figurative medium for the vision at the brink:

> 'I met a young child beside a dead pony
> I met a white man who walked a black dog
> I met a young woman whose body was burning
> I met a young girl, she gave me a rainbow . . .'

We have the start of many stories here, never to be finished, and in the very fact of this arrested promise an accurate rendering of the meaning of that awful apocalypse that may await us. Aptly, this style, which is so tuned to the reality, was actually dictated by it. For, as Dylan explains, 'Every line in it . . . is actually the start of a whole song. But when I wrote it, I thought I wouldn't have enough time alive to write all those songs, so I put all I could into this one.' Because of the precision of the tone and the adequacy of the vision, when it is over, and the respite won, the poet's resolve carries absolute conviction:

> 'And I'll tell it and speak it and think it and breathe it
> And reflect from the mountains so all souls can see it
> And I'll stand on the ocean until I start sinkin'
> And I'll know my song well before I start singin'
> And it's a hard, it's a hard, it's a hard, and it's a hard,
> It's a hard rain's a-gonna fall.'

I think Horowitz accepts too readily that Dylan's articulacy is not so much individual as traditionally 'skilful'; it assumes that Dylan's early work compliantly fits in his non-literal language according to the long-established literary rules.

This isn't the case. If you look from the *rules* to the work Dylan has produced you get entangled in listing Dylan's 'failures', or, to put it another way, in emphasizing Dylan's 'lack of sophistication' in handling language, or in defensively referring to his 'instinctive' talents.

Such entanglement will reveal, in fact, not *Dylan's* faults but a wrong perspective on the listener's or critic's part. Full as Dylan's work is of 'unsophisticated' imagery, the success – the eloquence and impact – of such language *in Dylan's hands* challenges any weighting of 'sophistication' as an evaluative term.

All the same, it is a feature of Dylan's early work that the good the bad and the ugly often go hand in hand. In *I'd Hate To Be You On That Dreadful Day*, for instance, bad things abound (Dylan never released a record of the song), like this:

> Well your clock is gonna stop at Saint Peter's gate,
> You're gonna ask him what time it is, he's gonna say
>   It's Too Late
> Hey hey, I'd sure hate to be you on that dreadful day.

I would imagine even Barry MacGuire would have rejected that; and yet the same song included this why-didn't-anyone-express-that-before idea:

> You're gonna have a nightmare and never wake up!
> Hey hey, etc.

As for the comparably gloom-ridden *A Hard Rain's A-Gonna Fall*, it is true that to a very large extent, Dylan's use of images is, as it happens, dictated by tradition. On the other hand, that makes it *un*characteristic of Dylan's early work; and in some ways even this song offers a special use of imagery.

Line upon line the pictures are piled up, some containing their own 'moral' via paradox:

Newport 1964, with John Hammond Jnr.

> I saw a new-born babe with wild wolves all around it . . .
> I saw guns and sharp swords in the hands of young children . . .
> Heard one person starve, I heard many people laughin' . . . ;

others with the same purpose but taking longer to say it:

> I met one man who was wounded in love,
> I met another man who was wounded with hatred . . . ;

and others which citing two pictures, offer an analogy or parallel:

> Heard the song of a poet who died in the gutter,
> Heard the sound of a clown who cried in the alley . . .

Then again, there are images which stand alone, entirely detached, and which do not apparently operate as direct moral diagrams:

> I bin ten thousand miles in the mouth of a graveyard . . .
> I saw a highway of diamonds with nobody on it . . .
> I saw a white ladder all covered with water
> I met a young girl, she gave me a rainbow . . .

The most interesting thing, perhaps, in terms of Dylan's achievement, is that although the fifth verse draws the morals almost specifically, and although the deliberate fragmentedness of the other verses does fit into a cohesive moral *theme*, the effectiveness of this theme still depends on the pictures rolling past, as if on and then off a screen, without opportunity of recall. In other words, there is a simple, strange sense in which for the song as a whole to succeed, each image within it asserts a segregated life of its own.

Even where Dylan does use traditional images (and there are many of them in his early work) he doesn't utilize them along traditional lines.

For example, think of the traditional rendering of someone's personality or spirit in terms of a 'light'. Someone's being referred to as giving out light is conventional, but the reference is normally indirect – like this perhaps:

> As Hartley's eyes swept the ballroom, his attention was called back, again and again, to the same animated face. Miss Satterthwaite (for indeed the face was hers) seemed to radiate an ethereal yet energetic light – and it was not long till Mr Hartley stood breathless in the glow of it.

The image of light there is almost asleep: it is a traditional image traditionally used. Dylan, employing it more casually, rejuvenates it by his non-traditional usage. He takes it from the context of third person narration and plunges it into a direct conversation: and so it emerges with a refreshing bluntness:

> It ain't no use in turnin' on your light, babe –
> That light I never knowed

and is given an effective extension:

> An' it ain't no use in turnin' on your light, babe –
> I'm on the dark side of the road . . .

A noticeably similar 'unsophisticated' bluntness is reapplied, years later, in that most eloquent 'Blood On The Tracks' song, *Tangled Up In Blue*, where he is handed the book of medieval poetry and describes his feeling that 'Everyone of them words rang true/and glowed like burnin' coal/Pourin' off of every page'. The cliché of 'words rang true' has its meaning re-activated by the physicality of the image that follows it: when words burn and pour, they really do *ring* too.

There is one further general point about Dylan's 'unsophisticated' imagery: where it *can* be called unsophisticated, it usually carries corresponding strengths.

Often, for instance, with Dylan's least subtle imagery, he relies on a combination of simplicity and *anger*, to yield a considerable effectiveness. This works well enough in *Masters Of War*.

> But I see through your eyes and I see through your brain
> Like I see through the water that runs down my drain.*

Consider too the *simple* effectiveness of the imagery in his *Ballad Of Hollis Brown*. There, the words are so riveting and so didactically visual that Dylan can even afford to echo the nursery-rhyme about the crooked man without this distracting us:

> You look for work and money
> And you walk a rugged mile
> You look for work and money
> And you walk a rugged mile . . .

---

* *Masters of War* also provides an example of Dylan's using an 'echo-image': that is, where the wording used to give one visual picture deliberately echoes other pictures, other moods – even another poet's voice: 'An' I hope that you die, and your death will come soon,/*I will follow your casket on a pale afternoon* . . .' The poet there, of course, is Eliot; and in recalling him, Dylan moderates his song's mood of anger with the Eliot tone of underlying sadness.

Neither are we distracted when we come to an apparently histrionic analogy like this:

> Your wife's screams are stabbin'
> Like the dirty drivin' rain.

The very lack of balance in the construction of that analogy enforces its realism. It is a way of the narrator saying 'I understand your desperation – *your* imbalance.'

And this relationship between narrator and subject gives the song a strength that is more widely distributed than the isolated quotation above can indicate. We can turn back to David Horowitz' article for more on this point:

> Technically speaking, *Hollis Brown* is a tour de force. For a ballad is normally a form which puts one at a distance from its tale. This ballad, however, is told in the second person, present tense, so that not only is a bond forged immediately between the listener and the figure of the tale, but there is the ironic fact that the only ones who know of Hollis Brown's plight, the only ones who care, are the hearers who are helpless to help, cut off from him, even as we in a mass society are cut off from each other.

When even such an early song as *The Ballad Of Hollis Brown* has such strengths, it is plainly useless to talk of his 'unsophisticated' approach – unless we use that adjective to be synonymous with 'honest'.

Horowitz also points to the power of the blues in Dylan's hands; and here too it is fruitless to measure his worth by traditional literary criteria. Horowitz argues:

> Indeed, the blues perspective itself, uncompromising, isolated and sardonic, is superbly suited to express the squalid reality of contemporary America. And what a powerful expression it can be, once it has been liberated (as it has in Dylan's hands) from its egocentric bondage!
>
> A striking example of the tough, ironic insight one associates with the blues (and also of the power of understatement which Dylan has learnt from Guthrie) is to be found in the final lines of *Hollis Brown*:

> > 'There's seven people dead on a South Dakota farm,
> > There's seven people dead on a South Dakota farm,
> > Somewhere in the distance there's seven new people born.'

> How much of the soul of contemporary American society and its statistical conscience is expressed in this sardonic image!'

When Dylan returns to the blues on his masterpiece album of the 1970s, 'Blood On The Tracks', he gives us this crowning example of spectacular simplicity – and wit:

> Buckets of rain, buckets of tears
> Got all them buckets comin' out of my ears

Dylan uses conventional figurative language to equal effect in one of the very earliest of his published compositions, *Song To Woody*, where he takes the obvious but worthwhile step of personifying the 'funny ol' world' which

> Seems sick an' it's hungry it's tired an' it's torn
> It looks like it's a-dyin' an' it's hardly bin born.

That reliance on twisting the conventions of the figurative recurs in the unreleased *Train A-Travellin'*, where we have an extended metaphor which uses a reality of pleasant associations to stand for an unpleasant ethos:

> There's an iron train a-travelin' that's bin a-rollin' through the years
> With a firebox of hatred and a furnace full of fears . . .
> Did you ever see its passengers, its crazy mixed-up souls?

The eloquence achieved by alliteration (in that second line) is typical of Dylan's 'unsophisticated' work. The use of the train metaphor is more complex: 'iron' is usually associated with an animate machine such as a train in an approving way – as a coloured term indicating strength (as it is, for example, in Dylan's own much later *Never Say Goodbye*, 1974, where 'my dreams are made of iron and steel'). In *Train A-Travellin'* it is associated with blindness, or stubbornness; it condemns a dogmatic quality (the direction of which is, of course, shown by that 'firebox of hatred').

This ultra-simplicity of imagery is partnered frequently by an *opposite* sort of quality to one of 'overriding anger' – partnered, that is, by an understatement. There is no anger here, and there is nothing complex either; but the effectiveness is undeniable:

> Oh a false clock tries to tick out my time
> To disgrace, distract and bother me
> And the dirt of gossip blows in my face
> And the dust of rumours covers me
> But if the arrow is straight
> And the point is slick
> It can pierce through dust no matter how thick:
> So I'll make my stand
> And remain as I am
> And bid farewell and not give a damn.
>
> (*Restless Farewell*)

None of those would be called complex images – or great ones – but in that an image's function is not to sit glistening for the critic's entertainment but rather to make more vivid the artist's idea, then they work perfectly. And they don't need the energy of a *Masters Of War* anger-blanket to help them.

They are far from clichéd: and yet they *are* standard images. The element of surprise, which gives them their force, is the shift from the clock image as the centre to the dust image – and so visually from the sharpness of the ticking to the smothering softness of that 'dust'.

This early simplicity of language often works in a different general direction. Rather than just ignoring traditional literary rules, Dylan often actually breaks them – and the effects are not then so simple.

Consider, for instance, these two tiny lines from *Eternal Circle*:

> Through a bullet of light
> Her face was reflectin'

They don't provide the visual image one might expect – because visualization is just about impossible. The picture given by 'bullet of light' is *contradicted*, and so cancelled out, by the reflectin' *face* – for face challenges, by its very roundness of shape, any idea of light like a bullet, which is to say, like a fast straight line. Yet if there is no visualization, there is still a response to that 'image', and still a purpose in its being there. It is a word-sound image; part of its strength is that its *sounds* are attractive – and they give the voice a kind of equivalent articulacy to the wiry strength of the accompanying guitar-sounds.

By the time of the fourth album, 'Another Side Of Bob Dylan', coming straight after *Restless Farewell*, one very characteristic type of image has emerged: images invoking the elements. Dylan notices winds, rains, and so on keenly, using them dramatically in the action of his songs. His presentation of them is distinctive – so much so that anyone familiar with even a few Dylan songs would recognize all the following lines as being from his work:

> The night comes in a-fallin' . . .
> The wind howls like a hammer . . .
> And the firing air it felt frozen . . .
> An' the silent night will shatter . . .
> Through the mad mystic hammering of the wild ripping hail . . .
> The stars one by one they're a folding . . .
> The sky is folding . . .

plus, to choose four lines together (from the unreleased *Walls of Red Wing*):

> As the night laid shadows
> Through the crossbar windows
> And the wind punched hard
> To make the wall siding sing

or, to add a phrase that only strays slightly from an imagery of the elements:

> . . . electric light still struck like arrows.

That line is from the fourth-album song *Chimes Of Freedom* which is in one way the central song of the album. Ostensibly, the opposite is true: it is the last explicit protest song: the words have a message. Yet the message is *not* the important point – and it is as if Dylan uses this apparent 'message song' to show his listeners that significance lies elsewhere. In doing that, the song offers the motto for the whole album. And indeed it has the album's 'sound', to note which brings us to what *is* the importance of *Chimes Of Freedom*: namely, that with this 'sound' – the echo, the voice, the chiselled word-*shapes*; the sculptured, hard-grained phrasing – Dylan creates a world. It is in notable contrast that in the later, more 'out-of-this-world' Dylan work, its force is, paradoxically, an interpretative one, not a sculptural.

So far, I have focused on a general *simplicity* in Dylan's language; but Dylan is far more famous (albeit due to misconceptions, on the whole) for the antithesis of this – a complexity of language that runs over (so the charge goes) – into the positively obscure. 'Another Side Of Bob Dylan' begins the development of the new complexity. The first hints of it come even earlier.

The previous album, 'The Times They Are A-Changin'', offers an interesting example of poetic transference. On the beautiful *One Too Many Mornings* the attributes of one thing are transferred onto another:

> And the silent night will shatter
> From the sounds inside my mind . . .

The prose equivalent, stripped of this transference, would be that the silence (of the night) will be shattered; as Dylan has it, the night will shatter.

This transference succeeds: it comes across as forceful and unforced. It urges the inseparability of the night and the silence. It gives us creatively, and with a terse economy, the idea that if the night were no longer silent, it would not be the same night.

There is a line in the unreleased *Long Ago, Far Away* (1962) which offers, in a sense, another instance of transference – one involving slighter implications but an arresting visual picture:

People cheered with bloodshot grins.

From the fourth album, perhaps the most historically interesting song is *Spanish Harlem Incident*; which begins with this:

> Gypsy Gal, the hands of Harlem
> Cannot hold you to its heat

which, as far as his figurative language is concerned, is like a stylish and immediately impressive declaration of independence on Dylan's part. It's a pretty good image, and very individual.

Thus with *Spanish Harlem Incident*, and that fourth album, we find the really substantial beginnings of Dylan's famous complexity – the beginnings of what 1965 brought out with an explosion, and what 1966 sustained in the 'Blonde On Blonde' double-album. (By the 1965 explosion, I mean that that year saw a huge list of great Dylan songs, great Dylan recordings: *Ballad Of A Thin Man*; *Can You Please Crawl Out Your Window?*; *Desolation Row*; *Farewell Angelina*; *From A Buick Six*; *The Gates Of Eden*; *It's Alright Ma (I'm Only Bleeding)*; *It Takes A Lot To Laugh, It Takes A Train To Cry*; *Just Like Tom Thumb's Blues*; *Like A Rolling Stone*; *Love Minus Zero/No Limit*; *On The Road Again*; *Outlaw Blues*; *Positively 4th Street*; *She Belongs To Me*; *Subterranean Homesick Blues*; and more besides – all from 1965. An amazing, breathtaking burst of prolific creativity.) *Spanish Harlem Incident* is therefore especially interesting – *historically* interesting because of its pioneering slot in Dylan's output.

> I am homeless, come and take me
> Into reach of your rattling drums.
> Let me know, babe, all about my fortune
> Down along my restless palms.

There, strikingly, is that individual style of impressionism which Dylan was to cultivate (and which attracted so many unfortunate imitations – including much from The Beatles, with their 'plasticine porters' and 'marmalade skies'). Dylan's impressionism works because in his imagery above, he begins simply enough with that non-literal, non-physical, 'homeless'; and while he moves to that apparently vaguer 'rattling drums' yet the adjective there has a precision of its own: one is shown how appropriate the phrase is to the spirit of the girl as Dylan sees her. Next, there is a precise function in the uniting of two ideas in 'my restless palms' – the validity of the fortune-telling allusion being sympathetically strengthened by its connection to the singer's admitted desire for hand-in-hand contact. And the wish implicit there harks back to that 'come and take me' in the earlier line.

> Gypsy Gal, you got me swallowed,
> I have fallen far beneath
> Your pearly eyes so fast an' slashin'
> And your flashin' diamond teeth.

There is nothing contrived here, as the context and the recording yield up those lines. 'Swallowed' works neatly, and the unobtrusive reversal of the usual teeth and eyes metaphors again strikes the listener as unforced, evoking a real idea of the girl the song addresses.

It is in terms of the girl that this near-Gothic effect works also:

> The night is pitch black, come an' make my
> Pale face fit into place, ah! please!

For such a girl, the night *would* make itself dramatic. Again, we feel that the girl's personality draws out this, in the final verse:

> On the cliffs of your wildcat charms I'm riding,
> I know I'm round you but I don't know where.

In fact the first of those two lines gives a perfect summary of how the writer stands for the creation of the song. His language, throughout, is intent on eliciting a captivating vision of those 'wildcat charms'; and the singleness of purpose places Dylan's impressionistic imagery a long way from the random hit-and-miss impressionism of the hosts of Dylan's imitators. Theirs is exhibited for its own sake and is its own reason for being; Dylan's is there to assist the communication of specific and personally realized themes.

Correspondingly, it is only when he has no such theme – when he is expressing nothing more personally valid than a recognizable public feeling – that he succumbs to a vagueness and sloppiness of language which resembles that of his imitators.

This happens in Dylan's archetypal protest song, *The Times They Are A-Changin'*. With that song, his aim was to ride on the unvoiced sentiment of a mass public – to ride, that is, as the spokesman for people who wanted to hear just such 'a fuck you of enraged self-assertion'. (That phrase is Elia Katz'.)

As a result, the language is weak – imprecisely directed and conceived too generally. It offers four extended metaphors, and makes no more than an easy politician's use of any of them. The four are: change as a rising tide; change dependent on the wheel of fate; the Establishment as an edifice; and yesterday and tomorrow as roads to be opted for.

People enjoy the song in the sense that they approve of its theory; it is a less satisfying alternative to Country Joe & The Fish's *Fish Cheer*, Woodstock Version – which was the ultimate fuck-you of self-assertion, and offered a mass public actually in on the speaking.

The Times They Are A-Changin' was certainly prophetic – but it has been outdated by the very changes the song itself threatened. Its message is *politically* out of date. On the one hand 'mothers and fathers throughout the land' are as ready as ever to criticize what they don't understand, and on the other hand the people who wanted change have rightly lost the optimism of expecting senators and congressmen to heed their political calls.

The Bob Dylan of the late 1970s fully acknowledged the way that the changing of the times had dated his song about them. When he sang it – for the first time in thirteen years – on his 1978 tour, he re-interpreted it as a sad, slow admission of his generation's failure. This version appears on the 'live' album 'Bob Dylan At Budokan', where there is even the inspired touch of a Duane Eddy guitar-sound to emphasize the anachrony of the song.

When The Ship Comes In prophesies a socio-political ideal future too – and offers us Dylan singing of the coming change in terms of an arriving ship – which seems as unsurprising as the use of roads, tides and so on in *The Times They Are A-Changin'*. Yet *When The Ship Comes In* has *not* been outdated by events. It survives because it is wisely unspecific; not out of vagueness, nor from an attempt to provide a common-to-everyone account. Necessarily and rightly, *its* references to coming changes are figurative to the point of allegory – because the important thing is (by contrast) the *personal* responses of the writer towards the anticipated future. The details, figurative, metaphorical, allegorical and symbolic as they are, define and illustrate *these* responses:

> Oh the foes will rise with the sleep still in their eyes

131

And they'll jerk from their beds and think they're dreamin'
But they'll pinch themselves and squeal
And they'll know that it's for real . . .

Oh the fishes will laugh as they swim out of the path
And the seagulls, they'll be smilin' . . .

Where *The Times They Are A-Changin'* gives us no sense of proximity to any individual's sensibility, *When The Ship Comes In* plainly offers a sincere vision. It puts us in contact with a real and *fine* sensibility. It doesn't lean on mass sentiment at any point; mass sentiment can, if it likes, lean on *it*.

That is why the song reminds me of the truly charming Richard Lovelace poem, *To Lucasta, Going To The Wars*:

Tell me not, Sweet, I am unkind
That from the nunnery
Of thy chaste breast and quiet mind
To war and arms I fly.

True, a new mistress now I chase
The first foe in the field;
And with a stronger faith embrace
A sword, a horse, a shield.

Yet this inconsistency is such
As thou too shalt adore;
I could not love thee, Dear, so much,
Loved I not Honour more.

Lovelace died in 1658, and wrote that poem in an age when its simplistic gallantry, chivalry and patriotism were just what the public approved of; yet Lovelace has offered not the *public* view but a highly *personalized* glimpse, so that the poem retains an impetus even today: and this despite the fact that the poem's attitude to war could hardly be more estranged from our own. Because Lovelace didn't lean on a *public* attitude, his poem has not been castrated by that public attitude's collapse. Something about it, through which its delicate self-reliance shines – still appeals.

Similarly, while *The Times They Are A-Changin'* has deteriorated, *When The Ship Comes In* is bound to last.*

Since *Spanish Harlem Incident* – fourth album – has been praised and *The Times They Are A-Changin'* – third album – disparaged, perhaps I have given the impression that by the time of that fourth album, Dylan had put bad writing behind him. This is not the case.

Ballad In Plain D, which is also from the fourth album, is a *very* bad song – partly because the words seem forced to fit the tune (and forced into rhymes also: 'Beneath a bare lightbulb/The plaster did pound/Her sister and I/In a screaming battleground/And she in between/The victim of sound.') and partly because words

---

* Another Dylan song that in this way resembles *The Times They Are A-Changin'* and contrasts with *When The Ship Comes In*, is the much less well known *Paths Of Victory*. Its language is total platitude: not a single fresh analogy breaks up the flow of cliché: 'The trail is dusty/And my road it might be rough/But the better roads are waiting/And boys it ain't far off –/Trails of troubles,/Roads of battles,/Paths of Victory/We shall walk.' An instantly forgettable and rather tiresome song – yet the theme is the same in basics as that of *When The Ship Comes In*. How erratic the standard of Dylan's use of language still was at the end of 1963!

With Susie Rotolo, 1963.

and tune so obviously *don't* fit. The lyric is full of Sensitive Teenage hysteria; the tune is Reflective and rather morose.

The hysteria shows a more fundamental fault: the telling of what is a tale of adolescent-love-frustrated is done not from outside, not with a detachment capable of reassessing the significance of the things experienced; but from the inside, so that the *assessment* is as teeny and entangled as the experience. Dylan could only have made the song worth having if he had handled his theme 'afterwards': if he could have judged from a non-adolescent perspective. The song deals with a stage of immature development and yet Dylan refuses to see it as such. His allegiance is to the state of mind which experienced the story; his attitude towards his own immaturity is a long way from mature.

There is, throughout the song, a pretence at the quality of assessment that is so patently missing.

> Myself for what I did
> I cannot be excused
> The changes I was going through
> Can't even be used.
> For the lies I told her
> In hope not to lose
> The could-be dream-lover
> Of my lifetime.

It doesn't convince. Somehow by the time we've got past 'The changes I was going through' we are aware of a sort of self-idealization on the narrator's part, enforced by that 'Myself . . .' as it is cushioned and coddled by the tune, and emphasized also by that hint of deliberate mysteriousness. We don't get told about the changes, nor about the 'lies', but their existence (and apparent importance) is thrust at us with an exaggerated solemnity we are supposed to take at face-value – to take with an equal solemnity.

The reliance on face-values leads Dylan to some embarrassingly bad lines:

> Of the two sisters
> I loved the young.
> With sensitive instincts
> She was the creative one.

Nothing in the song (and it has thirteen verses) *shows* us any of this: it is simply insisted upon.

There is, of course, another factor – Dylan's performance – which predictably goes a long way to minimizing the song's fault. With some lines, his voice can enhance sufficiently to give positive pleasure, as for instance at the very beginning:

> I once loved a girl,
> Her skin it was bronze . . .

and it is also true that there is one instance where the vagueness of imagery (which comes across, generally, as a kind of sulkiness) rolls back to give us an impressive glimpse of the boy-girl relationship gone wrong:

> Till the tombstones of damage
> Read no questions but Please,
> What's Wrong?
> What's Exactly The Matter?

which *is* detached enough to see the two lovers from the outside and observe the way that those sad questions get asked, as they so often do when our relationships are crumbling. Through the rest of the song, we have a dominant impression that despite that 'once' in the opening line, it all happened about two days before the song was set down, and that the motivation for the writing lay in the unsorted, ill-articulated

Dylan in New York, 1972, during the long gap between 'New Morning' and 'Pat Garrett', during which he guested on sessions for Doug Sahm, Steve Goodman and others.

aftermath of the experience.*

Only that motive could explain how such a bad song could have come from Dylan, especially at a time when so many good ones were emerging. Perhaps any transition period (as 1964 certainly was in Dylan's development) makes for vulnerability.

At any rate, 1965 was far more hectic and found Dylan's use of language in a far greater state of flux.

At one end we have *It's Alright Ma (I'm Only Bleeding)*, which is mainly a more circumspect re-working of, say, *Only A Pawn In Their Game*, yet merges this old approach to new language. Part of the song's impact is thereby its very patchiness – the way it keeps wowing from one sort of articulation to another. Thus Dylan makes even transitional experiment work for him not just as a way forward but as a procedure in its own right and for its own sake.

One minute the listener hears:

> Advertising signs that con you
> Into thinking you're the one
> that can do what's never been done
> that can win what's never been won
> Meantime life, outside, goes on
> all around you.

Very straightforward stuff. But then there's this:

> Temptation's page flies out the door
> You follow, find yourself at war,
> watch waterfalls of pity roar . . .

The struggle towards a complex figurative language keeps bursting through in flashes like this. The image that takes us to the edge of the waterfall, to the juxtaposition of 'pity' and 'roar' is only one of many 'deepening-points' in the song: it works and is abrasive in a more inward way than we would have expected from the earlier social-commentary songs. It is more real than the mirror of his older 'realist' songs.

This veering away from mere external (political) generalization goes hand in hand with a paradoxical change in external attitude. It appears (though not for the first time: *North Country Blues*, *The Lonesome Death Of Hattie Carroll* and others all have their personalized moments) along with a more resigned, accepting posture:

> It's all right, Ma, I can make it . . .
> It's all right, Ma, it's life and life only

and along with a more savage and jaundiced vision of what he bitterly calls 'people's games':

> Disillusioned words like bullets bark
> as human gods aim for their mark,
> Make everything from toy guns that spark
> to flesh-coloured Christs that glow in the dark
> It's easy to see without lookin' too far

* There's no greater contrast in levels of maturity (which is to do with turning an objective intelligence on oneself, and not to do with being 'grown up') anywhere in Dylan's work than that between the teen-petulance of *Ballad In Plain D* and the matchless lost-love songs on 'Blood On The Tracks' a decade later – *If You See Her Say Hello*, *You're A Big Girl Now* and *You're Gonna Make Me Lonesome When You Go*.

that not much
is really sacred.

All these changes seem to stem from Dylan discarding an anger that was the child of *optimism* – an indignation (as, for instance, in *Masters of War*) which could only be sustained so long as the belief in enlightened-congressmen-about-to-heed-the-call could itself be sustained. Dylan's graduation from the *Masters of War* approach towards real poetry – the poetry of real experience – can in this way be seen as prompted not by a change in political *belief*, nor by a *rejection* of politics (which is the same thing) but by a change in *assessment* of his political vision. To put it over-simply, Dylan became a more serious artist when profound political pessimism set in. The spectre of pessimism showed up pamphleteering songs as pitifully inadequate and rather silly. Dylan said so himself in *My Back Pages* and again in the song we've just looked at:

> While one who sings with his tongue on fire
> gargles in the rat-race choir –
> bent out of shape by society's pliers . . .

It's Alright Ma is not the last of Dylan's protest songs, but it is the last in which the vestiges of the old attitude remain – the last of the type wherein anger (and anger of the kind that pleads for help from senators) replaces analysis with accusation: and, like *My Black Pages*, it specifically abdicates the protest function. The con-temporaneous *Gates Of Eden* (see chapter 3) is very different in vision and organization and utterly different as an indicator of what Dylan had come to expect of himself as an artist.

This change seems complete by the time of *Desolation Row* – a classic illustration of the distinction between accusation and analysis. *Desolation Row* is a brilliant *political analysis* of American society, and shows vividly the connection between its pessimism and a seriousness of intent.

Dylan chooses to offer his narration from inside Desolation Row itself, and so he can communicate one part of his gloom in a personalized way:

> When you asked me how I was doing
> Was that some kind of joke?

The intention of the whole, however, is not to repeat the theme of, say, *North Country Blues*, which was basically the chronicle of a community's suffering in the face of encroaching penury. In *Desolation Row* Dylan is dealing with contemporary America in terms of its infection of human values. He is no longer treating a particular side-effect of capitalism as a sort of overlying weight which affronts the pockets of golden-hearted miners and the conscience of liberals. Dylan is recognizing a pervasive 'Amerika' (as it was called then), one that mutates all humanity and offers insinuatory as well as polarizing challenges: challenges against which the old liberal blueprints are worse than useless. Dylan no longer expects solutions to arise out of reforms or legislation. Neither does he see any point in rallying around the home-comforts of *We Shall Overcome*. There *is* no broad solution. The most Dylan looks for is that we can each try to develop, *individually*, an unwarped perspective:

> Right now I can't read too good
> Don't send me no more letters, no:
> Not unless you mail them from Desolation Row.

Excepting its final verse, the song is Dylan's necessarily tentative expression of such a perspective for himself.

On Lower 7th Avenue, New York, 1963. (The same tyre motif was to re-appear in the Nashville Skyline period).

He comes back to essentially the same stance on the 'Slow Train Coming' and 'Saved' albums of 1979–80. His prepare-to-meet-thy-maker warnings are saying again that at most (but also at least) one has the fundamental duty to oneself of keeping a clear head above all the poisonous waters of chaos and corrosion in which our society makes us swim.

On *Desolation Row*, Dylan emphasizes the complexity of the subject-matter, in the first place, by a sustained reversal of norms within the song: the beauty-parlour is filled with big hairy US Marines and it is the riot squad that needs putting down. Casanova, the sophisticate, is being spoon-fed; Romeo is moaning.

139

If nothing else on first hearings, the song is a striking and a sinister parade — and we come to see the chaos with clarity, come to see in the parade a barrage of folk-heroes in careful disarray: participants, victims and agents of a disordered, sick society.

The other general characteristic of the song is associated with the 'sinister' element: the song confronts us with recurring hints of imminent disaster. (Again, the similarities in 'Slow Train Coming' and 'Saved' are plain.)

For analysts of America committed to Big Bang Revolution, such hints are taken, of course, as signs of promise; but Dylan declines to go along with this approach (which, in order to simplify the 'solution', must warp the truth about the problems to be solved — must posit them as equally simple). In *Desolation Row* the imminent disasters are past and present as well as future. The verses pile up and pile up, the sinister intimations pile up with them, and there is no suggestion (no 'hope', in other words) that the crescendo will ever be curtailed.

If it wasn't for the last verse, with its different function, the song could be circular: which re-asserts that the parade could pass not once, or even several times but endlessly: timelessly. The very lengthiness of the song enforces this impression, as it is meant to, and so does the long and rather formless instrumental section which comes between the penultimate verse and the last.

This instrumental section takes the last verse away from the circular plane of the rest and sets it aside. Only on the page does it 'follow on' from the other verses; in reality it is off to one side, a satellite, alone but with a special focus which can be brought to bear on the rest at any point. When people consequently say that *Desolation Row* has two endings, they could more usefully say instead that it doesn't have an ending at all.

But though the climactic holocaust never quite comes, Dylan's intimations of disaster build up towards one. They come with ever-increasing intensity and there is, of course, in any case, a cumulative effect. At the beginning, the commissioner — who is blind — is tied by one hand to the tight-rope walker; the riot squad is bound to burst out somewhere; furtively, the ambulances move in and depart. Then we get these lines:

> Now the moon is almost hidden
> The stars are beginning to hide
> The fortune-telling lady
> Has even taken all her things inside . . .

Here Dylan carries us further into the darkness, linking the blanching of the moon and stars with the ominousness of the astrologer packing up and gravely going home after glimpsing the future. The neatness and power of these lines shows Dylan's success with a new economy of language.

What follows on has a neatness of not quite the same kind:

> All except for Cain and Abel
> An' the hunchback of Notre Dame
> Everybody is makin' love
> Or else expecting rain

and by this point in the song, we've had enough opportunity to note what a curious amalgam it is — part surrealism, part impressionistic metaphor, part allegory and part riddle: an anti-logic nightmare.

The most striking evocation of impending catastrophe is, however, achieved very simply — in the one arresting line

> The Titanic sails at dawn.

That summarizes concisely the tone and colouring of the whole song. For all its simplicity – perhaps because of it – the analogy does not take away from the complexity of the overall vision. Dylan takes the 'Titanic' to represent contemporary America: for the Titanic was the ship of the future, the 'proof' of man's civilization and progress, the unsinkable ship which, on her maiden voyage, sank. And, according to the best stories (and Dylan relies on their currency – a neat case of poetic licence) when the ship began to sink the passengers refused to believe it was happening. The palm-court orchestra kept playing and the people in the ballroom danced obliviously on.*

The different kinds of oblivion and denial in America – the various ways in which the dancing continues – are presented with an incisiveness maintained throughout the song. The focus on all this escalating malaise is kept strictly under control.

The cumulative effect mentioned earlier is, in this sense, fully allowed for. The swelling up of evil as we are given it never becomes histrionic: yet it operates powerfully as it grows through from the postcards of hangings, via the cyanide holes, and on past the factory

> Where the heart-attack machine
> Is strapped across their shoulders
> And then the kerosene . . .

The first two verses of the song are actually very general: introductory in a conventional way – 'Here is the parade'. It is when he gets to the third verse that Dylan begins to focus on specific components of the overall chaos and disease.

He fixes first on the modern liberal conscience:

> The Good Samaritan he's dressing,
> He's getting ready for the show
> He's going to the carnival tonight on
> Desolation Row.

By the time we meet this Good Samaritan the moon has already hidden and the stars are retreating. It is not the kind of darkness that should encourage dressing for dinner. Like everybody's making love, it is an inappropriate response. The wrong gesture at the wrong time. It is part of the lethal unawareness against which Dylan speaks out.

In their own ways, the other verses argue the same case – and the shift of perspective in the final verse just emphasizes and reiterates the point. It's a world of commissioners; we're all blind.

In the verse quoted just above, the argument applies – in so far as poetic language can be paraphrased down into particulars, which it mostly can't – in that the liberal conscience marries an indiscriminate humanitarianism to an equally effete set of fashionable reforming aims, never achieves sufficient vision to begin to transform society and thus gets nowhere. The Good Samaritan is blown from aim to aim and from idea to idea by the prevailing outrages and ailments of a society in flux. Dylan is

---

* The lines immediately following that 'Titanic' have their applicability too: 'Everybody is shouting/Which Side Are You On?' *Which Side Are You On?* was an intensely political song composed by one Florence Reece (then aged 12), the daughter of a miner in Kentucky. (The tune, incidentally, as Alan Lomax explains it, was a variant on the English *Jack Munroe*, the title phrase replacing 'lay the lily-o'). It later became a national union song. It is cited also in Duberman's political play *In White America*. Dylan, interviewed by *Playboy* in 1966, made his attitude clear: 'Songs like *Which Side Are You On?* and *I Love You Porgy*, they're not folk music songs: they're political songs. They're already dead.'

urging instead the primary need to recognize and assert essential human values which must ultimately be re-established. The one place where the possession, or rediscovery, of the necessary detachment and honesty of response is possible is, of course, on Desolation Row. It is worse than useless to go there in carnival mood.

Such blindness, manifest in other ways, comes under attack most urgently towards the end of the song, and in the eighth and ninth verses is given a kind of cause-and-effect examination.

The seventh verse berates the bourgeoisie ('Across the street they've nailed the curtains'; 'They are spoonfeeding Casanova ... poisoning him with words'); the eighth verse indicts the education system which that bourgeoisie has established. A system organized to enforce and perpetuate ignorance, Dylan paints it as a nightmarish machinery for bringing into line the potential enemies of the state – which is to say, of the *status quo* – the independent thinkers:

> Now at midnight all the agents
> And the superhuman crew
> Come out an' round up everyone
> That knows more than they do.

That is terrific. That 'crew' suggests, along with the opening phrase 'At midnight ...', the whole sinister morass of collective vandalism, political purges and press-gangs.

Those lines insist, equally acutely, on an overriding presence of violence; it is conjured up in the first two lines of that verse, so that we are forewarned of the 'heart-attack machine' and the kerosene; and impressed upon us too is the near-impossibility of escape. Dylan urges upon us anew a sense of the powerlessness of the individual ...

> ... brought down from the castles
> By insurance men who go
> Check to see that nobody is escaping
> To Desolation Row.

The allusion, clinched by that 'castles', to Kafka's visions, makes this pessimism unequivocally clear. Dylan has not merely *argued*, but has *created* for us, the powerlessness just mentioned. It is not a polemic but a vision that he leaves us with, and which insists that all *any* individual can do is hold to some integrity of personal perspective. And that, in the end, is exactly what *Desolation Row* offers.

An earlier chapter argued that, like T. S. Eliot, Dylan has challenged the validity of traditional distinctions between poetic 'seriousness' and levity; it is equally true that Dylan has challenged, by his switching of modes of language within a single song, the traditional conceptions of 'serious' (which is to say scrupulous) technique.

Not only *Desolation Row* offers this challenge: many of the songs that date from 1965 display a similar chaos of language – an amalgam to some degree of blues vernacular, impressionism, allegory and more.

Like A Rolling Stone is one such song. Its opening verse is straightforward, almost monosyllabic slang:

> Once upon a time you dressed so fine
> Y' threw the bums a dime
> in your prime, didn' you?
> People'd call, say Beware Doll,
> You're Bound T' Fall –
> you thought they were all

kiddin' you;
you used to laugh about
ev'rybody that was hangin' out
Now you don't talk so loud
Now you don't seem so proud
about havin' to' be scroungin' your next meal –

How does it feel?! Ah! How does it feel?! . . .

The brevity and crispness of the language – city language, straight from the streets – combines with the pile-up effect of all those internal rhymes, fired past the listener as from a repeater-rifle, establishing at once the tone of bitter recrimination. The tone is modified as the language changes, as it accommodates a broader theme, a heightened appreciation on the narrator's part of the girl's fall to 'homelessness':

You said you'd never compromise
with the mystery tramp, but now you realize
he's not selling any alibis
as you stare into the vacuum of his eyes and say
do you want to
make a deal? –

How does it feel?! Ah! How does it feel?!

Here the words are longer, those 'ize' sounds slow-fading, the phrasing much less colloquial, the 'meaning' – measured in prose terms – vaguer. This change of language keeps its momentum, and paradoxically, as the language gets 'vaguer' so the meeting of eyes between the narrator and Miss Lonely intensifies: they reach the point where understanding is searching and personal, and communication can be achieved at this pitch:

You never turned around to see the frowns on the
jugglers an' the clowns when they all did
tricks for you . . .

You used to ride on your chrome horse with your
Diplomat . . .

You used to be so amused
At Napoleon in rags and the language that he used –
Go to him now, he calls you, you can't refuse . . .

This calculated lack of specificity becomes, in Dylan's hands, a positive entity grown out of and beyond the specific; and it opens up the way for the re-creation of many different universal relationships. As this use of language becomes a dominant characteristic of Dylan's writing (as it does in 1965) so he provides a whole series of songs which are scintillating studies of human relationships. The listener is no longer just witness to incidents from Dylan's own life (as he was, say, with *I Don't Believe You*, *Girl From The North Country* and *Boots Of Spanish Leather*) nor just a witness to incidents from other people's lives (as with *North Country Blues*, *Hattie Carroll* and *Hollis Brown*). Just as Lawrence moved from making art out of direct autobiographical experience to making much greater art out of universal experience, so the Dylan of the mid-60s moved in a similar direction.

Perhaps the easiest song to clarify this is actually a later one, *Dear Landlord*: for the point of that song is that it doesn't matter 'who the landlord is' – it is simply 'Dear Someone'; the song captures the essence of a relationship we can recognize as possible between any two people. It no longer needs Dylan the man to take one of the parts.

But if this use of language (which is still in transition in *Like A Rolling Stone*) no longer offers us autobiography, its universal glimpses are of course rendered as through Dylan's eyes. And so, like any great artist, Dylan bequeaths us a part of reality we could not otherwise have received. To render things that are real in a genuinely new way (which takes more than an 'original style') is actually to have *created* something new and at the same time true.

Like A Rolling Stone is, naturally, not the only song from 1965 which is, in the sense discussed, transitional. *It's All Over Now, Baby Blue*; *Positively 4th Street*; *On The Road Again* – all these are half-way houses in the same sense. It is also true that many other Dylan songs from 1965 make no demands on the 'Napoleon in rags' type of language; and there are yet others in which that language is subjugated to themes still clustered around autobiography. Into these categories come, at a minimum, *Bob Dylan's 115th Dream*; *Highway 61 Revisited*; *If You Gotta Go, Go Now*; and *Subterranean Homesick Blues*.

There are also songs full of the calculatedly unspecific which operate differently again – as, for instance, *Ballad Of A Thin Man* (see chapter 3) and those two great songs *Love Minus Zero/No Limit* and *She Belongs To Me*, along with others in which words function mainly by helping Dylan's voice to be the masterpiece of rock-*musicianship* which it had become by 1965: in particular, of *From A Buick Six*.

Nevertheless, there is a general direction to which songs like *Like A Rolling Stone* are signposts.

The first one that truly marks the arrival of the new type was issued as a single (though with little commercial success): *Can You Please Crawl Out Your Window*. In this song, the language flashes and sculptures, takes a hundred different photographs, captures a human possibility which comes across as always having been there, recurring and recurring, but never detected or seen in focus before. It needn't be a relationship we have been through for it to impress us as true – as accurately stated and real; and only the most insensitive listener would feel a need to ask what the song 'means'.

It almost stands up just as words on the page; and yet the recording is one of the very finest things ever to come out of rock music (and actually there are *two* recordings – the unreleased one forming part of the 'Stealin'' bootleg tapes).

The language of the song, though, is at least as interesting as its music. Consider the phrase 'fist full of tacks'. Dylan uses that in at least three main ways. First, it gives us a visual image of sorts – it directs our awareness towards the man's hands: and these are implicitly kept before us when we come, later in the same verse, to his 'inventions' and again later when we come to 'hand him his chalk'. Second, 'fist full of tacks' gives us a vivid metaphor *at the same time* as yielding a neat juxtaposition.*
The juxtaposition is of course that in the first half of the relevant line we get the man and the sweep of the room and are then zoomed down to the (much more precise) tiny contents of his closed hand. The metaphor is characteristic of Dylan – and takes us all the way back to *Talkin' New York*, on his very first album, where he says:

---

* A comparable example is 'You walk into the room/with a pencil in your hand', from *Ballad Of A Thin Man*. That yields a visual incongruity by means of its juxtapositioning; it also uses the 'pencil' as a symbol – so that the two lines give us not only the man's entrance as others see it but also his own attitude (because, that is to say, to come in 'with a pencil in your hand' is plainly to be unreceptive to real life – to wish to be an observer and not a participant).

> A lot of people don't have much food on their table
> But they got a lot of forks 'n' knives
> And they gotta cut somethin'.

Those lines are explaining why his initial New York audiences were hostile: it is a figurative explanation. 'Fist full of tacks' operates similarly. It could be swapped, in a prose précis, with the word 'aggressively', and yet it does a lot more than the word 'aggressively' could do. The third way it works is in establishing a tone of verbal precision – it is an incisive, sharp phrase – which is important throughout the song. It influences the sound, later on in the song, of words like 'test' and 'inventions', 'righteous' and 'box', and links up, in effect, with that phrase 'little tin women' in the final verse. 'Little tin women' is of exactly corresponding brittleness and precision. This impression is enforced in the music, too, by the guitar-work in particular and by various zylophonic effects in general. Dylan provides a contrast to all this 'tin-tack' atmosphere – it is beautifully contradicted by that gangling (and warm) chorus line:

> Use your arms and legs, it won't ruin you.

where the words enact the motion, where the listener is actually a part of the flailing limbs swimming out of the window – where, in other words, the sounds and impressions are rounded instead of thin and soft rather than sharp. More generally, the whole of the chorus takes part in this exercise of contrast: the qualities of 'crawl', 'use', 'ruin', 'haunt', and Dylan's long-drawn-out 'want' are all antithetical to the qualities of that initial 'fist full of tacks'.

Another interesting ingredient in the same song is connected with that tremendous line

> With his businesslike anger and his bloodhounds that kneel . . .

because until we isolate that line, it doesn't occur to our visual response to have our murky, semi-existing bloodhounds actually *kneeling*. Dogs cannot easily kneel at all; yet in the sense that they are humble/faithful/servile etc, they are kneeling, figuratively, while they are standing. We meet the Dylan phrase accordingly: we visualize the *atmosphere* that corresponds to silent, standing bloodhounds ranged around the man – and ranged, in fact, around *his* knee. It is thereby the man's that comes into our picture, and not the dogs' knees at all.

There is, in this crucial mid-60s period, one song which seems to stand altogether alone in Dylan's output and outside any pattern that can be devised for tracing the development of his art. That song is *Farewell Angelina*. There is no available recording of this by Dylan himself, and the best-known version of it is by Joan Baez. One tends, therefore, to think of the song as really a poem – as words-on-the-page.

Doing so, it appears that the song *does* fit a pattern: it seems half-way from *Can You Please Crawl Out Your Window* to 'Blonde On Blonde'. Yet it isn't actually like that at all. *Farewell Angelina* seems to introduce surrealistic language with a bang: that is to say, in a new way for Dylan; and by the time of 'Blonde On Blonde' he has adjusted that language almost out of recognition. It is in this sense that *Angelina* stands alone. Where 'Blonde On Blonde' works as a sort of contemporary technicolour surrealist movie, *Farewell Angelina* seems like a black-and-white 1940 surrealist short (and *Can You Please Crawl Out Your Window* is not like a film at all):

> Just a table standing empty by the edge of the sea . . .

– that is the line that encapsulates the song – its essential tone and its distinctive kind of image. A strange song: and the fact that there are still things in it that do seem

145

characteristic of Dylan's other work does not make it, in overall effect, any the less strange – quite the opposite.

The melody *is* typically Dylan, if only minority-Dylan: it has a similar expansive lightness and brightness to the near-contemporaneous *Mr Tambourine Man*.

Some of the lines in the lyric add to this similarity:

> The triangle tingles and the trumpets play slow
> The sky is on fire, and I must go . . .

and

> . . . In the space where the deuce and the ace once ran wild
> Farewell Angelina, the sky is folding . . .

Perhaps the attempt to explain 'Angelina's' relation to other Dylan songs by means of a movies analogy is a clue to its very singularity – namely that unlike most of Dylan's imagery, that in *Farewell Angelina* is emphatically and fundamentally visual. It is, almost uniquely, simply a series of *pictures*, sometimes switching suddenly on and off, sometimes sliding into each other:

> King Kong little elves on the rooftops they dance
> Valentino-type tangos while the make-up man's hands
> Shut the eyes of the dead, not to embarrass anyone:
> Farewell Angelina, the sky is embarrassed, and I must be gone.

Even that remarkable 'the sky is embarrassed' is an assertion we visualize; we picture the sky, and picture it in relation to the song's other protagonists, throughout the song. And this is all that is offered or required; if we receive all the visual glimpses, if we really can, instantly,

> See the cross-eyed pirates sitting perched in the sun
> Shooting tin cans with a sawn-off shot-gun

then the song has worked.

It is on the 'Desire' album of eleven years later that Dylan returns to this photographic mode: on 'Sara', where we're offered snapshots again – '. . . them playin' with their pails in the sand/They run to the water, their buckets to fill/. . . the shells fallin' out of their hands/As they follow each other back up the hill' and 'Them playin' leapfrog and hearin' about Snow-White'.

When we come back to 'Blonde On Blonde' and this mid-60s progression, things are not so simple. We come to material where visual imagery is only one factor, and one that fluctuates enormously in importance even within a single song, and we come to a surrealist language distinctly *unlike* the surrealism of Dali or Magritte. In one important sense, Dylan's vision throughout 'Blonde On Blonde' much more closely resembles that of Bosch. There is no suggestion that the narrators in these 1966 songs stand, like Magritte, on the threshold of madness. On the contrary, they are sane men surrounded by the madness and chaos of other people and other things. The surrealistic pile-ups of imagery do not reflect the state of a narrator's (or Dylan's) psyche: they reflect the confusion which a calm and ordered mind observes around it.

In this sense, the album is a whole and the individual songs are only parts; and it

November 1965, San Francisco – a month later Dylan was completing his most prolific year recording some great unreleased rock material with The Hawks including the amazing She's Your Lover Now *and* Barbed Wire Fence.

doesn't matter that sometimes the chaos seems to be America and sometimes seems to be the city life of particular sorts of people. It doesn't even contradict the spirit of the whole that a couple of the songs evoke a chaos that is inside the emotions of the narrator – the chaos of happy infatuation in *I Want You*, or of non-comprehension in *Temporary Like Achilles*. *I Want You* propounds a relationship between the lovers and the outside world which fits the general pattern of the album well, in that it lends itself, as a dichotomy, to a relation between internals and externals – between chaos and order:

> The cracked bells and washed out horns
> Blow into my face with scorn
> But it's not that way, I wasn't born
> To lose you . . .
>
> . . . She is good to me
> And there's nothing she doesn't see
> She knows where I'd like to be
> But it doesn't matter –

The chaos is there all right. And *Temporary Like Achilles* bears some resemblance to this:

> Well I lean into your hallway
> Lean against your velvet door
> I watch upon your scorpion
> Who crawls across your circus floor

That 'your hallway' suggests a place of refuge, and so raises again the fact of there being a gulf between narrator and outside world. The *strength* of the sense of refuge-seeking urged on us ('your hallway' is followed up by the repetition of the possessive adjective – 'your velvet door', 'your scorpion', 'your . . . floor') has been established earlier in the song by the eloquence of this:

> Kneeling 'neath your ceiling
> Yes I guess I'll be here for a while
> I'm trying to read your poetry
> But I'm helpless, like a rich man's child.

And when we say that those lines *are* so very eloquent, we come to recognize them as having many of the characteristic strengths of Dylan's mid-sixties' work, and having emphatically the strengths of the 'Blonde On Blonde' collection.

In the first place, there is the refusal to incubate a 'serious' poetic language. How else could the slightly lugubrious voice relish its delivery of 'Kneeling 'neath your ceiling/Yes I guess I . . .'?

Thrown in for good measure, in the second place, is the sort of abrasive little generalization that epitomizes part of Dylan's intelligence: '. . . helpless like a rich man's child'. And this kind of side-remark is always an odd mixture of humour and high seriousness. It is there to bring a smile but it has an open moral insistence behind it. However lightly introduced, the contrast Dylan makes in this instance between her 'poetry' and a debilitating richness is made with real severity.

It is equally characteristic as a sample of 'Blonde On Blonde' in the way figurative language is the norm (as with 'your poetry') yet mixes easily with the literal.

It has also the vision of chaos which dominates all of 'Blonde On Blonde' – 'Kneeling . . . I'm trying . . . But I'm helpless' – and the richness of organization (all that internal rhyming and odd southern emphasis) and richness of

148

sound. The words purr across the airwaves to the listener: kneeling, 'neath, ceiling, while, poetry, child.

But *Temporary Like Achilles* is not the album's best song. A far better one – a truly superb song – is *Absolutely Sweet Marie*, in which the words are borne along on a sea of rich red music, bobbing with a stylish and highly distinctive rhythm. Dylan's voice is at its very best, handling the repeated line which caps each verse with as much alert variety in delivery as would be humanly yet still felicitously possible. Each time it arrives, the line is different – more insistent yet always spontaneously mooded.

Dylan's harmonica also excels itself with an invincible, searing solo that bequeaths new boundaries and new life to any concept of the blues.

The lyric overflows with all the qualities we specially associate with the 'Blonde On Blonde' collection.

> Well your railroad gate you know I just can't jump it
> Sometimes it gets so hard to see
> I'm just sitting here beating on my trumpet
> With all these promises you left for me
> But where are you tonight Sweet Marie?
>
> Well I waited for you when I was halfsick
> Yes I waited for you when you hated me
> Well I waited for you inside of the frozen traffic
> When you knew I had some other place to be
> Now where are you tonight, Sweet Marie?

The challenge to distinctions between 'serious' and 'light' poetic language is clear enough there, and so are the abrasive little philosophical points, flashed out with smiles:

> Well anybody can be just like me, obviously

is about as ambiguous as anything ever could be, and just as a joke pay-off line is clipped on to it, so later on in the song we come to this delightful alliance between sincere observation and jest:

> But to live outside the law you must be honest
> I know you always say that you agree . . .

Of course, to get the tone of that last-quoted line you need to go to the recording; and so do you to get the full and incredible richness of sound that comes not only from the swirling, oceanic music but also from Dylan's bending of the words, as he breathes indelible cascades of life into lines and phrases like these: 'your railroad gate you know I just can't jump it'; 'with all these promises'; 'And now I stand here, looking at your yellow railroad/In the ruins of your balcony/Wondering where you are tonight Sweet Marie'. Actually Dylan's handling of the single word 'balcony' shows how much and how appropriately he can reawaken our tired old vocabulary and language.

Absolutely Sweet Marie also has its share of the glimpses of chaos, the effective communication of which depends on largely figurative expressions. It is easy to see how the metaphoric technique lights up the chaotic vision:

> . . . I just can't jump it
> Sometimes it gets so hard to see
> I'm just sitting here beating on my trumpet . . .
> But where are you . . .? . . .

149

Paris, 1966. As with London, it was to be twelve years later before he performed here again.

> Well I don't know how it happened but the riverboat captain
> he knows my fate
> But ev'ybody else . . .

> . . . you see you forgot to leave me with the key.

The song also holds a characteristic richness of organization: a well-integrated, almost self-perpetuating system of internal rhymes and subterranean rhythms. These features work together perhaps most obviously in the second verse. And that verse also yields Dylan's humour, it is there in his self-conscious – almost self-parodying – rhyming of 'halfsick' with 'traffic'. The humour is there later in the song as well, in his mischievous matching of the ambiguous, ostensibly humble 'obviously' with that acidic fullstop on 'fortunately'.

(And Elvis Costello, let it be said, could have learnt all he knows about agile, tricksy rhyming if this was the only record he'd ever heard.)

But Dylan's humour in this song is not achieved at the expense of seriousness. Throughout, we are conscious and appreciative that the narrator stands for self-honesty. His message is be true to yourself, and as it is given in that epigrammatic 'to live outside the law you must be honest' its earnestness comes across.

150

It is also true that with each (freshly-delivered) return to the 'But where are you ...' line, we are returned to a mood appropriate to what is fundamentally an eloquent, outgoing love-song. All of the imagery works at maintaining this. The frustration of 'I'm just sitting here' is ennobled, on the quiet, by that 'trumpet'; the 'promises' tumble from the tune with a kind of reverential flutter and poignancy; and the reproaches all work, essentially, at widening our impression of the scope of the narrator's love – look, that is to say, at what he has been through. Even the use of what is probably, in intention, just drugs jargon gives us visual images of romance: '... the riverboat captain/he knows my fate' evokes, however illogically, glimpses of riverboat journeys on waters attended by weeping willows. The final verse perpetuates this romantic insistence, giving it Romeo's conclusive emphasis: 'In the ruins, of your, bal-cony ...'.

To turn from the romantic associations of 'balcony' in *Absolutely Sweet Marie* to the song that immediately follows it on the 'Blonde On Blonde' collection is to be given quite a contrast.

4th Time Around is more than just a parody of The Beatles' 'Norwegian Wood'. It begins as a cold, mocking put-down of a girl and a relationship untouched by love. For extra sarcasm's sake, it is set against a backing of fawning, schmaltzy guitar-work. But the drumming hints from the start at something more urgent and compelling than cold mockery, so that by the time the lyric switches attention to a second and love-tinged relationship, the tone of the song has been switched over too.

The contrast between the two women is plain enough:

> She threw me outside ...
> You took me in

but the perspective is not that simple. The vast majority of it focuses on the 'she' part – suggesting the narrator's personal weakness and perhaps vulnerability; and in consequence this majority consists of language soaked in coarse sexual innuendo that brings out Dylan's skill in pursuing the suggestive. (The songs on what's generally known as the basement tapes, recorded the year after 'Blonde On Blonde', indulge in the suggestive to an unprecedented extent for Dylan, with lines like 'I bin hittin' it too hard/My stones won't take', 'that big dumb blonde with her wheel gorged', and 'slap that drummer with a pipe that smells', plus the whole of *Please Mrs Henry*.)

The 1974 album 'Planet Waves' returned puzzlingly – more heavy-handedly and so less comfortably – to this coarseness. It is there in the Dylan-written sleeve-notes:

> Back to the starting point! ... I dropped a double brandy and tried to recall
> the events ... family outings with strangers – furious gals with garters and
> smeared lips on bar stools that stank from sweating pussy ... space guys
> off duty with big dicks and duck tails all wined up and voting for
> Eisenhower

and it is there in the otherwise admirable *Tough Mama*, where Dylan lazily offers this awkward analogy:

> Today on the countryside
> It was hotter than a crotch ...

Dylan's technique for delivering sexual innuendo is very interesting in *4th Time Around*. It is almost like a parody of a schoolboy reading Shakespeare aloud in class; instead of the frequently-required line overflow, there is a pause – encouraged, but not exaggeratedly, by the tune – at the end of odd lines in the lyric. Into each pause comes all the innuendo and ambiguity that Dylan can muster:

151

I
Stood there and hummed
I tapped on her drum
I asked her how come

And she
Buttoned her boot
And straightened her suit
Then she said Don't Get Cute.
So I forced
My hands in my pockets and felt with my thumbs ...

And after finding out I'd
Forgotten my shirt
I went back and knocked.
I waited in the hallway, as she went to get it
And I tried to make sense
Out of that picture of you in'your wheelchair that
    leaned up against

Her
Jamaican rum
And when she did come
I asked her for some.

The pause Dylan creates at the end of 'And I tried to make sense' has, of course, a different purpose. (And after it, the lapse back for that pointed 'come' has an added force – it seems in every sense uncontrollable on the narrator's part.) With 'tried to make sense' the pause is to allow a change of mood to begin impinging. The tone is no longer jaundiced. From here on it is open and alert and more sensitive; for from the midst of the imagery appropriate to the narrator's sexual, loveless encounter, Dylan – and here is the touch of genius – produces a clear and striking counter-image:

> ... that picture of you in your wheelchair

With that, he establishes the hint that here, in the offing, is something with a warmer potential – something for which it is worth the narrator's while to salvage his own sensibility.

Yet having produced this counter-image Dylan allows it to recede and settle at the back of the listener's mind. Only at the very end is it reintroduced, to fuse into one clear perspective all the different threads of feeling and of imagery which run through the song. It ends:

> And
> When I was through
> I filled up my shoe
> And brought it to you;
> And you,
> You took me in
> You loved me then
> You didn't waste time
> And I,
> I never took much
> I never asked for your crutch
> Now don't ask for mine.

That 'crutch' has all the complex functioning a pun can ever have. As we are presented, triumphantly, with the mental cadence from 'wheelchair' down to that 'crutch' at the close – in the sweep of which the 'picture' is brought sharply to life – we have one of those fine, rare moments in poetry where although the technical device is *seen* functioning it does so with such supreme calculation and panache that its 'intrusion' actually enriches the finished work.

However good *4th Time Around* is, and however clever, it is one of the minor works on 'Blonde On Blonde'. It is useful to look at others before coming to the major works on the album.

Just Like A Woman is one of Dylan's uncomfortably sentimental songs. The chorus is trite and coy and the verses aren't strong enough to compensate.

> . . . she aches just like a woman
> But she breaks just like a little girl.

This is a non-statement. It doesn't describe an individual characteristic, it doesn't say anything fresh about a universal one, and yet it pretends to do both. What parades as reflective wisdom ('. . . woman but . . . girl') is really maudlin platitude. It hasn't even engaged Dylan's skill in minimizing the badness. It would, for example, be less bad if the 'But' of the pay-off line was an 'And' – for at least we would then be spared so blatantly lame and predictable a 'paradox'.

On the other hand the part that we might as well call the 'middle-eight' is beautifully done:

> It was rainin' from the first an' I was
> Dying there of thirst an' so I
> Came in here
> An' your long time curse hurts but what's worse is this
> Pain in here, I can't
> Stay in here,
> Ain't it clear that
>
> I just can't fit . . .

Why that is so 'beautifully done' can be understood only from the recording. It is a question of delivery. Singing those words, those unit-construct lines, Dylan moulds and holds out to us a hand-made object, a sort of clever toy with a lot of tactile appeal. You need the recording for the indescribably plaintive resonance the voice yields up on those simple little words like 'rainin'', 'first', 'came' and even 'ain't'; and you need the recording above all because that long middle-line demands Dylan's own pronunciation, by which 'curse hurts but what's worse' becomes five equal fur-mouthed jerks and 'what's' rhymes gleefully with 'hurts'. You have to hear Dylan doing it.

Leopard Skin Pill-Box Hat is also a minor song, though far from a bad one. It's a good joke and a vehicle for showing Dylan's electric lead-guitar-work, and that's really all.

Right from the opening line, Dylan takes advantage of its blues structure. He uses a repetition of his first line *as if because the blues do that* in such a way as to make it a put-down, the repeated full description of the hat suggesting its owner's small mind:

> I see you got your brand-new leopard-skin pill-box hat
> Yes, I see you got your brand-new leopard-skin pill-box hat.

There are other smiles within the song – little flashes of malice and mockery – which don't depend on the blues structure but which ride along happily enough on its waves:

> Well I asked the doctor if I could see you:
> It's bad for your health, he said ...

and

> Well I saw him makin' love to you
> (You forgot to close the garage door)
> You might think he loves you for your money but
> *I* know what he really loves you for!:
> It's your brand-new leopard-skin pill-box hat.

The best thing in *Leopard-Skin Pill-Box Hat*, though, utilizes the blues structure devastatingly. It comes in the second verse, while Dylan is still disparaging the hat; he marries the long-downward trail of the standard blues third-line to this:

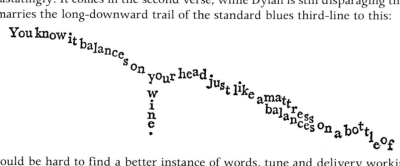

It would be hard to find a better instance of words, tune and delivery working so entirely together. They mimic what they describe to (literally) giddy perfection.*

The other song on 'Blonde On Blonde' that memorably draws on the blues – and rather more seriously so than does *Leopard-Skin Pill-Box Hat* – is *Pledging My Time* (the progression of which, incidentally, is echoed by Dylan's *It Hurts Me Too* on the 'Self Portrait' album) which for this reason is dealt with not here but in chapter 2.

Then there is *Obviously Five Believers*, which sounds as if it belongs on the 'Highway 61 Revisited' album rather than 'Blonde On Blonde' (just as the thing *aimed at* in *Outlaw Blues* was actually *achieved* on the later *From A Buick 6*) and is very much a rock song. It gives us a totally relaxed, in-command Dylan – so much so that he rightly hands over the harmonica part to Charlie McCoy, and the words don't matter one iota. The most that is really required of them is that they shouldn't interfere – and they don't. They even include lines already made familiar at the beginning of the album. The album starts with *Rainy Day Women Nos 12 & 35*, with its simple pun chorus lines:

> But I would not feel so all alone:
> Everybody must get stoned

and the first finish of the album (since the final side is in essence separate from the rest), falling on *Obviously Five Believers*, echoes that phrase explicitly:

> Guess I could make it without you honey if I
> Just did not feel so all alone.

As for the major songs in the 'Blonde On Blonde' collection, they strike me as being *One Of Us Must Know (Sooner Or Later)*; *Memphis Blues Again*; *Visions Of Johanna* and *Sad-Eyed Lady Of The Lowlands*.

---

*There is another attempt at a similar effect in another 'Blonde On Blonde' song, *Most Likely You Go Your Way And I'll Go Mine*. Lack of balance is treated there too, in middle-eight lines for which tune helps words by seeming to falter and totter appropriately in the delivery of lines which include 'But he's badly built/An' he walks on stilts/Watch out he don't/Fall on you...'

The greatness of *One Of Us Must Know* is to do with vague but dramatic impressions it carries in its music and its overall structure. It is manifestly, magnificently alive – like some once-in-a-lifetime party (and aptly the lyric impinges as if it is being delivered at a party, the voice rising and falling against a backdrop of bubbling noises and motion). The music flows over you in waves, so that linked to the party impression, the song is a rock equivalent, at least fleetingly, of the party Scott Fitzgerald describes in *The Great Gatsby*, where

> ... the orchestra is playing yellow cocktail music, and the opera of voices
> pitches a key higher. Laughter is easier minute by minute, spilled with
> prodigality, tipped out at a cheerful word. The groups change more swiftly,
> swell with new arrivals, dissolve and form in the same breath; already
> there are wanderers, confident girls who weave here and there among the
> stouter and more stable, become for a sharp, joyous moment the centre of a
> group, and then, excited with triumph, glide on through the sea-change of
> faces and voices and color under the constantly changing light.

One Of Us Must Know is like that – not in its people or its social orientation but as regards its rhythms, its movement: its life. It breathes with a kind of majestic sexual life; it holds your attention with a symphonic sort of warmth. The music never stops rising and falling and to complement this, ordinary little words, signifying little on their own, are caressed into a loving but subservient eloquence by Dylan's voice. Dylan singing the line

> But you said you knew me an' I believed you did

and words like 'personal' and 'understood' come across as merely part of the musical whole. A truly great song, and unlike Dylan's many beautiful songs celebrating the finding of a refuge, this one creates a relationship (sculptured by its narrator's implicit dialogue with the woman sharing it) but without putting the two lovers together against the world. The world whirls noisily around them, but is no threat. For once it does not howl like the wind: it jangles not intrusively but exactly *like* a party at which it feels OK to remain.

Beyond being an exciting rock-music performance, *Memphis Blues Again* should be regarded as at least as great as *One Of Us Must Know*. It shares with *Visions Of Johanna* and *Sad-Eyed Lady Of The Lowlands* a greater-than-average duration and a general high seriousness of intention. It also offers all those qualities noted earlier as being characteristic of the 'Blonde On Blonde' songs, including a drugs imagery that gets no special stress.

The narrator is someone just trying to get by in modern America: someone trying to get by, that is, without shutting off or closing up; someone who sees a lot happening around him but can't discern any pattern to it nor any constant but meaninglessness; someone who, in this situation, stays more outwardly vulnerable than he needs to because he retains a yearning, however vague, for some better kind of world.

All this comes through to the listener from disconnected visual glimpses: that is how the imagery works. The song begins with this:

> Oh the ragman draws circles
> Up an' down the block
> I'd ask him what the matter was
> But I know that he don't talk

and the visual dominance is such that we get a picture to cover the third and fourth lines – they don't just pass over as abstract reflection. We see the singer standing disconsolate, aware that there is no point in trying to communicate.

The same process of visualization – if that is a word – applies throughout the song. The narrator is there in front of us, avoiding 'some French girl who says she knows me well', confronting Mona, believing the railroad men, thinking about Grandpa, hiding under the truck, winning his argument with the teen preacher, staggering around stoned and telling us that we just get uglier, smiling at black-haired Ruthie, and sitting patiently on Grand Street ('where the neon madmen climb'). It is only with the heartfelt cry of the chorus,

> Oh! Mama! Can this *really* be the *end?!*
> To be stuck inside of *Mobile* with the Memphis *Blues* again!

that the visual predominance dies away. We only picture Dylan saying 'Oh! Mama!' – we don't picture Memphis Tennessee or Mobile Alabama at all. They are not part of the visual language; they are symbols, words that stand for other things – hope and despondency, potential and restraint. They are abstract ideas.

This song is interesting too in the way that Dylan, very typically, handles his moral point. He bestows an implicit blessing on some things and frowns on others. It is a question of drawing to the listener's attention that some things strike the artist as enhancing and others strike him as restrictive.

The narrator himself is also made to represent certain values, certain virtues (and since we can associate the narrator directly with Dylan, this is easy enough – and a useful instance of how Dylan uses his personal legend to assist his art). These amount to a frank and sensitive openness to life, even at the expense of sophistication and propriety:

> . . . An' I said Oh! I didn't *know* that! . . .

> . . . Ev'rybody still talks about
> How badly they were shocked;
> But me I expected it to happen,
> I *knew* he'd lost control! . . .

which is contrasted with the machinations of the senator

> Showing everyone his gun,
> Handing out free tickets
> To the wedding of his son

and to the neon madmen of the modern city – the ones who have settled into it all – and to the claustrophobic ladies who furnish him with tape, and so on.

The humour that breaks out beyond the histrionics of hamming up 'Oh! I didn't *know* that!' also aids the moral evaluation. The narrator only adds to our awareness of his virtue when he raps out

> Y'see, you're just like me.
> I hope you're satisfied.

Who wouldn't be?

Dylan ends the song with a disarming, memorable summary of the predicament he's been showing us that we are *all* in:

> And me I sit so patiently
> Waiting to find out what price
> Ya have to pay to get out of
> Going through all these things twice

The language of *Visions Of Johanna* has already been partly dealt with in chapter 3; and any amount more could be said. What should follow here is therefore doubly difficult to sort out.

The mixture of 'serious' and 'flippant' language; the mixture of delicacy and coarseness; the mixture of abstract neo-philosophy and figurative phraseology; the ambiguity that begins with the song's very title – because Johanna is not just a girl's name but also the Hebrew for Armageddon; the humour; the intensive build-up of the song's scope – all this is pressed into the service of a work of art at once indefinable and precise. It is, not for the first time, hard to say what the song is 'about' and yet it rightly impresses most people as saying a good deal, and in doing so it engages a great many of Dylan's distinctive strengths.

The effects are precise in the sense that the glimpses we get (as chapter 3 suggested with particular reference to the first verse of the song) are very strikingly accurate recreations of experience.

The character-sketches are very accurate too; for instance:

> ... Little boy lost, he takes himself so seriously;
> He brags of his misery, he likes to live dangerously ...
> He's sure gotta lotta gall
> To be so useless an' all
> Muttering small talk at the wall
> While I'm in the hall –

or

> In the empty lot where the ladies play blind man's buff
>   with the keychain
> An' the all-nite girls, they whisper of escapades out on
>   the D-train
> We can hear the night-watchman click his flashlight,
> Ask himself if it's him or them that's insane ...

Because the atmosphere there rebounds incisively off phrases like 'the empty lot', 'out on the D-train' and the 'all-nite girls', that nightwatchman comes across as vividly as a character in Dickens. That 'click' that Dylan provides him with is precisely the kind of tiny detail that is a large part of Dickens' touch. Dylan gives us the same cartoon-precision, deftly sketching in the nightwatchman's mannered essentials. We don't need to know what clothes he wears, or the colour of his hair, or the shape of his nose. He is real and we have truly seen him, and *felt* him doubt his sanity.

But the idea of Johanna is what dominates the song. In putting *this* across, Dylan's weighting of language, his economical fusion of simple words and tune, is amazing:

> And these visions, of Johanna,
> They've kept me up, past, the dawn ...
>
> But these visions, of Johanna,
> They make it all, seem so, cruel ...

The broadness of the song's scope is clinched by this fixed focal point. In effect, it is because the narrator returns again and again to the single idea of his relationship with Johanna, that he is able to be so receptive – to give an *equal* receptivity – to everything else he comes across. Thus (with an equal and splendid impersonality) the song can focus one minute on the coughing heat-pipes in Louise and her lover's room – where they are entwined and oblivious – and next minute on casual speculation about museums. Since Johanna is so much the centre of everything, the outer circumferences are all equitably regarded and rendered: all seen dispassionately as equally significant and insignificant. 'Jelly-faced women'; the secret of the Mona Lisa smile; the sounds of the night; they all flow with the same detachment through the narrator's mind, until

> The harmonicas play the skeleton keys in the rain

(a beautiful line – that connection between harmonica sounds and skeletons is a flash of real imaginative genius and fiery intuitive observation)

> And these visions, of Johanna,
> Are now all, that remain.

To turn from *Visions of Johanna* to *Sad-Eyed Lady Of The Lowlands* is not only, as earlier implied, to turn from one major song on 'Blonde On Blonde' to another; it is also to turn from a success to a failure – and a failure no more easily explicable than most things to do with Dylan's work.

It is unsuccessful, and rather grandly so, inasmuch as it is offered on the album as something of extraspecial importance and doesn't live up to its billing. It takes up the whole of the fourth and final side of the double-LP, despite lasting only about one minute longer than *Desolation Row*, which slots in with three other songs on a single side of 'Highway 61 Revisited'. *Sad-Eyed Lady Of The Lowlands* is not a more important song than *Desolation Row*. It's long, it's attractive, it's puzzling and ambiguous, and Dylan's voice on it is very beautiful – but it isn't one of Dylan's great songs. It is rather like sexy, fur-lined wallpaper.

All the same, the intention behind the song was clearly a major one, and the consequent recording is obtrusive enough to merit a special attention.

Let's begin by recognizing a few ambiguities. The chorus of the song is full of them:

> Sad-eyed lady of the lowlands,
> Where the sad-eyed prophets say that no man comes,
> My warehouse eyes, my Arabian drums –
> Should I leave them by your gate,
> Or, sad-eyed lady, should I wait?

The 'warehouse eyes' juxtaposition is a fine enough encapsulation, perhaps, to compensate for the indolent vagueness of those 'drums' and the corresponding 'gate'. Yet it is a little *too* encapsulated: like a diagram, from which the listener has to fit the bits together by himself: a sort of Poetic Language Kit that needs to be built up at home. As for the rest of the chorus: the line preceding 'warehouse eyes' means absolutely nothing. It's just there for neatness' sake (which inevitably means that it is not *artistically* neat at all) – for mood-setting repetition and rhyme. And the title-line itself stands for – what?

It shouldn't matter. The lady's sad eyes are just as much warehouses as the narrator's; Dylan passes his myriad perspectives in front of those eyes, and what the song tries to communicate is the world which therein confronts them – the world that makes them sad. So 'she' is just a convention – a sort of camera.

But in the vain hope of cutting down on our perplexity in response to the whole, we *do* find that the identity of the title person, or title symbol, matters to us.

The camera-shots, the perspectives: do they create more than wistful but nebulous fragments? Do they add up to any kind of vision, as the whole presentation, duration and solemnity of the song, imply that they should? No. Dylan is resting, and cooing nonsense in our ears (very beguilingly of course).

The only thing which unites the fragments is the *mechanical device* of the return to the chorus, and thus to the title; because there is nothing to suggest a particular significance to that title (as, say, there is in *Visions of Johanna* and *Memphis Blues Again*), its intended function of holding things together virtually fails. It is, in the end, not a whole song at all, but unconnected chippings, and only the poor cement of an empty chorus and a regularity of tune give the illusion that things are otherwise. The structure makes the song seem a complete entity; the sense of the song denies it.

All the same, these disunited parts are interesting, and the spreadeagled 'Blonde On Blonde' recording offers many of the features of Dylan's artistry.

Dylan delivers it like slow-motion waves, unfurling the phrases with a strung-out concentration that is at once committed, intense and yet mellow. He breathes out the lines – lines full of alliterative emphasis, melting and echoey atmosphere, and obscured, nebulous pictures:

> The kings of Tyrus with their convict list
> Are waiting in line for their geranium kiss
> And you wouldn't know it would happen like this
> But who among them, really wants, just to kiss you?
> With your childhood flames on your midnight rug
> And your Spanish manners and your mother's drugs
> And your cowboy mouth and your curfew plugs
> Who among them do you think could resist you?
> Sad-eyed lady of the lowlands? . . .

The fourth line there offers a much cheaper cynicism than Dylan normally exhibits; and the rhyming eighth line is unusually weak. The other six lines of that verse are more demanding.

The opening couplet gets much of its force from its elaborate alliteration and internal rhymes – and how nicely the tune holds back fittingly on the word 'waiting' in line two. The power of the *imagery*, though, is fundamentally untraceable – for it is basically surrealistic, and thus not susceptible to rationale or analysis. For me, 'the kings of Tyrus' is hardly visual at all; 'their convict list' is not really visual either – but it is distinctly atmospheric: it increases my sense of sadness, it suggests perhaps an irretrievable past. The 'waiting in line' gets disregarded almost entirely: it is just the outstretching hand that presents that marvellous 'geranium kiss'. Why try to explain the impact of that? And it is only natural, correspondingly, to give up on 'your cowboy mouth and your curfew plugs' – which yield perhaps less unadulterated impact but a great deal of unadulterated aesthetic pleasure. The singer's 'ru-u-u-ug' and 'dru-u-u-ugs' is perhaps a necessary device for lending the relevant couplet its impression of parallels, but beyond that 'midnight rug' makes those 'flames' literal and visual, and is in itself evocative enough; and that sixth line:

> And your Spanish manners and your mother's drugs

brings in, with a skilful kind of equipoise, pleasantly conflicting ideas of elegance and tragedy – and lends both a harmony and counterpart to the misty moods of the whole verse.

Lines in other verses operate in much the same essentially surrealistic ways –

> With your mercury mouth in the Missionary Times . . .
> And your matchbox songs and your gypsy hymns . . .
> To show you where the dead angels are that they used to hide . . .

yet some operate less intensively. There are lines and lines of largely explicable simile, where the listener's problem is merely how to glean from them the moral 159 slant. Is this sort of thing intended as praise or condemnation or neither (or indeed both)?:

> . . . your eyes like smoke and your prayers like rhymes
> And your silver cross and your voice like chimes . . .

They seem morally neutral because they are uninspiring; as the similes grow more distinctive – largely through becoming cliché, paradoxically enough – they lose their neutrality. By the time we have had 'your face like glass' (a classically back-handed compliment) and we reach 'your saint-like face and your ghost-like soul', we can't fail to be aware of Dylan's/the narrator's severity. His condemnation comes so powerfully through the line just quoted that the question which follows – ostensibly reverential rhetoric – comes across as a fairly heavy sneer:

> Who among them do you think could destroy you?

And yet – and yet – he seems to mean it all *nicely* – which means that at base, it is just badly written.

The concluding verse's second line, with its clever and derisive piece of shorthand description of

> . . . your magazine husband who one day just had to go

seems the only line that really isn't muzzy in its import.

In the end, whatever the song's attractions and clever touches, they have been bundled together, and perhaps a bit complacently, without the unity either of a clear and real theme or of cohesive artistic discipline.

Dylan, later, seems to have been aware of this: seems to have abandoned the song – never singing it in concerts, and using the mention of it only as a calculatedly poignant tug in the much later, desperate special-pleading song *Sara*. It is also directly after *Sad-Eyed Lady Of The Lowlands*, in the chronology of his released recordings, that Dylan draws back from this ever-thickening undergrowth of surreal, allusively complex use of language. After it, he begins, in general, the harder process of paring down toward a new simplicity.

With 'The Madonna' – Joan Baez and Dylan at Newport, 1964.

Chapter 6
Dylan's Use of Language
Towards A New Simplicity

Love is so simple
(To quote a phrase)
You've known it all the time
I'm learnin' it these days
(from Dylan's *You're A Big Girl Now*)

In contrast to 'Blonde On Blonde', Dylan's surrealism is stripped down to a chilly minimum on 'John Wesley Harding'—the most dramatic example being in that central song *All Along The Watchtower*.

If *Desolation Row* can be seen as a circular song, with its parade going on forever, so too can *All Along The Watchtower*—which is, among other things, a more economical, and far more chilling, restatement of the same theme. But how does it end, this song? There are two alternatives. Either it gets an added element of menace from the very *endlessness* of the nightmare vision offered, as the song goes round and round, so that the helpless cry 'There must be some way out of here' *recurs after* 'The wind began to howl'. Or else, if it is not circular in that way, then it ends, as Richard Goldstein argued in a *Village Voice* review, on an emphatic full-stop—indeed, a terrifying full-stop. Just three clean, razor-sharp verses, with an end that signifies the end of *everything*:

> Outside in the distance
> A wild cat did growl
> Two riders were approaching
> The wind began to howl.

As Goldstein says, the suggestion of menace in those lines is far too ominous and powerful for them to be concluded with a series of dots.

The general nature of the language in a song like this is impressionism revisited, and no longer reflecting summer tension in the city, as did 'Blonde On Blonde', but reflecting wintertime in the psyche instead.

By the time of the 'Nashville Skyline' album, we find, not unexpectedly in view of its terrain, no trace of surrealistic imagery at all. The images on this album rest as firmly in logic and plain speaking as would be consistent with imaginative expression. They are founded in the logic of traditional rural life, dependent on that life's unvarying rhythms and verities—seasons, the processes of agriculture, growth, replenishment and death:

> Turned my skies from blue to grey...
> Tonight no light will shine on me...
>
> Once I had mountains in the palm of my hand
> And rivers that ran through every day...

The impetus for lines like those is less a matter of image-coining than the use of idiom—idiom that is a natural product of rural culture. And those lines quoted above, if we regard them as holding images, comprise the sum total of imagery on the 'Nashville Skyline' album—with four rather special exceptions.

First, that awkward, uncharacteristically saccharine pair of lines:

> Whatever colours you have in your mind
> I'll show them to you and you'll see them shine

which doesn't sound like Dylan writing, and which stands out of the song in which it occurs – *Lay Lady Lay* – in the same way that the chorused phrase 'Take me down to California baby' stands out in the basement-type song *Yea! Heavy & A Bottle Of Bread*.

Second, that imagery which is integral to deliberately selected cliché, as with 'You can have your cake and eat it too' – again from *Lay Lady Lay*.

Third, the images that are images *only* in the sense that they yield snapshots of the narrator-predicament – as with, for instance, 'If there's a poor boy on the street' (from *Tonight I'll Be Staying Here With You*) or 'Shake me up that old peach tree' (from *Country Pie*).

The fourth and final exception is again from *Lay Lady Lay* (an exceptional song!) and is here:

> His clothes are dirty but his hands are clean . . .
> And you're the best thing that he's ever seen . . .

That reverses the expected moral weighting. The Noble Workman has honorably *dirty* hands – and in the west, clean hands belong only to the no-good gamblin' man. But this is not a double-edged commentary from Dylan, such as we had on the song *John Wesley Harding*: it is a plain statement of praise. What is surprising is that while you expect the image to work, as most of the album does, within the country music milieu, in fact 'clean hands' takes its ethic not from the mid-West but from the Bible: from the 24th Psalm, which is a Psalm of David:

> Who shall ascend into the hill of the Lord?
> Or who shall stand in his holy place?
> He that hath clean hands, and a pure heart.

That short catalogue above shows the exceptional – in the sense of uncharacteristic – moments on 'Nashville Skyline': the broad mass of it is without surrealism, without any imagery at all indeed, and uses a language of extreme simplicity.

It was, after all, quite a shock, on a first play of 'Nashville Skyline' back in 1969, to hear Dylan singing lines like

> For your love comes on so strong . . .

And when we come to the middle-section of the same song (*Tonight I'll Be Staying Here With You*) we find Dylan coming on even stronger with this 'new' language:

> Is it really any wonder
> The love that a stranger might receive?
> You cast your spell and I went under
> I find it so difficult to leave . . .

This compares closely with the middle-section of the later song *Hazel*, from 'Planet Waves':

> Oh no I don't need any reminder
> To show how much I really care
> But its just making me blinder and blinder . . .

The joke-rhyming of 'wonder' and 'under', and even more so of 'reminder' and 'blinder and blinder', combined with the playful vacuousness of the melodies of both those sections, suggest the milieu of the Hollywood musical more than

162

anything. They'd go comfortably inside *On The Street Where You Live* from 'My Fair Lady'. Not exactly Dylan terrain.

So what is he playing at?

A useful comment was offered by a review of the 'Self Portrait' album by Geoffrey Cannon, in the *Guardian* (June 26, 1970). Cannon dealt with the 'You cast your spell and I went under' kind of language by saying this:

> '. . . the coup of 'Nashville Skyline' [was] to demonstrate that proverbs are aphorisms when used (as they always are, except in books) by a particular person to a particular person, in a place and a time. It's human context, not verbal dexterity, that lets words, especially words of love, work.'

That account is a little dangerous, of course: we shouldn't be talked into gracing any old pop clichés with the accolade of being 'aphorisms'; nor should we forget that using clichés in a careless way trains people to *think*, as well as speak, in platitudes, and so trains people not to think at all.

But Cannon's argument does apply to Dylan's work in the 'Nashville Skyline' context. When Dylan sings 'For your love comes on so strong', he is effectively saying that that phrase will do as well as any to cover the part of his feelings that can be put into words. And in saying that, he is rejecting a self-image of Dylan the brilliant poet in favour of a concept of himself as an ordinary man coping with love. That is how such phrases work. This is not Dylan patronizing the ordinary mind; it is a confession, candid and accepting, that he is, in ways that it matters to be honest about, an ordinary man himself. And it is an off-loading of the Dylan Myth—which he was to do all over again from a different direction when he came to 'Slow Train Coming' and 'Saved' a decade later.

If 'Nashville Skyline' began this off-loading process, and if its language was kept deliberately mundane, then the next album, 'Self Portrait', pushed things very much further.

Now, seen in the long back-projection of his work, it isn't gruellingly important that the album was so second-rate—but of course when it was new, in 1970, the adjustments necessary to come to terms with 'Self Portrait' seemed enormous. Dylan was demanding more and giving less with this album.

At first hearing, much of the work was trite, rutted and simplistic: and that, in itself, had huge and perplexing impact. Here was an apparently third-rate collection of work from a man who, rightly or wrongly, had become accepted as the genius of our generation.

There were, of course, people who didn't face these difficulties—those who simply listened and enjoyed; and Dylan has always been on their side, against classification, with those who, in his view, know 'too much to argue or to judge'.

All the same, the question 'How should we respond to this album?' was a common one among those whose concern isn't disproportionately with Dylan's *music* at the expense of a concern with the words.

First, there is a blandness of defeat about it. It is there in the hoarse way he delivers that shouted, descending chorus-line that breaks through at the end of the live *Like A Rolling Stone* like a rattling of chains; and this feeling of defeat spreads across everything on the album.

This sense of listless defeat comes across most clearly through Dylan's voice. It conveys, especially in the 'happy' songs, a sort of choking caution (just listen, for instance, to *I Forgot More*)—an impression that Dylan has walked, Godlessly, close to 'the valley of the shadow of death' and dare not now explore beyond the simplistic verities adhered to by Nashville, Tennessee. It is not so much mental plumpness as

Fourteen years apart, but same stance: Dylan at Carnegie Hall Hootenanie 1962 and with the Rolling Thunder Revue in Houston, Texas, 1976.

an exhaustion of courage – as if the Dylan of 'Self Portrait' has placed himself under house-arrest because the old Insanity Factory is too close to his gates.

And while this kind of rest/retreat is understandable enough in the *man*, it doesn't do much for his art.

The parallel with the Born-Again Christian albums 'Slow Train Coming' and 'Saved' (especially 'Saved') is very strong (whereas the minor albums of the mid-70s just show Dylan the artist coasting): on 'Slow Train Coming' and 'Saved', Dylan's panic at Godlessness has him clinging not to Nashville's country verities and simplicities but to the gospel ones of the Bible Belt. The main virtue of *Saving Grace* is that it confesses this need-to-cling, just as *Watching The River Flow* was to do not long after 'Self Portrait'.

Yet, on the positive side, just as 'Slow Train Coming' and 'Saved' are good enough to repay countless plays, so too 'Self Portrait', albeit a very minor Dylan work, has its own riches; and now that the album is well into the past, it is easier to enjoy them.

First, the album does not lack warmth; and second, its self-deprecation can be seen as showing an egolessness which is, now and then, a welcome ingredient in Dylan's largely ego-emphatic output. As Bill Damon put it (*Rolling Stone*, September 3, 1970):

> With all of its unity and inclusiveness, 'Self Portrait' is too complex to have a point of view . . . It is Eastern in its egolessness . . . Dylan does remind us on this album of all the ways we have known him . . . but Dylan's image serves only his music.

Go on, admit it – even the cover painting has its virtues. It is enjoyable for its childlike technique and colouring, a relief from image-building ad-man photography, and interesting also because, like the painting Dylan did for The Band's 'Music From Big Pink' album, it owes a lot to the pen-and-ink sketches of Woody Guthrie. (Dylan's debt in this respect became clear to anyone who has seen Guthrie's drawings when Dylan published *Writings And Drawings By Bob Dylan* in 1973).

Quite a throwback – and on one level, the whole album is a throwback. It is not, as Richard Williams maintained at the time, 'an attempt at the Great North American Album', but it is a deliberate package of Golden Oldies, from folk to country to chart-climbing pop – and this in itself tells us something about how unprepared to be complex Dylan is in his use of language.

I Forgot More is a country classic, and Dylan sings it like Roy Orbison would. *In Search Of Little Sadie* and *Little Sadie* are based on an older song, which Johnny Cash recorded as *Transfusion Blues* when he was with the Tennessee Two on the Sun label and as *Cocaine Blues* on later CBS recordings (one studio, one live with a prison audience). The story-line has remained much the same – it tells of an escape, arrest, trial and jailing. But while Cash plods through a lifeless narrative, congealing in his artificial Manliness, Dylan ditches the worst platitudes, transforms others, by his timing, into wit, and fills his narrative with creative idiosyncrasy. While Cash sings 'overtook me down in Juarez, Mexico' a (place already associated with Dylan in song, from *Just Like Tomb Thumb's Blues)* Dylan has it 'They overtook me down in Jericho', which gives, as Geoffrey Cannon wrote, 'an echo of his persistent references to places of abstract myth. Cash places the arrest: Dylan puts it anywhere.'

Dylan's use of 'Jericho' makes allusion to something else from the Golden Oldie past, too. One of the little witticisms in the performance is the way Dylan's voice goes *up* as he sings the word '*down*'; and this is exactly what Elvis and the Jordanaires do with the same word in their classic version of *Joshua Fit The Battle Of Jericho* on the 'His Hand In Mine' album of 1961, of which I've no doubt that Dylan is extremely fond.

The other oldies on 'Self Portrait' are Gordon Lightfoot's *Early Morning Rain*; *Like A Rolling Stone*; *Copper Kettle*; *Gotta Travel On*: *Blue Moon*; Paul Simon's *The Boxer*; *The Mighty Quinn*; *Take Me As I Am (Or Let Me Go)*; *She Belongs To Me* and two Everly Brothers hit songs, *Take A Message To Mary* and *Let It Be Me*.

With *The Boxer*, Dylan's minimal re-write of the lyric is very telling – and typical of Dylan's ability to say more with less. He simply changes one word, from:

> And he carries a reminder
> Of every glove that's laid him down

to:

> Of every blow that's laid him down.

That 'blow' means we actually see the boxer better: we comprehend that outside the ring as well as inside it, his life is a series of defeats.

The inclusion of two Everly Brothers songs was more striking at the time than it is now, since in recent years, through rock 'n' roll revivals galore, they have been acknowledged as crucial figures in the pre-Dylan era; but when 'Self Portrait' came out, you weren't supposed to still like or even remember that old stuff – you were supposed to be Progressive and despise the 3-minute single.

People still take too much for granted the achievements the Everlys pulled off. They first topped the US charts in 1957 (with *Wake Up Little Susie*) and from then till some time in the earlyish '60s they were constantly in the charts, it seemed. They were very commercial and they were very good. At a time when most people 'found a sound' by accident, they developed one deliberately and intelligently, bridging what gap there was between pop and modern country music. And at a time when pop's understanding of music was near-retarded, the Everlys were consistently alert and curious. They handled their own arrangements and they had taste. By 1967 they were extremely passé.

At that point, Dylan wrote *them* a song, *The Fugitive*, which the Everlys never actually put out, though it turns up in Dylan's catalogue as *Wanted Man*. His recording of their two hits on 'Self Portrait' repeats his compliment to their deserved stature and to their undoubted influence. *Let It Be Me* is a perfectionist's re-drafting of the Everlys' version, in effect; Dylan stays very faithful to their wistful and solid pop world. With *Take A Message To Mary*, Dylan returns the song (again, Bill Damon said it first) 'back to the Code of the West'.

It is a timely reminder that Dylan would not have been revisiting Nashville if the Everly Brothers had not brought it to all of us a decade earlier – long before either Dylan *or* Gram Parsons thought they were 'going country'.

The writers of so many of the Everlys' hits, Felice & Boudleaux Bryant, also wrote *Take Me As I Am (Or Let Me Go)*, which appears on 'Self Portrait', and which has a title, though not a style, so appropriate to Dylan: it sounds like his motto from way-back-when. Yet it redrafts the presentation of that motto, removing from it the big contradiction, the huge inconsistency, that used to apply. On the old tracks where Dylan was saying Accept What I Am, Tolerate, he said it without much tolerance at all, and delivered his message with a bitter impatience. (The only exception, I think, is *All I Really Want To Do*).

With *Take Me As I Am* that paradox has gone. Gently, he re-states, having learnt to practise what he pleads for:

> You're trying to re-shape me in a mould, love
> In the image of someone you used to know
> But I won't be a stand-in for an old love
> Take me as I am or let me go.

For 'someone you used to know', read 'someone I used to be': the old love is the younger Dylan.

So what of the handful of 'Self Portrait' songs that Dylan wrote himself? How do they fit these messages of harking-back and of stressing simplicities?

Living The Blues is, in concept, a Golden Oldie in itself. It's less like the Guy Mitchell/Tommy Steele hit *Singing The Blues* than people said at the time, but it's far from new. The structure is Tin Pan Alliance, and Dylan had debuted it earlier, on CBS-TV in 1969 – a much faster version than the album one, drawing splendidly on Fats Domino piano-work. The album version draws correspondingly on the Jerry Lee Lewis not so much of *High School Confidential* and *Great Balls Of Fire* (though Dylan bows briefly to those on his earlier *Down Along The Cove*) as of his early-60s country work: B-sides like *Fools Like Me* and *Cold Cold Heart*.

Belle Isle ('a model of non-linear narrative', Bill Damon called it) is effectively a Very Oldie too. It is deliberately unoriginal in story, language, structure and overall ethos – and is a terrific parody of the Celtic ballad. I think it still the highlight of the album.

It can be seen as a link to the much earlier, beautiful *Boots Of Spanish Leather*. They are both love *dialogues*, the latter ending with an estrangement and *Belle Isle* ending as its sequel, with an imagined spiritual reconciliation: a neatening-up of existential history. Yet, granted its traditional Gallic model, *Belle Isle* is also self-sufficient and self-contained. Like an island, in fact.

It's hard to avoid words like 'exquisite' in assessing the song: but it isn't that shallow. The tune flows out lightly and gracefully, like the gown billowing out around the maiden in the story; but the accompanying strings are sombre: more so than any appropriate Gallic mist would demand. Dylan treats the subject and the tradition it springs from with respect and a sympathetic mockery simultaneously; yet there is also a tone in his voice that takes up that foreboding suggestion in the strings. There is a darker presence around the edges of this Romance.

This disperses for a little while near the end (before the strings impinge to bring it back again) when the full sunshine of Dylan's comedy bursts through:

> Young maiden I wish not to banter
> 'Tis true I come here in disguise
> I came here to fulfil my last promise
> And hoped to give you a surprise!
> I own you're a maid I love dearly
> And you've bin in my heart all the while . . .

That first line is joyously funny because through the archaism, it *is* graceful, and the poise is kept so beautifully all the way to that 'banter': and Dylan singing these archaisms is the aural equivalent of A Sight To Be Seen. The second line, with its force falling so gleefully on 'disguise', makes it radiantly clear how far into the Gallic story-world Dylan is taking us, while the third line has a well-contrived calming influence – its words float down in a gentle spiral – so that the imminent absurdity of what follows doesn't overbalance and come too soon. The fourth line brings the fall – that ludicrously bad distribution of syllables, the awfulness of the rhyme and the bathos of the hope expressed (itself accentuated by the rush of syllables given over to its expression). It has all been perfectly timed. It is brilliant clowning, like that 'unbalanced' line from *Leopard-Skin Pill-Box Hat* on 'Blonde On Blonde': 'You know it balances on your head just like a mattress balances on a bottle of wine'.

Moreover, Dylan doesn't leave it there, on *Belle Isle*, like some broken Humpty Dumpty. With the lines that follow, all is restored. That 'I own' enacts the first flourish towards a restoration, as Dylan's voice gently hams up a bewildered search for the right note; the hush through 'you're a maid I' begins to get it back; the slowing-down on 'love' gives the necessary foothold; 'de-e-ear-ly' acts as one last wobble; 'And you've bin in my heart' is oh-so-nearly back in balance; and the eventual resolve of the voice's note with the music, at the end of 'all the while', announces the firm restoration of the balance. So then, as the firm, emphasized beat comes down on the word 'me' in the line that follows:

> For me there is no other damsel

—where the voice and the music are precisely synchronized—Dylan re-sets the tone of the song, right there at the end. And in re-setting the tone there, and in the music that follows to close over the song, Dylan draws all its elements together: the sombre quality, the humour and the traditional Romance. The sum of these parts is, in *Belle Isle*, mystery. And mystery, as Dylan said in 1966,

> ...is a fact, a traditional fact ... traditional music is too unreal to die. It doesn't need to be protected. Nobody's going to hurt it ... All these songs about roses growing out of people's brains and lovers who are really geese and swans who turn into angels—they're not going to die.

Likewise *Belle Isle*. Its mystery, as much as its Gallicness, is what makes it a traditional song and a brilliant achievement.

But there is something else to be said in relation to the kind of language Dylan deals in on 'Self Portrait' (and 'Nashville Skyline')—and it's a point that relates also to Dylan's consistent independence of rock modishness. 'John Wesley Harding' is, as we noted earlier, a dramatic gesture of distancing; so too is 'Self Portrait'. It is very much out on its own, and one main way this is emphasized is in Dylan's rejection of the *language* of a modish rock-culture here.

Before 'John Wesley Harding', Dylan's language had been scattered with the old familiar phrases: hung up, where it's at, and so on, along with much hip drugs-terminology. With 'John Wesley Harding' this disappears. 'Nashville Skyline' shows a careful reliance on the language of 'ordinary men' and 'Self Portrait' stays with this change of tack.

In 1966, Dylan said that he'd been unhappy with aspects of his use of language before *Like A Rolling Stone* because:

> I was singing words I didn't really want to sing. I don't mean words like 'God' and 'mother' and 'President' and 'suicide' and 'meat-cleaver'. I mean simple little words like 'if' and 'hope' and 'you'.

With 'Self Portrait', as with 'Nashville Skyline', Dylan is reconciled to such words.

Patrick Thomas, commenting on this shift (while reviewing the 'Nashville Skyline' album for *Rolling Stone*, 1969) wrote: '...the "new" Bob Dylan lyrics, which wring out responses from words like "suitcase" and "rumours", are simply recognition of the fact that not all Americans feel the dead-weight of thrice-throttled, TV-choked English.' And he contrasts this 'new' Dylan language to the 'constant overstatement of urban vernacular'.

On 'Self Portrait', more than ever before, Dylan is using his 'ordinary language' with a dignity of expression which involves much of that weapon of the great artist, *understatement*.

The Dylan of the 1970s, after 'Self Portrait', returns overwhelmingly to singing his own, rather than other people's, material. From 'New Morning' through 'Blood On The Tracks', 'Desire' and on through to 'Saved', he has shifted with fascinating agility through many modes of language, in all of which he has developed his use of understatement, established his artistry, and, with a wholly mature intelligence, freed himself from any obligation to cling on down any one linguistic track.

His basic instinct, though, all through this second decade of his work, has been towards a new simplicity of language.

'New Morning' arrived just a few months after 'Self Portrait' and while in singing-style and timbre, it shows something like a return toward 'Blonde On Blonde' modes of expression, it signalled just the same that the new simplicity of language was not being abandoned by Dylan.

Creatively, perhaps, beyond this chiselling of language, 'New Morning' confirmed that, as he entered the 1970s, the rock poet genius of the 1960s was resting.

On it, Dylan has lost that amazing urgency of communication – that arresting quality, that abrasive presence – and has nothing much to say. Obviously the two things are connected, though one is a matter of delivery, of performance, while the other is a matter of vision. But the lack of one always betrays, in Dylan's art, the lack of the other.

Dylan sounds tired and abstracted and not really 'there' by his own standards. There is even a deterioration in his use of cliché – from, say, the obvious sharpness of 'Blonde On Blonde' 's

> You say you told me that you
> Wanna hold me but you
> Know you're not that strong . . .

On the pleasant, slight *If Not For You*, the cliché is still knowingly offered – as if Dylan *were* back in 1966 – and carried to the point of self-ridicule:

> Winter would have no Spring,
> Couldn't hear the robins sing;
> I just wouldn't have a clue –
> Anyway it wouldn't ring true –
> If not for you

yet the emptiness is as prominent as the confession of it.

When we come to *The Man In Me* (not a Dylan song with much appeal to feminists, fairly enough), there is, because of this sort of emptiness, an added dimension of irony (which again, Dylan's own awareness of does not dissolve) in the lines

> The man in me will hide sometimes
> To keep from being seen
> But that's just because he doesn't want to
> Turn into some machine . . .

and it is reasonable to feel that the artist in Dylan, at least, ought not to be so much in hiding. The song has its own strengths, but it has no commitment. And really, it is a pretty pointless joke to have, in the middle section, Dylan pushing even closer to *On The Street Where You Live* than he had done an album or two earlier, as cited earlier in this chapter, by almost quoting it exactly, in words and tune, here:

> But oh! what a wonderful feeling
> Just to know that you are near

and similarly, when, in *Winterlude*, he strokes the listener with

> Winterlude, this dude thinks you're fine

we're likely to feel that we've had enough songs now from 'this dude' and that we'd 169 prefer to return to those of the genius whose best talents lurk somewhere under this blithe and stereotyped 'dude' personality.

The trouble is that Dylan loses control over this 'dude' persona, to the extent of letting two different selves get mixed up.

This happens on *Sign On The Window*. To rhyme

> Build me a cabin in Utah

with

> Have a bunch of kids who call me Pa

would be immaculate, with all that doubt about this formula-for-happiness shown up in Dylan's delivery, *if*, when he came to the word 'Pa', the note was laid down firmly, like a trump-card. That would be the real Dylan way—and however stylized, and therefore *personally* insincere, it would have flawless *artistic* sincerity.

But Dylan quite simply delivers it wrong (something I don't think he'd ever done before, and almost never since). He gives the word 'Pa' a wobble on the voice—a really awful tremolo-gentility. It's embarrassing, and it happens because Dylan mixes himself up with 'the dude'.

Dylan's lack of anything much to say shows itself too, on 'New Morning', in his conformity to what became a general trend in the pre-New Wave 1970s: namely, the careful gathering up of whole clusters of ever-more-famous, ever-more-'professional' session-musicians. No one could deny their abilities, but Dylan's earlier albums show how unnecessary these extra battalions are for him and his art.

This trend was being identified long before New Wave declared it lethal and destroyed it in 1977 (except in California, where they were too busy eating and dieting and eliminating thought from the shopping-list of things that interested them, and where, in consequence, the music has been unlistenably dull ever since).

Back in 1971, in the first edition of this book, I wrote that: 'the whole trend reveals, right across the scene, a huge disparity between the tiny amount the 1960s stars have left to communicate and the vastness of their access to the best studios and the very best supportive facilities, as a result of their previous (more primitively achieved) attainments. There they all are—George Harrison, Eric Clapton, Crosby, Stills, Nash, McCartney, Kantner, and more—all laying down increasingly trivial material, decorated and supported by increasingly exquisite, "professional" accompaniments. And Dylan (on "Self Portrait" and "New Morning") is right there with them.

'It becomes, before long, a spurious sort of panacea and, since it relies more and more on the ordinary listener possessing extraordinarily good stereo (or, imminently, quadrophonic) equipment, it is debatable whether, under these conditions, technology is the servant or the master of the music'.

All this, of course, was punctured admirably by punk. It had got to the point where no one in Britain dared get on a stage, even in a pub, unless they had monstrous megawatt equipment and could play fifteen chords. The punk bands were important because they saw that for the nonsense it was, and did something about it—and the boom that is still continuing in 1981, whereby hundreds of obscure singles of very primitive technical quality are issued on hundreds of tiny independent labels, is a demonstration that when you feel you do have something to say, the technology is not going to inhibit you.

Now Bob Dylan knew all this perfectly well all along, and most of his recordings, all through his career, have disregarded those debilitating 'standards' of technical production that came into vogue at the end of the 1960s: and that is why the way that these impinge on 'New Morning' is especially irksome.

170

And it does impinge: one's awareness of the technology—the ever-present sense that it is *there* — impinges on the music.

This is, at the very least, ironic when, as happens on the title-track of the album, it is used to extol the virtues of watching rabbits in the great outdoors.

Moreover Dylan's specializing, at the start of the 1970s, in songs of rural simplicity, in which he comes on again and again in a Happy Family Man role as singer/narrator — confirms that he feels he has little to say.

Even in the album's rock song, *One More Weekend*, there is a facile combination of country-sounding slide guitar and noticeably cosy lyrics:

> We'll go some place unknown
> Leave all the children home;
> Honey why not go alone
> Just you and me . . .

This compares directly with *Leopard-Skin Pill-Box Hat*:

> If you wanna see the sunrise
> Honey I know where
> We'll go out and see it sometime
> We'll both just sit there and stare

and the change in the later song (which parallels the earlier one in structure and music too) to a married-couple situation is far from artless. Nor are the details of the realization. While the vagueness of the exhortation in *Leopard-Skin Pill-Box Hat* pithily evokes the narrator's deliberate callousness, the corresponding specificness of the plan suggested in *One More Weekend* evokes only a timidity on Dylan's part; and while 'Honey' is used almost as belittling sarcasm on the '66 song, the same word comes across very differently on the 1970 revisit. Here, used immediately after the situation reveals itself, it half-suggests 'honeymoon', while the whole proposal urges what is precisely a second honeymoon. No wonder it's a slightly weary track, and that its rock harshness does not convince.

Dylan's Happy Family Man role, irrespective of how it applied, at the time, to his private life, is unconvincing in his art. You don't render a vision of happiness by insisting that you're happy, or simply by using a bland voice.

This is what Dylan attempts, wrongly, on 'Nashville Skyline' and 'Self Portrait', and he does so again on 'New Morning' — yet with a significant difference in how it comes out.

Self-awareness of this fault shows through, on tracks like *If Not For You*; the accompanying self-effacement, sometimes self-apology, makes for an odd contradictoriness not found in Dylan's other work.

First, Dylan slips into imitating himself — a trap many distinguished writers fall into, from Wordsworth to Mailer: trying to reach the floor and the door in *If Not For You* just like in *Temporary Like Achilles*; re-writing *Leopard-Skin Pill-Box Hat* as *One More Weekend*; roughing up his voice again so as to echo 'Blonde On Blonde' rather clumsily; the 'old crossroad sign' in *Winterlude* just like back in *One Too Many Mornings*; the déjà vu allusion to romantic, mid-60s-style chaos in *The Man In Me*, where

> The stormclouds are ragin'
> All around my door . . .

and the blatant nostalgia of that line in the middle of the flawed but fabulous *Sign On The Window*: 'Sure gonna be wet tonight on Main Streeeeeet . . .'; plus, perhaps finally, what is in effect a reassurance that yes, after all, he still remembers Bob the young folkie rebel, when he ends *Went To See The Gypsy* with this utter non sequitur:

> So I watched the sun come risin'
> From the little Minnesota town
> From that little Minnesota town.

On top of all this, there is a marked expression of explicit doubt about the family-man-countryman role. Thus the element of self-parody is far more apparent than on the two previous albums – to the extent, even, that birds become 'birdies' (echoing, in the process, Jerry Lee Lewis' *Livin' Lovin' Wreck*) and the wife-and-children become merely a possible formula to try out:

> Build me a cabin in Utah
> Marry me a wife, catch rainbow trout
> Have a bunch of kids who call me Pa...

And to clinch it, this is followed not only by a patently unconfident remark (made less positive still by its being repeated, as if for self-persuasion):

> That must be what it's all about
> That must be what it's all about

but also by the capping touch of genius – that intentionally ingenuous little 'Oh-oh-oh-oh!' which Dylan puts over the end of the riff that follows.

Throughout the album, also, there is a subtle but sustained falsification of the rural/patriarchal ideas: a persistent kind of Midas touch which deliberately makes the picture an idealized and therefore not a real one.

It shows in his going not to 'the hills' at the end of *Day Of The Locusts* but to the American hills most artificialized by Tin Pan Alley, 'the black hills of Dakota'. It suggests Dylan rushing off to Doris Day; it makes his escape to the hills just a story, by making it just a joke – mere fictional allusion.

Then, just as the next song, *Time Passes Slowly*, takes up the story *in* the hills, so also it takes up the unreality suggested in the earlier track:

> Time passes slowly up here in the mountains
> We sit beside bridges and walk beside fountains

warbles Dylan – and plainly, as he's testing whether we'll notice, there aren't any fountains up mountains. The very word suggests the Ideal, not the real. It offers a kind of exquisite, ethereal, pastoral conceit: a sort of Greek Mythology-land, an Elysium. Something not there.

Then, out of the disjointed but compulsive evocation of the strange and fragmentary *Went To See The Gypsy*, comes

> Outside the lights were shining
> On the river of tears...

which fits the rest of the song less than the album as a whole: its function is to ally and associate with the Elysian motif established in the earlier songs.

In *Winterlude* the unreal becomes dominant and explicit. The title itself implies that the album is all a show, like, in this sense, *A Midsummer Night's Dream*. The rhythm is waltz-time; the clichés focus on a dreamworld of romance – denying any corresponding 'real life' romance – the kind that sparkles through the Dixie Cups' record *Chapel Of Love*:

> ...my little apple
> Winterlude let's go down to the chapel

And it's not only a waltz – it's a skating song. It's Dylan On Ice.

That carries a further suggestion of the unreal: the ice-top as merely a precarious covering, a sheet hiding and transforming something else. Alongside this, the lyric reveals the snow on the sand – the shifting sand.

We can see this urged unreality through the rest of the album too: in *New Morning* itself, with its intentional things-aren't-what-they-seem touch of

> a country mile, or two . . .

and in even the obvious theatrical mystique of the title of the next track *Sign On The Window*, while *The Man In Me* has as its theme the message keep-it-all-hid.

As for *Three Angels* – it impresses straight away as being not only *sur*real but as echoing that pop classic of *false* religiosity, Wink Martindale's *Deck Of Cards*. It also echoes closely a short, striking passage from Genet's 'Our Lady Of The Flowers':

> But neither of the two seemed to care whether Divine was absent or
> present. They heard the morning angelus, the rattle of a milk can. Three
> workmen went by on bicycles along the boulevard, their lamps lit, though
> it was day. A policeman on his way home . . . passed without looking at
> them.

As there, but more so, 'the real world' in Dylan's song passes like a pageant below the gaze of the narrator and his rather ungainly angels. Dylan's making them ungainly – keeping them perched up on poles wearing 'green robes, with wings that stick out' – is another wry confession of his intent.

The cumulative effect of all this carefully-established unreality is to make 'New Morning' very different, in its vision, from any other of Dylan's albums. It begins to express a new optimism-through-doubt. He may have little to say but he has the courage to know it – and to make, to pass his time, an intelligent critique of what he *doesn't* believe in anymore. 'New Morning' says for his country persona what *My Back Pages* said about his protest persona.

And what it says about his use of language is that as he steps out beyond the utter simplicity of 'Nashville Skyline' and 'Self Portrait' toward a new simplicity that can bear the demands of the creative artist Dylan cannot help but be, he is here already showing how the simple can encompass the subtle.

That Dylan could be directly touched by something very much from the *urban* world was shown by the single that he issued at the end of 1971: *George Jackson*.

Dylan starts the song very simply by declaring this response, and using the classic blues opening-line to say so:

> I woke up this morning

and then tightening up at once into the particular and the special – personalizing it:

> There were tears in my bed
> They killed the man I really loved
> Shot him through the head.

It is exactly like the pre-1964 protest-songs – even down to the formula of a guitar-backing till the end of the penultimate verse, then a harmonica solo laid on top, then guitar alone again through the last verse, then back with the harmonica for the fade-out.

What is *not* like the pre-1964 protest material is this:

> They were frightened of his power
> They were scared of his love.

That is the post-mystic Dylan—the post-acid Dylan; and in the light of Steven Goldberg arguing (see 'Lay Down Your Weary Tune: Drugs And Mysticism') that after 'Nashville Skyline' Dylan's post-mystic politics would be reactionary, it is interesting to find those mystic traces in the middle of this committedly radical song.

It's also interesting to see the way the end of the song shows Dylan's most Blakeian simple language deliberately echoing one of George Jackson's most spirited (and unBlakeian) remarks. Jackson says in one of his letters that from now on, he's just going to divide people into the innocent and the guilty.

As Dylan re-states this, it is Us and Us, not Us and Them:

> Sometimes I think this whole world
> Is one big prison yard
> Some of us are prisoners
> The rest of us are guards.

Then, after a long gap, comes the magnificent 'Planet Waves' album, which reveals a Dylan not so willing to have jumped back into a purely urban milieu.

It is demonstrably a Dylan album of the '70s in managing to bind together elements of the city-surreal-intellectual world from which 'Blonde on Blonde''s language derived, with a new willingness to re-embrace older, folksier, rural strengths.

Going Going Gone shows this binding together admirably. Here is the city language:

> I'm closin' the book
> On the pages and text
> And I don't really care
> What happens next . . .
> I bin hangin' on threads
> I bin playin' it straight . . .
> I bin livin' on the edge . . .

and here is the urging of an older, simpler wisdom:

> Grandma said 'Boy go follow your heart
> I know you'll be fine at the end of the line
> All that's gold doesn't shine
> Don't you and your one true love ever part.'

Back on *Memphis Blues Again* (on 'Blonde on Blonde'), 'grandpa' was just a joke; in *Going Going Gone*, 'grandma' has insights to offer. She represents something stable and reliable (and, by the implication of her age, something resilient). And her old, simple wisdom is deftly stressed by Dylan having her speaking that truism, that neat opposite of 'all that glisters is not gold'.

Through the rest of the song, Dylan presses on with this forging together of the two different worlds he'd previously walked through separately. He brings in an echo of his old folk-singer days with a near-quote from *Don't Think Twice, It's All Right*—'I bin walkin' the road'—and he binds a rural, backwoods image and vaguer, mid-60s-Dylan language together in the opening verse:

> I've just reached a place
> Where the willow don't bend . . .
> It's the top of the end
> I'm going, I'm going, I'm gone.

Back on the streets of New York, 1972.

The whole album devotes itself to revisiting, as the adult with the mid-60s surreal achievement behind him, the Minnesota landscapes and feelings from which he had emerged in the first place. *Hazel* deals with the girlfriend he'd had long before he ever first set out for New York City; and in *Something There Is About You* he says it carefully and clearly:

> Thought I'd shaken the wonder
> And the phantoms of my youth
> Rainy days on the Great Lakes
> Walkin' the hills of old Duluth . . .
> Somethin' there is about you
> That brings back a long-forgotten truth . . .
> I was in a whirlwind
> Now I'm in some better place.

This same theme, of the inexorable tug of the past and the struggle to wed it to the present, runs through the album. It is there in *Wedding Song*, and, coming at the end of the album, these lines, with their chilling full-stop, emphasize the desperation the whole song examines:

I love you more than ever
Now that the past is gone.

An earlier image in the same song echoes across the years from 1965's *Farewell
Angelina*:

I've said goodbye to haunted rooms
And faces in the street
To the courtyard of the jester
Which is hidden from the sun . . .

and *Dirge* similarly says goodbye to old haunts – to the old folk days of Greenwich
Village, such that the song acts as a re-write of *Positively 4th Street*:

Heard your songs of freedom
And man forever stripped
Acting out his folly
While his back is being whipped . . .
I can't recall a useful thing
You ever did for me
'Cept pat me on the back one time
While I was on my knees . . .
No use to apologize –
What difference would it make?

So there is a lot of tension explored here, all stemming from the contradictory
ways in which the past reacts upon the present. The chill desperation of *Wedding
Song* and the distanced vitriol of *Dirge* show one side of the process; the enriching
feelings of re-visiting on *Something There Is About You* and *Hazel* and *Never Say
Goodbye* show the other side. What all the songs reveal is this tension in the language:
this struggle on Dylan's part to reconcile the city-surreal-intellectual approach to
language with the newer, simpler approach.

As much as in *Going Going Gone*, for instance, you can trace the ebb and flow of
these two previously separate modes of expression through a song like *Tough Mama*.
And it works well here: Dylan is beginning to succeed with his project of fusing the
two –

Tough Mama
Meat shakin' on your bones
I'm gonna
Go down to the river and get me some stones
Sister's on the highway
With that steel-drivin' crew
Papa's in the big house
His workin' days are through . . .

With 'Planet Waves', without a doubt, Dylan has come a lot closer than he had on
'New Morning', to forging his own new resources of language.

With 'Blood On The Tracks' his progress suddenly shows through in a
tremendous, unexpected leap forwards and upwards. This album is almost certainly
his best, and puts the constant struggle between 'Blonde On Blonde', or 'Highway 61
Revisited', and 'Nashville Skyline' – the struggle enacted in 'New Morning' and
'Planet Waves' – dramatically behind him. There is no longer an ebb and flow
between those two extreme modes of expression. There is, on a whole new plateau,
as it were, a successfully-attained, fresh language which *is* the new simplicity – and

in which, as ever in the best of Dylan's work, simplicity is deceptive, communicating more by being able confidently to say less.

'Blood On The Tracks' gives us, also, Dylan's scorching *urgency* at its very best, utterly free from the chains of the 1960s.

For this reason alone, its historical importance is immense. When it was first released, in 1975, its effect was colossal. An adjustment was needed, critically, to the fact that Dylan had so dramatically broken free of the decade with which he was so deeply associated by virtue of having so profoundly affected it. Some adjustment was necessary to Dylan's generation's consciousness, from the fact that with 'Blood On The Tracks' it was Bob Dylan who had produced the most strikingly intelligent, apposite and entirely contemporary album of the 1970s.

Most people had assumed that, in effect, Dylan's decline at the end of the decade he had made his own, the 1960s, froze seminal work – 'Highway 61 Revisited', 'Blonde On Blonde', the basement tapes, 'John Wesley Harding' – into an historical religious object which one had to choose, by the mid-70s, either to put away in the attic or else to revere perhaps at the expense of more contemporary artists. Instead, 'Blood On The Tracks' legitimized Dylan's claim to a creative prowess – a power capable of being directed at us effectively for perhaps another thirty or forty years.

The common conception of how rock music moves forward needed to be adjusted too. That conception has always been that artists come and go in relatively short time-spans, with careers peaking early. 'Blood On The Tracks' challenged that idea. Here was a masterpiece fully ten years after Dylan's first major 'peak', 'Highway 61 Revisited' – and one as different and as fresh as it possibly could have been. It addressed the post-1960s world, and our darkness within, with a whole arsenal of weapons.

Its creative genius is still very much an undiminished thing of the present. It has as much sheer freshness as Dylan's, or anyone else's, first album; as much genuine urge to communicate; as much zest. Yet it combines them all with a sharp wit and corrosive intelligence, and an impeccable judgement, so that the sum of these parts is a greater whole than any of Dylan's other achievements.

Like 'Planet Waves', 'Blood On The Tracks' deals, among much else, with the overlaying of the past upon the present – but gone, utterly, is any element of Dylan's myopic early-70s insistence on eternal love and on its wholesome cocoon. In its place is a profoundly-felt understanding of our fragile impermanence of control – so that in dealing with the overlay of past upon present, Dylan is dealing also (unlike 'Planet Waves') with the inexorable disintegration of relationships, and with the dignity of keeping on trying to reintegrate them against all odds.

Tangled Up In Blue deals with the way in which many forces – past upon present, public upon privacy, distance upon friendship, disintegration upon love – are further tangled and reprocessed by time. It's a scintillating account of a career and a love affair and of how they intertwine. It becomes a viable history of fifteen years through one man's eyes, and in its realism and mental alertness it offers a vigorous challenge to all the poses of wasted decay that most 'intelligent' rock has been marketing since the fall from grace of the 1960s optimism.

As it would need to be, Dylan's writing here is chiselled by the full concentration of his artistry. He can coin a new mode of expression with an almost in-passing agility:

> Later on when the crowd thinned out
> I was about to do the same

– and there is the wit, tossed out as if it were easy, and there too is the bubbling spontaneity which Dylan achieves within the disciplined limits of a strikingly precise verse-structure.

He makes this work for him so well. There is, for instance, a rhyming spill-over toward the end of each verse, like this:

> I was standin' on the side of the road
> Rain fallin' on my shoes
> Headin' out for the east coast
> Lord knows I paid some dues
> Getting through —
> Tangled up in blue

It is there as that fourth line (rhyming with the second) spills over into the short fifth line (which rhymes with the sixth).

As we listen to the song, these short spill-overs become more and more stabbing in their emotional effect as they become at the same time more and more agile and clever as rhymes. As here:

> She studied the lines of my face
> I must admit I felt a little uneasy
> When she bent down to tie the lace-
> -s of my shoe —
> Tangled up in blue

and finally, triumphantly, here in the last verse:

> But me I'm still on the road
> Headin' for another joint
> We always did feel the same
> We just saw it from a different point
> Of view —
> Tangled up in blue.

Beyond that wonderful use of a formal, limiting shape and structure to yield scintillating leaps of feeling and expression, *Tangled Up In Blue* contains a whole assortment of verbal spikes and explosions that all operate not as distractions from the main body of *feeling* in the song but as ways of evoking the emotional complexity and urgency of it all. That Dylan can make time, in the course of what is delivered as a fast, breathless narrative, for flashes like this:

> I had a job in the Great North Woods . . .
> But I never did like it all that much
> And one day the axe just fell

shows an alertness and mental dexterity that augments the emotional seriousness and depth of the song. And there is an accompanying dexterity of sketching in, quick as a flash, a whole range of universally recognizable moments in fresh, intensely accurate strokes of language, from the evoked dialogue with inbuilt self-mockery here:

> She lit a burner on the stove
> And offered me a pipe
> 'I thought you'd never say hello,' she said
> 'You look like the silent type'

to the very funny sureness of touch in this summary of that common feeling of whatever-happened-to-*those* people:

> Some are mathematicians
> Some are carpenters' wives
> Dunno how it all got started
> I dunno what they're doin' with their lives

where that last line communicates the inevitable ambiguity of feeling – sadness at time's destruction of friendships and at the same time, truly, an indifference to where or what those people are now.

Tangled Up In Blue, then, opens the album at a pretty high level of intensity and brilliance. *Simple Twist Of Fate* carves out its own indelible impression on the mind, and *You're A Big Girl Now* presses on still further with the unsparing examination of whether a decaying relationship can withstand the strains of time and other lovers; and then with *Idiot Wind* we return to these themes again but with a yet greater intensity.

Seen first as a sort of Positively 4th Street Revisited, it is not the album's most successful song. The too-personal bone-scraping jars:

> Someone's got it in for me
> They're planting stories in the press . . .
> I haven't known peace and quiet
> For so long I can't remember what it's like . . .
> You'll find out when you reach the top
> You're on the bottom . . .

It also produces, in Dylan, a need to step back from that extra-personal quality somehow: and he does so in the wrong way, by stylizing his delivery of the anger, so that his voice at those points comes across with a faked-sounding passion.

Yet this is a small element in the song. It deepens into one of infinitely greater emotional range than a *Positively 4th Street*. The idiot wind that blows is the whole conglomerate of things which assail our integrity and of love that renders us hapless and out of control. The song locks us in a fight to the death, in a contemporary graveyard landscape of skulls and dust and changing seasons. Destruction and survival again.

The preoccupation with this just-possible survival one must fight for is urged most eloquently in this tremendous, evocative stanza:

> There's a lone soldier on the cross
> Smoke pourin' out of a box-car door
> You didn't know it
> You didn't think it could be done:
> In the final end he won the war
> After losing every battle . . .

That is matched, later in the song, by the extraordinary tugging wildness of this – a triumph of poetic strength:

> The priest wore black on the seventh day
> And sat stone-faced while the building burned
> I waited for you on the runnin' boards
> 'Neath the cypress tree while the springtime turned
> Slowly into autumn:
> Idiot wind
> Blowin' like a circle around my skull
> From the Grand Coulee Dam to the Capitol . . .

(And what a rhyme!)

The 1976 return to TV to aid the cause of Ruben 'Hurricane' Carter.

Then, in total contrast, we have the lightly-sketched humane straightforwardness of *You're Gonna Make Me Lonesome When You Go*, which represents yet another fully-fledged success for Dylan's new simplicity of language. This is a conscious reversing of all those 1964ish Dylan songs where he leaves his lover for the road. This time, she leaves him for the road. The strength of the song lies in its tone of lively philosophic acceptance: there is no self-absorption, much less self-pity. His love for her comes through from the way in which he accepts that she must go and so tells her his feelings unreprovingly:

> I've seen love go by my door
> (Never bin this close before) . . .

Much of the song is thus delivered – so lightly as to suggest that it's in brackets, with the same sparkling, *generous* humour. I think it astonishing that a man who, by the time he made this album, had been monstrously famous for over a decade and had been acclaimed as a genius before he was twenty-five, could have the down-to-earth self-knowledge to throw out, in this song, so ordinarily humorous and puck-ish a phrase as the one that ends this stanza:

> You're gonna make me wonder what I'm doin'
> Stayin' far behind without you
> You're gonna make me wonder what I'm sayin' –
> You're gonna make me give myself a good talkin' to . . .

Again, as ever on this unsurpassed album, the simplicity of language represents the opposite of a dullness of emotion. Throughout, from the deft movie-script of *Lily Rosemary And The Jack Of Hearts* to the scrupulously checked-in intensity of *If You See Her, Say Hello* (a marvellous re-write of *Girl From The North Country*) and from the flawless blues of *Meet Me In The Morning* to the barbed sanity of *Buckets of Rain*, 'Blood On The Tracks' is the work of an artist who has never been of sharper intelligence nor more genuinely preoccupied with the inner struggles and complexities of human nature. Dylan's sensibility here is 100 per cent intact. He is also an artist who has lost, on 'Blood On The Tracks', not one iota of his devotion to, nor expertise with, a wide range of American music.

180   'Desire' (1976), the album that follows, inevitably has a narrower range, though

Dylan's use of language on it—most of these songs were written, totally un-characteristically, in collaboration, on the lyrics, with Jacques Levy—is another (and distinctive) success for the new chiselled simplicity.

The movie-spinning of *Lily Rosemary And The Jack Of Hearts* is continued on *Black Diamond Bay* and on *Joey*, which works only if you take it as the classic American gangster movie in song, and not as a straight Dylan narrative twisted badly by an obviously phoney moral weighting. The featherweight pop song is back in Dylan's repertoire with *Mozambique*. The protest song is back in *Hurricane* (the weakness of which is shown by how much better the music is than the ideas behind the words; the hollowness of 'He could have bin the champion of the world' was assured, years and years earlier, by Dylan's own youthful *Davy Moore*). And on the more substantial songs on 'Desire' there is, regrettably, a distinct falling-away from the surgical incisiveness of the 'Blood On The Tracks' collection by virtue of Dylan's shift of preoccupation, away from an engaged concentration on the corrosions of time and failures of love, and toward a more mystical, religious focus. (As this applies in *Isis* it is dealt with in the last chapter of the book.)

Oh Sister has this new emphasis:

> We grew up together from the cradle to the grave
> We died and were reborn and left mysteriously saved—

and also stands as a pretty clumsy attempt at dialogue with the new 1970s generation of liberated woman. It is clumsy not least in making bluntly clear, from lines like

> And is our purpose not the same on this earth
> To love and follow His direction?

that he has not been listening to a word they've been saying.

Romance in Durango is another pop song—but it is utterly marvellous, right from its flinty, glistening opening line:

> Hot chili peppers in the blistering sun

which gets a supercharged impact from the minimal melody, the stabbed bunching of the syllables and the desert-burn of Dylan's voice. Pop song it may be—it is splendidly the heir of Marty Robbins' *El Paso*, and parodies that song's death-scene magnificently—but it raises the pop song onto an undreamt-of high plane, through the compression of what is really skilful concentration in language. It has a strange dynamism, derived from interweaving long syllable-crammed lines—

> We'll drink tequila where our grandfathers stayed

—and sudden oases of more spacious lines in which, as often before, Dylan says more with less:

> The dogs are barking
> And what's done is done

All of this—the sternness towards a song like *Oh Sister* and the near-damning with faint praise of a song like *Black Diamond Bay* or *Romance in Durango*—is to under-rate the 'Desire' album, in ways that are invited more by the fact of its coming after 'Blood On The Tracks' than because of its own weaknesses. These, after all, are largely the result of its limitations of scope and intention.

More importantly, the album has exploratory strengths of its own which are easy to overlook and less easy to write about. Never before has Dylan so utterly made his word-content the servant of his music. The precise, almost mathematical interlock-ing of the two is primarily what concerns him on this album. He is serving an

181

apprenticeship here, at something new. Who else would do that, after scoring so total a success as 'Blood On The Tracks'?

I cannot indicate the nature of this apprenticeship – of honed communication of feeling, emotion sparked off at the innate mystery of things and places and sounds – half so well as Allen Ginsberg does on his sleeve-notes to the album. They merit several re-readings and they make a lot of unpindownable sense. In exactly the same way as the album itself, which is thus unique in Dylan's repertoire.

Being unique, and in the ways I'm suggesting, means that it lacks some of Dylan's use-of-language trademarks. One of these is his very special use of cliché, which is apparent throughout the rest of his work and which deserves some consideration in this chapter here and now.

'Dylan', wrote Richard Goldstein, 'approaches a cliché like a butcher eyes a chicken.' It is a useful starting-point. There are indeed moments when, with a sudden flash, the knife comes down:

> You say my kisses are not like his
> But this time I'm not gonna tell you why that is.

But this setting-up of the tired old bird and then killing it in front of us is comparatively rare. Usually there is no explicit butchery. Dylan just *displays* the clichés, holding them up in relish of their absurdity and allowing them to fall over, squawking in the mud, of their own accord:

> Well Frankie Lee he sat back down
> Feeling low and mean
> When just then a passing stranger
> Burst upon the scene
> Saying, 'Are you Frankie Lee, the gambler
> Whose father's deceased?
> Well if y'are there's a fella callin' ya down the road, an' they
> Say his name is priest.'

Dylan also gives us many pictures where clichés help provide sympathetic sketches of human foibles, human weakness, people who wrap up warm in absurd but plausible self-deception.

These sketches flash past without warning, in the most unexpected places, the most unexpected songs. In *Maggie's Farm*, for instance (1965) – where suddenly, after three verses of bitter complaint explaining why the narrator 'ain't gonna work on Maggie's Farm no more', the half-figurative language of the exposition gives way to this genuinely compassionate summary of Maggie's ma:

> Well she talks to all the servants
> About Man and God and Law
> Everybody says she's the brains behind pa
> She's sixty-eight but she says she's fifty-four
> Ah! I ain't gonna work for Maggie's ma no more.

So, as we see, she's an impossible puffed-up old battle-axe rasping out dreadful philosophic homilies, and doubtless she takes advantage of her hick sons and workmen most unscrupulously (you can just see them all going about their labours muttering sullenly, and darkly telling this new hand, Dylan, that they reckon she's the brains behind pa). But all the same we smile for her on catching her at that little impotent touch of pretence, patting her hair into place and claiming to be 'only' fifty-four.

Dylan in the crowd at the Mariposa Folk Festival, 1973.

Even in the love-vision of *Love Minus Zero/No Limit*, in which Dylan exalts his raven-woman, he has time to infuse his observation of ordinary mortals with compassion as well as sharp observation:

> In the dime stores and bus stations
> People talk of situations
> Read books, repeat quotations
> Draw conclusions on the wall . . .

That finely-set condemnation – using to the full the shoddy and sad associations yielded by 'dime' in that first line – is tempered by a corresponding sadness *for* them.

In other songs, Dylan uses the clichés for a more simple comic effect: they help to establish an image of Chaplinesque naïvete for the narrator – and since we see Dylan himself, tousle-headed and jerky, as the narrator, the clichés contribute to our seeing a Dylan of comic innocence:

> Mona tried to tell me
> To stay away from the train-line
> She said that all the railroad men
> Just drink up your blood like wine
> An' I said *Oh*! I didn't *know* that! . . .

Later in the same song – *Memphis Blues Again*, from 'Blonde On Blonde' – Dylan plays for a very similar effect, except that this time the contrast between the two levels of conversation glimpsed is not merely a contrast of figurative and literal language but also of the sophisticated and the hick:

183

> When Ruthie says come see her
> In her honky-tonk lagoon
> Where I can watch her waltz for free
> 'Neath her Panamanian moon
> An' I say Awh! C'*mon* now!
> Ya know ya know about my debutante . . .

The figurative – which is to say, in this case, the surrealistic – language surrounding Ruthie all suggests a sophisticated personal elegance in her. The words iridesce around her like a rich man's party – almost as if she had stepped suitably unreal out of a Leonard Cohen song. The very name 'Ruthie' fits perfectly the ethos of the lagoon, the fanciful moonlight waltzing and the necessarily sophisticated sensibility that would alight on 'Panamanian' (and it is *her* Panamanian moon!). And all this contrasts so beautifully with the inarticulate, ignorantly sceptical world of 'Awh! C'*mon* now!' – cliché as robust rejoinder, as deflater of pretence.

Dylan is equally capable of mocking *these* values, where he finds them over-simplified and tired: when, to return to the point about cliché, he finds them adhered to via automatic thought (i.e. non-thought). Hence, in *Motorpsycho Nitemare* (1964), when the narrator comes to beg a sleeping-place for the night from a curt and intransigent boor of a farmer, we are shown the farmer eyeing him suspiciously, and then we get this:

> Well by the dirt 'neath my nails I guess he knew I wouldn't lie
> He said 'I guess you're tired', (He said it kinda sly) . . .

Oh that good old working-man's dirt beneath the nails!

As Dylan has moved through the 1970s, he has increased the versatility of his use of cliché.

'Planet Waves' gives us this robust bumping-together of two clichés, which wakes the sleeping meaning of each:

> You angel you
> You got me under your wing

The much later *We Better Talk This Over* partly works by a similar bumping together, unexpectedly, of two phrases of common currency:

> Oh child
> Why you wanna hurt me?
> I'm exiled
> But you can't convert me

and it's generally true that the 'minor' songs from 'Street Legal' – particularly *We Better Talk This Over* and *True Love Tends To Forget* – are dazzling successes at conveying much through saying little.

Perhaps the deftest of all his touches, as far as *using* cliché (and not being used by it) is concerned, is the one Dylan brings off here (in *True Love Tends to Forget*):

> You're a tear-jerker baby
> But I'm under your spell
> You're a hard worker baby
> But I know you well
> And this weekend in hell
> Is makin' me sweat . . .

The first four lines lay the trap impeccably – they pile up the clichés so that the

Left: *1978 — a sixteen-year repertoire revisited, including remarkable re-interpretations of* Don't Think Twice It's All Right, I Want You, Tangled Up In Blue *and* The Times They Are A-Changin' *among others.*

Below: *Paris 1978.*

Right: *1976 was a year of experimental headgear.*

Below: *The song and dance man at Blackbushe, 1978. The first use of the top hat since 1965.*

listener starts mentally snoozing. Dylan catches us off-guard, and at that moment sets off the detonation of

> . . . this weekend in hell
> Is makin' me sweat.

It is one of Dylan's all-time-best uses of cliché as drama, as subversion, as wit, and not least as understatement. His success at thus speaking volumes through saying little underlines just how well he brings this most individual use of cliché into the service of his fight, in the 1970s, for a new creative simplicity of language.

Yet when Dylan experiments again with a *complexity* of language not unlike that of the 1965–6 songs, the one album he does it on is the one containing those two songs just quoted – the magnificent, much underrated 'Street Legal' (1978).

This album has Dylan's best band and its rich musical swirl is as unifying and affecting as that of 'Blonde On Blonde' twelve years earlier. And while Dylan's delivery carries incomparably more authority, sureness and toughness on 'Street Legal', his use of language is at times similarly dense and wild – packed tight with characters, incident, Biblical allusion, surreal flights of fantasy and a restless emotional thrust.

The album establishes its own vocabulary, such that there is an identifiable wholeness here. It is one of the album's strengths.

Unlike 'New Morning', the comparisons 'Street Legal' prompts with 'Blonde On Blonde' and the re-alighting on familiar techniques and preoccupations is not the result of either tiredness or a suspect willingness to please. This is a major collection from a Dylan on top creative form.

It is a Dylan, too, whose confidence is matched by his urgency. A kind of direct impatience burns through the whole work, from the harsh blues of *New Pony* to the re-affirmation of youthful self-confidence that flashes through the middle of *Is Your Love In Vain?*:

> I have dined with kings
> I've bin offered wings
> And I've never bin too impressed . . .

The same sureness of his own worth (a quality people always enjoy when it is exhibited with panache) strikes us in the opening song, *Changing of The Guards*:

> 'Gentlemen', he said,
> 'I don't need your organization
> I've shined your shoes
> I've moved your mountains and marked your cards . . .'

and equally in the closing song, *Where Are You Tonight?* Even on the James Dean level, this has as much flair as anything from 'Blonde On Blonde':

> If you don't believe there's a price for this sweet paradise
> Just remind me to show ya the scars;   .

while these two extracts hold the authentic voice of the anarchic master-thief of the mid-60s:

> I'd have paid the traitor and killed him much later
> But that's just the way that I am

and

> It felt out of place, my foot in his face . . .

Self-assurance also bristles through the audacious rhyming, in which Dylan often delights, but never more so than on this collection:

> Senor, Senor
> Can ya tell me where we're headin'
> Is it Lincoln County Road or Armageddon

and:

> I'm lost in the haze
> Of your delicate ways
> With both eyes glazed

and:

> She was torn between Jupiter and Apollo . . .
> And I couldn't help but follow

and:

> I was lying down in the reeds
> Without any oxygen
> I saw you in the wilderness
> Among the men

and most triumphantly and sustainedly in the breathtaking *No Time To Think*. The song uses a profusion of slick, tricksy internal rhyming – and its repetitious effect – to enforce the sense of a whirling merry-go-round created by the music's clockwork 6/8 rhythm:

> I've seen all these decoys
> Through a set of deep turquoise
> Eyes and I feel so depressed:
> China doll, alcohol,
> Duality, mortality . . .
>
> The bridge that you travel on
> Goes to the Babylon
> Girl with the rose in her hair
> Starlight in the east, you're finally released
> Suspended with nothing to share

The album's rich swirl provides more of those classic epigrams – or mottoes/quotes that function as epigrams – such as were coming thick and fast from the mid-60s Dylan: 'To live outside the law you must be honest'; 'Don't follow leaders, watch your parking-metres'; etc, etc. This parade is joined, on 'Street Legal', by the hilarious, poky 'son this ain't a dream no more, its The Real Thing!', and 'I don't have to be no doctor, babe/To see that you're madly in love'.

Baby Stop Cryin' contains a couple of notable back-references too. The offer made to Queen Jane Approximately – 'when ya want somebody ya don't have to speak to, won't you come see me Queen Jane' becomes, in the newer song, reversed into the more conventional

> Or if you just want a friend you can talk to

– with Dylan deliberately exposing this conventionality as part of his evocation of a much more hapless narrator figure. *Baby Stop Cryin'* also uses exactly the same I-know-and-you-know motif in its chorus as did the gloating, vicious *Tell Me Mama* of

1966 – again underlining in how different a relationship to the woman the song addresses its narrator now stands. He is no longer the hard, detached Brando figure ('Waddaya want me to do – send you some flowers?': 'The Wild One') of those days; he is locked in helpless love this time around – coaxing, pleading, entirely entangled.

Finally there is, in *Baby Stop Cryin'*, that magnificent sharp dart of humour, Dylan taking a moment out of the general bogged-downness of the song to flash us a little display of his deftness, here:

> Go down to the river babe
> Honey I will meet you there
> Go down to the river babe
> Honey I will pay your fare

– which parallels the same double-take of subject-matter we find in 1975's 'Blood On The Tracks' song *You're A Big Girl Now*:

> Bird on the horizon
> Sitting on the fence
> He's singin' his song for me
> At his own expense . . .

(and also, come to that, parallels what is at heart the same double-take process here, in the very much earlier *Lay Down Your Weary Tune*:

> The cryin' rain like a trumpet sang
> And asked for no applause.)

If, then, Dylan strays, on 'Street Legal', from his overall 1970s pursuit of a new simplicity of language, he does so only partially, and there is no disputing that he returns to it on 'Slow Train Coming' and 'Saved'. These albums are examined in the final chapter of this book.

Back with Joan Baez 1976: on stage in Houston, Texas as part of the Rolling Thunder Revue.

Chapter 7
Lay Down Your Weary Tune
Drugs & Mysticism

Reporter A lot of the young people who admire you
seem to be mixed up in a lot of drug taking and so forth.
What are your views on this problem?

Dylan Oh I don't have any of them views;
I sure wish I did – I sure would like
to share them with y'all.
(Isle of Wight Press Conference, August 1969)

Drugs and mysticism go together in the West because most of us are far from natural mystics. We need drugs to open Blake's doors of perception (as Huxley acknowledged). The very word 'high' suggests the connection – to be high all the time would be to hold on always to a transcendent vision. It is being high, not the brute possession of drugs, which totalitarian law-and-order should make illegal, because as it is their Dream Police let the Blakes through the net.

Dylan is not a natural visionary in the sense that Blake is. Being an artist, he has vision, but that vision has not encompassed mysticism unaided. Everyday concerns abound in his work – his early self-immersion in the blues, his absorbed concern for music generally, and his songs of socio-political comment: songs full of the signs of competitive ego, surface ideology and western logic, and infused with Old Testament concepts of vengeance. No way is Dylan's mind intrinsically eastern. Dylan's mysticism must have come through drugs as well as literature.

It follows that, as with most of us, for Dylan 'the mystical experience' was surely sparked off by 'the acid experience'. The West has a million mystics now.

This sort of claim provokes a curious antagonism. We, who think ourselves so much finer than the Victorians, adhere still to their mistrust of the painless and the instant – and yet we adhere inconsistently. We still like to believe in 'love at first sight'; we find plausible the instant conversion of Paul on the road to Damascus; we trust photographs which snatch up scenes and situations in a fraction of a second; and yet we use 'instant' as a derogatory term, even where it misleads and over simplifies to use it at all.

Acid only works 'instantly' in that it clarifies: what it clarifies is a wealth of experience and feeling acquired as slowly as life itself unfolds, assembled and blended gradually over the years.

Huxley's idea as to the way such a drug works seems very reasonable: that we operate 'normally' with a brain that filters the information we receive, obscuring much of the actual, so that we glean only a narrow apparition of reality. The idea of the everyday filter is not, even in English literature, a twentieth-century idea. George Eliot wrote in 'Middlemarch' that most of us walk about well-wadded in stupidity necessarily, because otherwise 'we should see the grass grow and hear the squirrel's heartbeat, and we should die of that roar which lies on the other side of silence'. For Huxley, mescalin rolled back the filter. Acid appears to do the same. It is in this sense that it clarifies: it allows the receipt of perceptions and distillation of experience unwarped by the blinkers of the everyday brain.

From this acid starting-point, it makes sense to attribute 'the mystical experience' to Dylan, as Steven Goldberg does in a contentious article in *Saturday Review* ('Bob Dylan and The Poetry of Salvation', May 30, 1970, USA).

He doesn't mention drugs once – and wonders whether Dylan's 'young audience' knows what Dylan is 'singing about' – but he makes some good points anyway.

He writes of Dylan's 'preparing to become an artist in the Zen sense' and explains:

> '... he was searching for the courage to release his grasp on all the layers of distinctions that give us meaning, but, by virtue of their inevitably setting us apart from the life-flow, preclude our salvation. All such distinctions, from petty jealousies and arbitrary cultural values to the massive, but ultimately irrelevant, confusions engendered by psychological problems, all the endless repetitions that those without faith grasp in order to avoid their own existence – all of these had to be released.'

Acid releases. The barriers and masks we construct in 'coping' with our 'psychological problems' drop anyway. We release our grasp.

Goldberg's article continues:

> The strength, the faith, necessary for this release was ... a major theme of Dylan's for ... three years. In *Mr Tambourine Man*, an invocation to his muse, he seeks the last bit of will necessary for such strength.

That seems both pertinent and clumsy. Dylan is *not*, in *Mr Tambourine Man*, asking for courage to give him 'the strength, the faith': he has the faith already. It shines through the song with a celebratory optimism directed at what he anticipates finding upon the 'magic swirling ship'. Yet the very next line of the song shows the pertinence of Goldberg's commentary, as Dylan sings 'my senses have been stripped'.

(Why, having reached this point, does Goldberg still not mention drugs? Why hide behind that vague phrase 'an invocation to his muse'? It is obvious that in *Mr Tambourine Man*, drugs are the focus of Dylan's 'invocation'.)

Goldberg goes on to explain how he sees Dylan striving toward a mystical vision from 1964 onwards – and, like all critics, Goldberg gets interesting only when he looks hard at specific work, as here:

> About the only redeeming virtue of Dylan's pre-visionary songs had been an attractive empathy towards the outsider. While Dylan was not to achieve the complete suffusion of vision with compassion until 'John Wesley Harding' in 'Highway 61 Revisited', he did begin to feel that the eternally incommunicable nature of the religious experience did not render human contact irrelevant. If his attentions were not loving, at least he was attempting to reconcile man's existence with his vision ...*Like A Rolling Stone*, which is probably Dylan's finest song and most certainly his quintessential work, is addressed to a victim who has spent a lifetime being successfully seduced by the temptations that enable one to avoid facing his [*sic*] own existence.

Goldberg goes on:

> Dylan's poetic talents are at their zenith in 'Blonde On Blonde'. Vision overwhelms him less than before, and he concentrates on finding peace through the kinds of women he has always loved: women of silent wisdom, women who are artists of life, women who neither argue nor judge but accept the flow of things...

In 'John Wesley Harding', Dylan reiterates his belief that compassion is the only secular manifestation of the religious experience; any code which demands more than pure compassion is generated in the imperfection of experience and does not flow only from a vision of God. Indeed, while change in Dylan's universe is the natural form of egotism: it is an individual's setting himself apart from the flow ... 'John Wesley Harding is not a political philosophy and our attempting to view it as such is to drain it of the wisdom it has to offer. This album is Dylan's supreme work; it is his solution to the seeming contradiction of vision and life. His vision continues to preclude a political path to salvation, but finally overcomes the exclusion of humanity that had plagued his previous visionary songs ... the creative manifestations of a life infused with God, gentleness and compassion replaces bitterness and cynicism. Where once there was confusion, now there is peace. Dylan has paid his dues. He has discovered that the realization that life is not in vain can be attained only by an act of faith ... To the children of Pirandello, drowning in their ennui and relativism, Dylan sings:

> 'There must be some way out of here
> Said the joker to the thief
> There's too much confusion
> I can't get no relief ...
>
> No reason to get excited
> The thief he kindly spoke
> There are many here among us
> Who feel that life is but a joke
>
> But you and I we've been through that
> And this is not our fate
> So let us not talk falsely now
> The hour is getting late'

The only way in which any of us can hope to play the thief, can ignite the faith of another and rob him of his confusion, is through love and compassion.

To me, however, the most interesting part of Goldberg's article is his citing of *Lay Down Your Weary Tune* as a signal of Dylan's changing from politics to mysticism. (This song was published in 1964 – the year of the 'Another Side Of' album, which also had that signal-song, *My Back Pages*; unfortunately, Dylan's recording of *Lay Down Your Weary Tune* has never been released.)

It isn't amazingly astute of Goldberg to point it out as signalling some change – a song more strikingly different from Dylan's earlier output would be impossible to imagine. All the same, it's a song that has received less attention than almost any other in the whole of Dylan's repertoire, so that it's of interest that Goldberg should focus on it at all. And no other song could enforce, for me, so strong a sense of the acid-mystic equation's validity. Goldberg cites it in terms of mysticism; I would cite it as Dylan's first acid song – the first concentrated attempt to give a hint of the unfiltered world, and a supremely successful *creation*. Goldberg refers elsewhere in his article to Dylan's having 'heard the universal melody'. Nothing could better substantiate the spirit of such a claim than *Lay Down Your Weary Tune* – one of the very greatest and most haunting creations in our language.

What strikes home immediately is its distance from what we know as acid-rock music. There is more here than the evocation of a feeling or mood: the song's chorus

1965: the year of his last solo concerts, two BBC-TV shows, the 'Don't Look Back' film, access to the pop charts with Subterranean Homesick Blues *and an astonishing array of new songs revolutionary in their impact on the folk scene, the new left, the campuses and the music business.*

posits a philosophy through compassionate incantation and the verses deal with an enchanted existence, wholly realized.

The tune, in A Major, runs through a simple 14-bar structure which, after its initial chorus statement, is repeated nine times – always with delicate variation.

By the device of having one self-renewing tune to serve both chorus and verses, Dylan doubles the sense of unity which covers the whole song, and its images, as Harunobu's umbrella shields his lovers in the snow. We find an impression of perfect balance not only between verse and chorus but between the opposites focused by the words – between the night that has gone and the morning announced by its breeze; between the trees and the earth to which their leaves descend; between the ocean and the shore; between the rain that sings and the listening winds.

The melody seems to entwine itself around us, in allegiance to the associations of 'wove', 'strands', 'waves', 'unwound', 'unbound', and 'winding strum' in the lyric. And by its very impingement it urges the felicity of Dylan's analogies between nature's effects and the sounds of musical instruments. As it flows through each line, with a graceful and liquid precision, the melody nurtures and sustains in us an awareness of how involving and creative such analogies are made to be. The tune, in fact, offers itself as an embodiment of 'the river's mirror'; its water smooth does indeed run like a hymn.

In contrast, the solo guitar accompaniment involves itself less with the verses than with the chorus. Based on the three simple chords of A, D and E, it does offer a strength in its strings. Paradoxically, it achieves this strength through strumming: and this maintains a rhythm that is at once flexible – responsive to Dylan's voice – and insistent – almost marching (as on a pilgrimage) – in its beat.

Dylan's voice on this track is as expressive as ever of distilled, unspecified experience and a fine sensibility, totally engaged. Handled by anyone else, it would   193 not be the same song – which also means that the words of the song have a complexity that demands such a voice as Dylan's. For the whole song, words, music *and* performance are all central.

Bearing that in mind, as usual, we do need the whole lyric here in front of us to look at properly, (the chorus is repeated after the first three verses and again at the end):

> Lay down your weary tune, lay down,
> Lay down the song you strum,
> And rest yourself 'neath the strength of strings
> No voice can hope to hum.
>
> (chorus)

> Struck by the sounds before the sun,
> I knew the night had gone.
> The morning breeze like a bugle blew
> Against the drums of dawn.

> The ocean wild like an organ played,
> The seaweed's wove its strands,
> The crashin' waves like cymbals clashed
> Against the rocks and sands.

> I stood unwound beneath the skies
> And clouds unbound by laws.
> The cryin' rain like a trumpet sang
> And asked for no applause.

> The last of leaves fell from the trees
> And clung to a new love's breast.
> The branches bare like a banjo moaned
> To the winds that listened the best.

> I gazed down in the river's mirror
> And watched its winding strum.
> The water smooth ran like a hymn
> And like a harp did hum.

Never before or since has Dylan created a pantheistic vision – a vision of the world, that is, in which nature appears not as a manifestation of God but as containing God within its every aspect. (The nearest Dylan comes to such a view elsewhere – and it isn't really very close – is in *When The Ship Comes In*. There, many aspects of nature are seen as indicators of a deity's feelings: the rocks, sun, sea-gulls and so forth function as signs that God is on Dylan's side.) In *Lay Down Your Weary Tune*, though, the pantheistic vision is complete.

Underlying an exhilaration so intense as to be saddening, there is a profound composure in the face of a world in which all elements of beauty are infused with the light of God. Rejecting, here, the Wordsworthian habit of mixing poetry with explicit philosophizing, so that it is explained, in a prose sense, that the divine light shines through everything, Dylan registers the same conviction with true poetic genius – making that dissembled light a felt presence throughout the song.

The words not only work as images but also as symbols:

> Struck by the sounds before the sun
> I knew the night had gone.

The night, there, is both real and metaphorical: and so is the morning that follows. Dylan uses the same symbolism in *When The Ship Comes In* (and that song calls to mind *The Ancient Mariner* by the supreme English pantheist Coleridge), which looks forward to the triumph of righteousness when

> . . . the mornin' will be a-breakin'.

This in turn relates closely to the chorus of *I Shall Be Released*:

> I see my life come shinin'
> From the west unto the east

(where morning breaks)

> Any day now, any day now
> I shall be released.

It is, of course, a conventional metaphor, but a none the less effective one in the context of the song we're discussing, because its very conventionality prevents it from obtruding. The song would be much less powerful if the symbols were not contained within their corresponding realities – the symbolic within the real night, and so on.

(A far more original means of expressing the same antithesis between hope and despair, in *Memphis Blues Again*, cleverly avoids comparable obtrusiveness by its very centrality to the song:

> Oh! Mama! Can this really be the end:
> To be stuck inside of Mobile

– despair –

> With the Memphis Blues Again.)

The morning Dylan sings of in *Lay Down Your Weary Tune* is heralded by a breeze: and again, Dylan accommodates the conventional associations – associations of freshness and change.

The 'bugle' at once alters the complexion of the line. It places the morning more specifically – because the bugle is not commonly a secular instrument – within a context of salvation.

In the following verse, this religious complexion is supported by the 'organ', with its obvious associations with worship and later confirmed by the 'trumpet', by 'like a hymn' and 'like a harp'.

The pantheistic idea is also implicit in the rejection of all distinctions. Each part of nature focused is given equal weight: to no part is any directly qualitative adjective or adjectival phrase ascribed. The nearest Dylan comes to such ascription is with the 'clouds unbound by laws' and the rain that 'asked for no applause' – and these confirm the idea of God as an evenly-distributed presence by suggesting a moral gulf between divinity in nature and the reductive inadequacy of man. The perception of this gulf is upheld by the last line of the chorus, which, were the implicit made explicit, would read 'No *human* voice can hope to hum'.

The song also rejects evaluative distinction between the various facets of nature by uniting them all in the central motif of the orchestra: each 'instrument' contributes towards an overall sound; each is concerned with the one divine melody.

This unity is substantiated by a wealth of onomatopoeic words within the song – strum, hum, bugle, drums, crashin', clashed, moaned and smooth. It is further developed, becomes multi-dimensional, because in response to this enchanted world the singer's senses (and therefore ours also) mix and mingle. An open acceptance of

Baudelairean *correspondences* is involved.* There is a huge tracery of this sense-mingling in the song. What constitutes the strength of strings? Their sound? Their physical vibration? Their vertical parallel lines? Their tautness? Their recalling of classical Greece (the lute of Orpheus, the melodious divinity of Pan's music)?

The *emotion* experienced as dawn appears corresponds to the *sound* of drums: and mingling such as this helps give the verse its haunting pull on the listener – an effect far beyond the simple dynamics of alliteration in that

> ... breeze like a bugle blew
> Against the drums of dawn.

'The ocean wild' produces an image of movement – a thing felt as well as seen (and the cadence of that phrase as carried by the melody emphasizes the sensation) – and corresponds not only to the sound but also to the physical act of playing the organ. The correspondence between ocean and organ depends also for its total effect on the similarity of sound between the two words and on the striking antithesis between an ocean's being clean and sharp and an organ's seeming musty and somehow imprecise; yet at the same time the antithesis is resolved by the impression of depth (again, metaphorical as well as real) common to both.

Part of the sense-mingling achieved by 'the cryin' rain like a trumpet sang' is surrealistic. Fleetingly, we get a visual image of the rain becoming a trumpet. This belies the effect of that 'cryin'' because to transform itself (from silver-grey to gold) into a singing trumpet, the rain must pour out, if not upwards, horizontally, like musical notes on a sheet of manuscript. It is a tribute to Dylan's achievement that we can accept, in passing, this strangeness of effect without finding it a distraction.

Again, the cadence of the melody works perfectly: the notes that carry the words 'rain like a' ascend so that they enact the pressing down of consecutive trumpet stops. Not only that, but the 'a' is held, extended, so that the 'trumpet' emerges on resolving notes; and we accept the image readily because the music that presents it returns us to base. To produce the 'trumpet' image on homecoming notes lends it a certain familiarity. The image remains striking, but not incongruous.

The cadence is equally cooperative in the first line of that same verse, where again it enacts what the words describe: it allows a graceful unwinding of the voice from the cushioning effect of that 'unwound', where the second syllable lingers, in the air, and dissembles into the cascading fall of 'beneath the skies'.

In fact not one phrase in the lyric fails to gain an extra power from the cadence – which shows how delicate and responsive Dylan's variations are within his 'simple' and economical 14-bar melody.

(None of these devices, or course, depend for their effectiveness on the kind of identification-parade attempted above. Being poetic devices, they work inwardly and unseen. The song only needs its listener to have an open responsiveness to nuance.)

The song is enriched in another small way: it echoes the Elven songs that celebrate Lothlórien in Tolkien's *Lord Of The Rings*.

Like Dylan's world in *Lay Down Your Weary Tune* Lothlórien is pastoral. ('Pastoral', of course, is most pointedly applicable to the Dylan song in that conceit which opens the fourth verse. The idea of leaves forsaking the branches – arms – of

---

* *Il est des parfums frais comme des chairs d'enfants,/Doux comme les hautbois, verts comme les prairies,/ – Et d'autres corrompus, riches et triomphants,/Ayant l'expansion des choses infinies ...'* And certainly, drugs like acid, or even hash, can give those of us less sensitive than Baudelaire an equivalent multi-sensual awareness.

their first love for the welcoming breast of the earth is a surprising one for Dylan: surprisingly traditional. It seems to have escaped from a poem by, say, Wordsworth, or Thomas Hardy, or even Matthew Arnold.)

Like Dylan's world, too, Lothlórien is a paradise, spiritual because real. Colours and sounds are ennobled and enhanced; and that there is an ethereal quality which caresses everything is no denial of the intense reality. It is an extra quality, endowed by the light – which Dylan manages to suggest in his world also.

That *Lay Down Your Weary Tune* does echo Tolkien is first apparent when Legolas sings 'a song of the maiden Nimrodel, who bore the same name as the stream beside which she lived long ago . . . In a soft voice hardly to be heard amid the rustle of the leaves above . . . he began:

> An Elven-maid there was of old,
> A shining star by day:
> Her mantle white was hemmed with gold
> Her shoes of silver-grey.
>
> A star was bound upon her brows,
> A light was on her hair
> As sun upon the golden boughs
> In Lorien the fair.
>
> Her hair was long, her limbs were white,
> And fair she was and free;
> And in the wind she went as light
> As leaf of linden-tree.
>
> Beside the falls of Nimrodel,
> By water clear and cool
> Her voice as falling silver fell
> Into the shining pool.'

You can at once hear Dylan's voice breathing the right kind of delicate life into those lines; that fourth verse, in particular, shows a similar (if much simpler) sort of writing, as regards mood and focus and technique – and beyond that, it's clear that the whole of the Legolas song fits Dylan's tune.

There are (less precise) connections too, between the Dylan song and this:

> I sang of leaves, of leaves of gold, and leaves of gold there grew:
> Of wind I sang, a wind there came and in the branches blew.
> Beyond the Sun, beyond the Moon, the foam was on the Sea . . .

(Again, the Dylan tune fits exactly.) That is a part of the song of 'Galadriel, tall and white; a circlet of golden flowers . . . in her hair, and in her hand . . .a harp.' And there we come across a similarity even between Dylan's song and Tolkien's prose.

Tolkien's prose is of interest – the prose that gives us the description of the land of Lorien, largely through Frodo's eyes – because it brings us back to Steven Goldberg's thesis and the mystic-acid equation. And just as Dylan's vision in *Lay Down Your Weary Tune* corresponds to Frodo's perception of the land of Lorien, both correspond, in turn, to an aspect of what an LSD vision can offer, by transforming an ordinary world into an earthly paradise. Anyone who ever dropped acid will recognize this:

> . . . Frodo stood awhile still lost in wonder. It seemed to him that he had
> stepped through a high window that looked on a vanished world. A light
> was upon it for which his language had no name . . . the shapes seemed at

once clear cut, as if they had been first conceived and drawn at the uncovering of his eyes, and ancient as if they had endured for ever. He saw no colour but those he knew, gold and white and blue and green, but they were fresh and poignant, as if he had at that moment first perceived them and made for them names new and wonderful. In winter here no heart could mourn for summer or for spring. No blemish or sickness or deformity could be seen in anything that grew upon the earth. On the land of Lorien there was no stain.

He turned and saw that Sam was now standing beside him, looking round with a puzzled expression ... 'It's sunlight and bright day, right enough,' he said. 'I thought that Elves were all for moon and stars; but this is more Elvish than anything I ever hear tell of. I feel as if I was inside a song, if you take my meaning.'

... Frodo felt that he was in a timeless land that did not fade or change or fall into forgetfulness ... he laid his hand upon the tree beside the ladder; never before had he been so suddenly and so keenly aware of the feel and texture of a tree's skin and of the life within it. He felt ... the delight of the living tree itself.

... Frodo looked and saw, still at some distance, a hill of many mighty trees, or a city of green towers; which it was he could not tell. Out of it, it seemed to him that the power and light came that held all the land in sway. He longed suddenly to fly like a bird to rest in the green city.

Frodo, like Dylan, stood unwound beneath the skies and clouds unbound by laws: without confusion, in the discovery of release, attuned to the holy chord.

Steven Goldberg contends that Dylan returns to this position from 'Nashville Skyline' onwards. Goldberg was writing before the release of any of the albums of the 1970s but his account includes predictions about 'the future', and no doubt he'd be happy for his remarks to extend at least to 'Self Portrait' as much as to 'Skyline'. This is his concluding paragraph:

It is only in the light of all that came before that ... 'Nashville Skyline' can be truly understood. Perhaps this is a failure of the work; certainly one would think so if he [sic] insists that any great work of art must stand alone. Alone, 'Nashville Skyline' is a tightly written, cleverly executed series of clichés that would seem to be merely a collection of nice songs by a Dylan who has gotten a bit mentally plump. As the final step in Dylan's search for God, however, it is a lovely paean. Dylan's acknowledgement of the joy of a life suffused with compassion and God. If this does not make the album particularly illuminating for the man who is unaware of Dylan's cosmology, to others it is evidence that he has finally been able to bring it all back home. He has heard the universal melody through the galaxies of chaos and has found that the galaxies were a part of the melody. The essence that Dylan has discovered and explored is a part of him at last. There will be no more bitterness, no more intellectualization, no more explanation. There will only be Dylan's existence and the joyous songs which flow naturally from it.

Is there any real basis for applying these last remarks of Goldberg's to Dylan's recent work? What of the other albums of the 1970s? Predicting the future is hazardous and Goldberg might have known better than to do it in regard to Bob Dylan. 'No more bitterness, no more intellectualization, no more explanation' indeed. And 'Nashville Skyline' as 'the final step in Dylan's search for God' – hah!

Chapter 8
The Coming of the Slow Train

Though thou loved her as thyself,
As a self of purer clay,
Though her parting dims the day,
Stealing grace from all alive;
Heartily know,
When half-gods go,
The gods arrive.
(from Emerson's *Give All To Love*)

Bob Dylan has always given us songs that burned with a moral sense. This was true in 1962 when he was transcribing the morality of Woody Guthrie:

Now a very great man once said
Some people rob you with a fountain pen
It don't take too long to find out
Just what he was talkin' about.
A lot of people don't have much food on their table
But they got a lot of forks 'n' knives
And they gotta cut somethin'.

and it has remained crucial in Dylan's work ever since. He was happy to transcribe also an *Old* Testament vengefulness in the early gospel-influenced material:

Tell me what you gonna do
When the devil comes creepin' in your room?

(from the unreleased *Watcha Gonna Do*) and, from *Masters Of War*:

Even Jesus will never forgive what you do

while the unissued *Quit Your Low-Down Ways* includes this:

You can read out your Bible
You can fall down on your knees
Pretty mama and pray to the Lord
But it ain't gonna do no good . . .

The Biblical quotations and allusions pour readily out of the early 'protest' songs such as *The Times They Are A-Changin'*, *A Hard Rain's A-Gonna Fall* and *When The Ship Comes In* too. But it is in the more creative work that burgeoned in the mid-60s that Dylan the moralist asserts himself forcefully with a new complexity which people have commonly mistaken for an amorality, or a denial of moral judgement.

The songs that included 'she knows too much to argue or to judge', 'there are no sins inside the gates of Eden', 'to live outside the law you must be honest', 'don't follow leaders' and so on – that favourite side of Bob Dylan was never urging on us the unimportance of moral clarity. He was arguing that to achieve that clarity, the individual must shake off the hand-me-down conventional moral codes, and the judgements we make thoughtlessly from them. He was pressing his generation to take the solo-flight of responsibility for arriving at its own morality.

This is everywhere in Dylan's work from 1964 to 1978. When, in 1979, Dylan declared himself Born Again, the turnabout was in his acceptance, after all those years, of an outside, handed-down moral code – the Bible accepted as the authentic voice of God and Jesus embraced as the true son of God. It was a complete volte face from

> live by no man's code

to

> There's only one authority
> That's the authority on high.

It was *not*, however, a sudden change from the hip amoralist to the priest: Dylan had seized on a new code, but remained utterly consistent in his preoccupation with struggling *for* a code.

Along with this unfailing sense of the need for moral clarity, Dylan's work has also been consistently characterized by a yearning for salvation. In fact the quest for salvation might well be called the central theme of Bob Dylan's entire output. To survive, you must attain that clarity of morality: you won't even get by without going that far; and then you must go beyond – get rescued from the chaos and the purgatory and find some spiritual home.

This is the constant theme. It is as strong in the 'Blonde On Blonde' period as in any other:

> And me, I sit so patiently
> Waiting to find out what price
> You have to pay to get out of
> Going through all these things twice.

That is how *Memphis Blues Again* ends; and the chorus of that song emphasizes this felt need to pass from one place to another – from one quality of life to another:

> To be stuck inside of Mobile
> With the Memphis Blues Again!

Twelve years later, he is waiting and yearning again:

> This place don't make sense to me no more
> Can ya tell me what we're waiting for
> Senor?

(from *Senor: Tales Of Yankee Power* on the 1978 'Street Legal' album) – and in the interim we've had the same quest for salvation echoed again and again, from 1967's *I Shall Be Released* to 1974's 'Planet Waves':

> In this age of fiber-glass
> I'm searching for a gem
> The crystal ball upon the wall
> Hasn't shown me nothing yet
> (*Dirge*)

and

> My dreams are made of iron and steel
> With a big bouquet of roses hanging down
> From the heavens to the ground
> (*Never Say Goodbye*)

and

> I was in a whirlwind –
> Now I'm in some better place
> (*Something There Is About You*).

200

The same quest for salvation permeates the whole of the 'John Wesley Harding' album (1968) and 'Blood On The Tracks' (1975) too.

It is the focus that shifts. Dylan's quest, as it is unfolded in the songs, has always been a struggle within him between the ideas of the flesh and the spirit, between love and a kind of religious asceticism—between woman as the saviour of his soul, and woman's love seen as part of what must be discarded in the self-denial process necessary to his salvation.

In the early days, woman's love was not enough; all those gotta-move-on songs resulted. By the beginning of the 1970s, Dylan was focusing in the other direction, following the tenets of the 'Nashville Skyline' album:

> Love is all there is
> It makes the world go round
> Love and only love, it can't be denied
> No matter what you think about it
> You just won't be able to do without it
> Take a tip from one who's tried . . .

By the time of *Wedding Song* on 'Planet Waves', Dylan is even more specifically disavowing the asceticism of the 'John Wesley Harding' collection, declaring that he chooses a woman's love rather than religion as his path to salvation:

> What's lost is lost, we can't regain
> What went down in the flood
> But happiness to me is you
> And I love you more than blood.

(More, that is, than the blood of the lamb on which, later, he is to become so keen.)

Effectively, then, tracing the way that from 'Blood On The Tracks' onwards, Dylan shifts back again away from woman as saviour is also to trace his slow train coming—his quest for salvation refocusing itself into a quest for Christ.

On 'Blood On The Tracks' and the next album, 'Desire' (1976), Dylan is trying to do a balancing act—trying to fuse God and Woman:

> In a little hilltop village
> They gambled for my clothes
> I bargained for salvation
> And they gimme a lethal dose
> I offered up my innocence
> Got repaid with scorn
> Come in she said I'll give ya
> Shelter from the storm . . .
>
> If I could only turn back the clock
> To when God and her were born
> Come in she said I'll give ya
> Shelter from the storm.

The 'Desire' album follows this through:

> Oh sister . . .
> . . . is our purpose not the same on this earth:
> To love and follow his direction
>
> We grew up together from the cradle to the grave
> We died and were reborn and left mysteriously saved.

What has to be said, drawing on the biographical evidence that's been available, is that the twists and turns between woman and God and trying to fuse the two – all these different focuses within Dylan's quest for salvation – are, from the mid-1970s onwards, crucially connected with Dylan's own separation from, reconciliation with, and divorce from, his wife Sara. She is the central figure around whom Dylan's struggle revolves – and Dylan himself made this clear and public, not only with by that title *Wedding Song* but yet more openly, on 'Desire', with the naming of a song *Sara*.

What happens essentially is that Dylan's struggle to keep Sara ends up as his struggle to renounce her: his conversion to Born Again Christianity is the last step down a long road he's been travelling for years.

The fact that it has been so personal a journey – not an objective narrator (The Artist) musing on Woman Versus God As Salvation in theoretical, philosophical terms – makes it more complex than the transitional songs I've been quoting suggest. The personal intensity adds other strands, which it is part of Dylan's struggle to try to interweave. Not only are we seeing Dylan-the-moralist move from the upholder of individual conscience to the priest passing on God's word; not only are we seeing a consistency in a Dylan whose songs have always been rich in Biblical allusion and language; not only are we tracing Dylan's tussle between woman as sensual mystery and God; we are also seeing, as the albums of the 1970s unfold, Dylan's increased preoccupation with the idea of betrayal.

This strand begins to appear on 'Planet Waves' – 'I ain't haulin' any of my lambs to the market-place anymore' – and it produces in Dylan's work something which at first comes across as an astonishing leap of arrogance: that is, that Dylan quite clearly starts to *identify* with Christ. He begins to do this not in the conventionally-taught sense – that of Jesus is my friend, sent by God to be human just like me – but in the sense of *confusing* himself with Christ.

From 'Blood On The Tracks' onwards, we are given parallel after parallel between Dylan and Christ: both charismatic leaders, both message-bringers to their people, both martyrs because both *get betrayed*. In retrospect, it is as if Dylan eventually converts to Christianity because of the way he has identified with Christ and understood His struggles through his own.

Dylan had had one eye on Jesus ever since the motorcycle crash of 1966 (or ever since, as he confessed in *Sara*, he had 'taken the cure' the same year). The unreleased *Sign On The Cross* from the 1967 'basement tapes' declared:

> . . . I know in my head
> That we're all so misled
> And it's that old sign on the cross
> That worries me . . .
> You might think you're weak
> But I mean to say you're strong
> Yes you are
> If that sign on the cross
> If it begins to worry you

but it is from 'Blood On the Tracks' onwards that Dylan's *identification* with Christ begins in earnest.

> I came in from the wilderness . . .
>
> She walked up to me so gracefully
> And took my crown of thorns . . .

Warfield Theatre, San Francisco, November 1980.

Below: *Back to that gospel plow, 1980. He did a great unreleased song at this time, called 'I Ain't Gonna Go To Hell For Nobody', which had probably been recorded for the 'Saved' sessions but didn't end up on the album.*

Left: *November 1980 in San Francisco: still giving audiences a challenge fifteen years on from the Newport Folk Festival controversy of 1965.*

Below: *Dylan at Memorial Hall, Hartford, Connecticut, May 9th 1980. One of the small-halls religious concerts done between the release of 'slow Train Coming' and 'Saved'. A very strange audience.*

> In a little hilltop village
> They gambled for my clothes . . .

Those lines from *Shelter From The Storm* are matched, in *Idiot Wind*, by:

> There's a lone soldier on the cross
> Smoke pourin' out of a box-car door
> You didn't know it, you didn't think it could be done
> In the final end he won the war
> After losing every battle . . .
> I've been double-crossed now for the very last time

(and the reference to that 'box-car door' not only reminds us of the image Dylan is to choose later of the 'slow train coming' but also reminds us that the links to his earliest influences are still there: Woody Guthrie's autobiography, *Bound For Glory*, is so titled because it is a quote from 'This train is bound for glory/This train . . .' and part of the soundtrack from Dylan's film 'Renaldo & Clara' consists of him singing a song popularized by those other early idols of his, the Staple Singers: 'People get ready/There's a train a-comin'' which uses the same train image to stand for the coming of the Lord.)

There is another unreleased song, performed by Dylan at an impromptu guest-appearance during a Jack Elliott set in New York in July 1975, that brings us back to Dylan's process of struggle for salvation in the terms we begin to see it from 'Blood On The Tracks' onwards.

Dylan starts to feel the slow train coming – starts to feel that, pushed on by what he sees as Sara's betrayal of him, he cannot continue to seek salvation through man-woman love. He is extremely reluctant to pull away from this direction, but he begins to recognize a compulsion within himself to seek salvation elsewhere.

The song he sang at the Jack Elliott gig includes this:

> I didn't hear the turning of the key
> I've been deceived by the clown inside of me
> I thought that you was righteous but it's vain
> Somethin's tellin' me I wear a ball and chain . . .
>
> I march in the parade of liberty
> But as long as I love ya, I'm not free
> How long must I suffer such abuse?
> Won't you let me see ya smile before I cut ya loose . . .
>
> My head says that it's time to make a change
> But my heart is telling me
> I love you but you're strange . . .
>
> Let me feel your love one more time
> Before I abandon it.

This is the pivotal theme of all Dylan's major work of the 1970s. Dylan's journey is from Sara to Jesus.

The work this theme prompts is least interesting at either end – when the Dylan of the mid-70s is simply pleading for Sara to stay with him, and when the Dylan of 1980 is rather smugly declaring himself saved.

The interesting work falls in the middle, when Dylan is in the thick of the dilemma just described:

> My head says that it's time to make a change
> But my heart is telling me
> I love you . . .

On the 'Desire' album, in this respect, the crucial song is *Isis*:

> Isis oh Isis oh mystical child
> What drives me to you is what drives me insane.

The song is a long parable – thirteen verses – and Isis is the woman in his life, the Hebrew goddess who also stands for the sensual and material worlds. She is the woman who was the sad-eyed lady of the lowlands, the woman who offered shelter from the storm

> With silver bracelets on her wrist
> And flowers in her hair;

the woman whom, in *Idiot Wind*, he followed

> Down the highway, down the tracks
> Down the road to ecstasy
> I followed you beneath the stars
> Hounded by your memory
> And all your ragin' glory.

She is the woman in whom he has invested a spiritual significance which he knows, underneath, that he is beginning to doubt:

> I married Isis on the fifth day of May
> But I could not hold onto her very long . . .

The narrator in this parable goes off in search of something else – he does not know what – but he searches mistakenly in the same old material world:

> I was thinkin' about turquoise
> I was thinkin' about gold
> I was thinkin' about diamonds
> And the world's biggest necklace
> As we rode through the canyons
> Through the devilish cold
> I was thinkin' about Isis . . .

He goes with a grave-robber to plunder a tomb, still wrong-headedly concerned with the material world:

> I broke into the tomb
> But the casket was empty
> There was no jewels, no nuthin'!
> I felt I'd bin had!

He is tugged back to Isis, still hoping that salvation lies in her:

> I came in from the east
> With the sun in my eyes . . .

and then follows a marvellous verse in which we're invited to understand, as the narrator has yet to, that the return to Isis is not enough, and can only be another temporary shelter before he sets off on the real, final quest. This is the undercurrent to the verse, but it works so well by evoking the re-embracing of Isis with magnificent tempting humanness. It also pins down in a few brief, deft strokes, a whole welter of comment on relationships in an age in which faithful monogamy is regarded as impossible – something one cannot maturely expect. 'This is a song about marriage,' said Dylan, introducing the live version in 'Renaldo & Clara':

> She said 'Where you bin?'
> I said 'no place special'
> She said 'you look different'
> I said 'Well, I guess . . .'
> She said 'you bin gone'
> I said 'that's only natural'
> She said 'you gonna stay?'
> I said, 'if you want me to, YES!'

That is a truly great piece of writing.

After *Isis*, after 'Desire', we come to the really central album in the whole pattern of Dylan's journey from the

> Love is all there is

of 'Nashville Skyline' to the

> But to search for love – that ain't no more than vanity:
> As I look around this world, all that I'm finding
> Is the saving grace that's over me

of 'Saved'.

The truly central album is 'Street Legal' (1978) – on which every song deals with love's betrayal, deals with Dylan's being betrayed like Christ, and deals head-on with Dylan's need to abandon woman's love.

'Street Legal' is one of Dylan's most important, cohesive and complex albums – and it warns us, as pointedly as art ever should, of what is to come. It prepares us for Dylan's conversion to Christianity just as plainly as the end of 'John Wesley Harding' prepares us for the country music of 'Nashville Skyline', and just as plainly as 'Bringing It All Back Home' signals what is just around the corner on 'Highway 61 Revisited'.

'Street Legal' brings it all together – Dylan the consistent moralist, Dylan the writer who draws heavily on the Bible, Dylan caught in the struggle between the flesh and the spirit, Dylan ending his relationship with Sara, Dylan the betrayed victim both of what he sees as Sara's love-in-vain and of all of us.

Consummately, Dylan does pull all these strands together on this album, both on its minor songs and its three outstanding major works, *Changing Of The Guards, No Time To Think* and *Where Are You Tonight (Journey Through Dark Heat)*.

New Pony, the first minor song, is Dylan's farewell to the world of sensual pleasures – his fond goodbye to the dirty blues ethic he is so good at and so fond of. It is the dark, deliberately nasty, revelling counterpart to that sad final blues from 'Blood On The Tracks', *Buckets Of Rain*, in which, coming after the new-deal precariousness of a relationship in which he notes that

> I know where I can find you
> Up in somebody's room
> That's the price I have to pay . . .
> (*You're A Big Girl Now*)

he concludes that

> I like the smile in your fingertips
> I like the way that you move your hips
> I like the cool way you look at me
> Everythin' about you is bringin' me misery.

New Pony is the dark, spiteful corollary of that blues mood. It is there to remind us   207 that Dylan is not quitting the world of sex and sin because he can't cope with it – *New Pony* shows him on top form, as good in that milieu as ever he was – he is quitting because it isn't enough. As the gospel chant in the background repeats, over and over, his feeling underneath is

How much longer?
How much longer?

And of course that counterpointing of Dylan's sexy, sleazy blues voice by the gospel plea for deliverance is a brilliantly economic, forceful way of evoking the tussle between flesh and spirit that Dylan meets head-on throughout this album.

Then there is *Senor (Tales of Yankee Power)*, which on one level deals with something else entirely. Having an unusual narrator-stance for Dylan, the voice here is post-Vietnam America, confusedly asking the Third World to reveal the way things really are. The white narrator seeks answers from the 'senor' – the Mexican/South American. The sub-title, 'Tales Of Yankee Power', is a nice irony.

Can you tell me where we're headin'
Is it Lincoln County Road or Armageddon? . . .
Will there be any comfort there, senor? . . .
Can't stand the suspense any more:
Can you tell me who to contact here, senor? . . .

Let's overturn these tables
Disconnect these cables
This place don't make sense to me no more
Can you tell me what we're waiting for, senor?

But while it stands as a classic post-Vietnam song – expressing a very different American instinct for survival and progress from the desperate instinct that has put Ronald Reagan in the White House, *Senor* operates also on what Dylan elsewhere calls 'a whole other level'.

Like the rest of 'Street Legal', it concerns Dylan's personal salvation-quest as well as the one America ought to be embarking on. Here he seeks guidance in the attempt to make the leap from worldly meaninglessness to a new higher ground.

Let's overturn these tables

is the Christ-gesture, a swift allusion to the routing of the money-lenders in the temple; and nothing could be clearer than

This place don't make sense to me no more

or the familiar theme of wishing he didn't have to wait any longer.

Baby Stop Crying re-presents the themes of betrayal and salvation.

You bin down to the bottom with a bad man, babe

is the dark, accusing opening line. The song goes on to try to reach the woman, despite the felt betrayal. It is urging her to join him down the new road to salvation, with Dylan still loathe to walk that road alone without her:

Go down to the river babe
Honey I will meet you there.

This plea that she understand the need for a new baptism and the need to

Opposite: *Still retaining that Chaplinesquerie which attracted attention when he first arrived in New York seventeen years before.*

renounce – this plea that she accept his need for spiritual journeying, that she come along too – is developed in the album's major songs, which we come to later.

Is Your Love In Vain, a song that has Dylan asking a new suitor some plain, urgent, selfish questions, again evokes the struggler, the man unable to stop yearning for an earthly salvation, despite his rating earthly pleasures low:

> Well I bin in the mountains
> And I bin in the wind
> I bin in and out of happiness
> I have dined with kings
> I bin offered wings
> And I've never bin too impressed.

That also gives us another paralleling of Dylan with Jesus, by reminding us of Christ being tempted as he gazes down from the mountains with the devil as salesman at his side.

Again, *Is Your Love In Vain* deals concretely – especially in the light of the sordid financial wrangling well-publicized around the Dylans' divorce – with the betrayal theme:

> All right I'll take a chance
> I will fall in love with you
> And if I'm a fool you can have the night
> You can have the money too . . .

This forcefully re-echoes that accusatory stab Dylan makes on the unreleased first version of *Idiot Wind* on 'Blood On The Tracks':

> You can have the best there is
> But its gonna cost ya all your love
> You won't get it for
> Money.

Back on 'Street Legal' the betrayal theme – and the spiritual restlessness – is continued in *True Love Tends To Forget*. Love has failed in both ways, and this song attempts to bid failed love goodbye. But Dylan's resolve is not yet strong enough:

> You told me that you'd be sincere
> But evidently you like playin' Russian roulette
> True love tends to forget.

> I was lying down in the reeds without any oxygen
> I saw you in the wilderness among the men . . .

There is the betrayal – and, suggested by that 'wilderness', the love's failure in any case to provide a fulfilment of the spirit. True love is not going to offer him salvation; yet he still wants to try that route and cling for it:

> You belong to me baby without a doubt
> Don't forsake me baby
> Don't sell me out
> Don't keep me knockin' about
> From Mexico to Tibet . . .

It's possible that, aside from keeping up his tradition of using place-names to distinctive effect, Dylan is here using the Mexico-Tibet see-saw to stand for two choices he can no longer accept: the warm, southern world of the sensuous and a cold, eastern religious asceticism. Dylan knows he must reject, and soon, both his lover and the fashionable zen-maintenance so popular as a refuge for displaced rich Americans, neither of which offer a way forward to the saving of his soul.

It is a typically audacious leap for Dylan that he can use Mexico as the symbol of earthly pleasures in this song while using it as an opposite symbol in *Senor (Tales Of Yankee Power)*.

The song that follows *True Love Tends To Forget* has Dylan a stage further on in his resolve. *We Better Talk This Over* is his announcement, not to us but to his partner, that they must break up.

It dwells on the betrayal theme again, of course, but it shows Dylan mustering enough artistic detachment to evoke a truly credible narrative 'spontaneity', as if the lines of the song catch him veering between the planned we-must-split-up speech and unplanned, impulsive expressions of feeling. It is a great rendition, fired by a devastating straightforwardness. It begins:

> I think
> We better talk this over
> Maybe
> When we both get sober . . .
>
> Let's call it a day
> Go our own separate ways
> Before we decay

and it's as clear from the tone of voice here as from the words themselves that this Dylan is indeed on the brink – and a great deal more in control of his destiny than he had been on the immediately previous studio album, 'Desire', when he was singing that buffeted, desperate song *Sara*.

We Better Talk This Over continues with this resolute yet untruthful bravado:

> You don't have to be afraid
> Of lookin' into my face
> We've done nothing to each other
> Time will not erase.

Plainly, that is expressing his consciousness of her *ineradicable* effect on him.

The feeling of betrayal floods in again:

> I feel displaced
> I got that low-down feelin'
> You bin two-faced
> You bin double-dealin'

and prompts his re-affirmation that in pinning his faith on this world's love, he had been wrong:

> I took a chance
> Got caught in a trance
> of a downhill glance . . .
> I'm lost in the haze
> Of your delicate ways
> With both eyes glazed.

In the midst of those two clusters of rhyming lines, as the narrator's emotions urgently switch to and fro, we get this neat deftness of touch:

Oh child
Why you wanna hurt me?
I'm exiled
But you can't convert me

And then, having voiced that conviction of the two lovers' separateness and estrangement, he switches again – to trying to reassure, and to suggesting gently that she too should consider seeking salvation along lines other than man-woman love:

You don't have to yearn for love
You don't have to be alone
Somewheres in this universe
There's a place that you can call home.

Then comes the sad, small line

I guess I'll be leavin' tomorrow . . .

This is very different in import and impetus, isn't it, from the declarations of leaving in the early-60s songs. In those, the gotta-move-on instinct was to do with a restlessness that he wanted to indulge, not resolve and a markedly different awareness of the restrictiveness of a relationship.

Then the needle of betrayal injects itself back into the song:

The vows that we kept
Are now broken and swept
'Neath the bed where we slept

and is only just withdrawn in time to end the song with warmer, more friendly resolutions of acceptance and departure:

Don't think of me and fantasize
On what we've never had
Be grateful for what we've shared
Together and be glad . . .
Time for a new transition
I wish I was a magician
I would wave a wand
The time would be gone
And we'd have both gone beyond.

This whole fundamental struggle, and how Dylan begins to confess that it is Christianity that is beckoning – it being *that* to which his yearned-for 'new transition' points him – is developed and played-out in the three major songs on the album: *Changing Of The Guards, No Time To Think* and *Where Are You Tonight? (Journey Through Dark Heat)*.

They chart Dylan's voyage from Sara to Jesus very clearly indeed, in writing as absorbing, complex and vivid as anything Dylan has ever given us.

It is in these songs too that the writer's comparisons between himself and Christ come thick and fast, as Dylan pulls all these themes and strands together and prepares the way unhesitatingly for the 'Slow Train Coming' and 'Saved' albums.

Changing Of The Guards is the first of these songs. It opens with Dylan reflecting on his own career: the time and energy spent; and at once we are back on the betrayal theme – but here it is betrayal by the world, not one woman.

Sixteen years

is the opening line, and is as economic a statement of Dylan's career-span, and the weariness felt, as it would be possible to make.

The second verse looks back to the beginning of that career:

> Fortune calls
> I step from the shadows to the market-place

and we know from that line that betrayal is being evoked. It deliberately echoes those other memorable lines on the same theme which *Tough Mama* gave us on 'Planet Waves' and which I've already quoted once:

> I ain't haulin'
> Any of my lambs to the market-place anymore.

Changing Of The Guards develops this theme in several ways.

> Renegade priests
> And treacherous young witches
> Were handing out the flowers
> That I'd given to you.

Those lines, addressed to Sara, express the sadness felt at seeing his love-songs misappropriated.

These lines, on one level, deal equally reprovingly with the record-company – the people whose work puts Dylan in that market-place:

> Gentlemen, he said,
> I don't need your organization
> I've shined your shoes, I've moved your mountains
> And marked your cards . . .

But the betrayal, as in the other songs on this collection, is personal too. Beneath a 'cold-blooded moon'

> The captain is down
> But still believing
> That his love will be repaid

and Dylan, recognizing with supreme regret that it will not be repaid, that it must be put in the past, recollects

> The palace of mirrors
> Where dog-soldiers are reflected;
> The endless road
> And the wayladen chimes

(an allusion to his old *Chimes Of Freedom* and as such, an echo of that passage in the unreleased *My Heart Is Telling Me* which we looked at earlier: 'I march in the parade of liberty/But as long as I love ya, I'm not free/How long must I suffer such abuse?')

The recollecting continues:

> The empty rooms
> Where her memory is protected,
> Where the angels' voices whisper
> To the souls of previous times.

Her memory is all that can be held onto, in those empty rooms; she herself has been waylaid by the forces of worldliness:

213

> They shaved her head
> She was torn between Jupiter and Apollo ...
> I seen her on the stairs
> And I could not help but follow
> Follow her down past the fountain
> Where they lifted her veil

and Dylan follows this immediately with a wild, potent evocation of feeling that shows him creatively in command of language and its freshness:

> I struggle to my feet
> I run past destruction in the ditches
> With the stitches still mending
> 'Neath a heart-shaped tattoo.

This imagery from what is the first song on the album is echoed brilliantly on its final song, where Dylan sings:

> If you don't believe there's a price for this sweet paradise
> Just remind me to show you the scars.

Changing Of The Guards involves too the Dylan-Christ parallel as he comes to deal with the present-into-future – his own rebirth:

> She wakes him up
> Forty-eight hours later
> The sun is breaking
> Their broken chains
> Mountain laurel and rolling rocks
> She's begging to know
> What measures he now will be taking
> He's pulling her down and she's clutching
> Onto his long golden locks.

That 'what measures he now will be taking' is a marvellous flash of mischief : in the midst of repainting the resurrection, Dylan has the confidence and control to point up and laugh at the gulf between the power of Biblical language and the cold jargon of contemporary life.

The song ends with a gentle attempt on Dylan's part to explain – and to urge Sara's acceptance of – what is to come from 'the new transition'. The times they are a-changing, he insists, in a radically different way from before.

To the world, to the 'gentlemen' of 'the organization', and to his lover too, he sings that the change must come now:

> But Eden is burning
> Either get ready for elimination
> Or else your hearts must bear the courage
> Of the changing of the guards.

It can be OK in the end:

> Peace will come
> With tranquillity and splendour
> On the wheels of fire

but there will be no worldly gain – no instant material dividend to be had from surrendering the old false life. It must be done anyway:

214

>   Peace will come ...
>   But will offer no reward
>   When the false idols fall
>   And cruel death surrenders
>   Between the king and the queen of swords.

The embattled lovers must stop their self-destruction and accept the new regime in which truth of spirit is its own reward.

No Time To Think has Dylan still on the merry-go-round – the noisy, mechanical going-nowhere of 'real life'. The hypnotic yet ridiculous waltz-rhythm underlines this, as do the incandescent jingle-jangles of internal rhyme:

>   Lovers obey you but they cannot sway you

and so on.

So here we have Dylan back on the edge, knowing he must make the leap, resist old love and old earthly niggling, yet with the disputatious voices of love and money and public and pleasure and politics and philosophy all trying for his attention, leaving him no time to think.

It is an incredible song and certainly one of the most important he's ever written. Definitely up there with *Desolation Row* and the other major epics. And in the context of the predicament Dylan ascribes to himself on 'Street Legal', it is a clear, brave, unequivocal song.

It opens with the clear statement of his conviction that without a re-birth, we are among the walking dead:

>   In death you face life with a charm and a wife
>   Who sleepwalks through your dreams into walls

– and 'walls' suggests both the wraithlike quality involved in walking through them *and* the restrictiveness of their presence.

The voices call him back, with their bamboozling choices, their shallow temptations and their abstractions:

>   Loneliness, tenderness,
>   High society, notoriety
>   You fight for the throne and you travel alone
>   Unknown as you slowly sink
>   And there's no time to think.

There ends the first chorus. The second verse brings in the motif of the tarot, and the hint of the now-familiar betrayal theme:

>   In the Federal City you've been blown and shown pity
>   One secret for pieces of change
>   The Empress attracts you but oppression distracts you

– the Empress standing, in the tarot pack, for an earthly wisdom, while that great phrase 'the federal city' stands for the glittering superficial world we all inhabit.

The chorus that follows develops the betrayal theme, and *this* is where the Dylan-Christ duality comes in solidly and without compromise:

>   Memory, ecstasy,
>   Tyranny, hypocrisy –
>   Betrayed by a kiss on a cool night of bliss
>   In the valley of the missing link ...

It is astonishing writing – tight, searing, and in full imaginative bloom in spite of the limits imposed by so strict and double-edged a rhyme-scheme.

The struggle out of the valley of the missing link is evoked again in the third verse:

> I've seen all these decoys through a set of deep turquoise
> Eyes, and I feel so depressed

and in its chorus:

> China doll, alcohol,
> Duality, morality –
> Mercury rules you and destiny fools you
> Like the plague, with a dangerous wink . . .

Then comes a reprise of the betrayal factor within Dylan's predicament:

> Your conscience betrayed you and some tyrant waylaid you
> The lion lies down with the lamb
> I'd have paid the traitor and killed him much later
> But that's just the way that I am
>
> Paradise, sacrifice . . .

How was it that we were so surprised when Dylan 'turned Christian' when these songs so specifically forewarned us?

In the next chorus, the tarot motif itself contributes to the betrayal theme:

> But the magician is quicker and his game is much thicker
> Than blood and blacker than ink
> And there's no time to think.

The Christ references are augmented in the next verse with another deft touch that reverberates back through even the most atheistic listener's memories of Bible stories:

> Vermin and jealousy's all that he sells as he's
> Content to put you under his thumb;
> Madmen oppose him your kindness throws him

and this is capped by this inspired way of trying to cope with these myriad jangling pressures:

> To survive it you play deaf and dumb.

The pressures are remorseless, just the same:

> You glance through the mirror
> And there's eyes staring clear
> At the back of your head as you drink
> And there's no time to think.

What a lot that conjures up. First, there is Dylan's perennial fascination with mirrors and the odd, playful way in which they call reality into question – as they have done in life and art over many centuries. Dylan shares with Alice the idea that you should be able to pass through mirrors to another reality on the other side. And here, not for the first time, he presents this notion as being of spiritual import. He did this on the 'John Wesley Harding' album, at the end of *I Dreamed I Saw St Augustine*, in which the 'I' figure, the narrator, sees himself as part of the world of blind cruelty which victimizes the saint. That song ends with Dylan therefore unable to pass through the mirror:

> I put my fingers against the glass
> And bowed my head and cried.

On the later album 'New Morning', we're given this, in that odd little song *I Went To See The Gypsy*:

> He can drive you from your beer
> Bring you through the mirror
> He did it in Las Vegas
> An' he can do it here . . .

There is more to the image in *No Time To Think*. There is the vivid captured moment (of recognition) – of suddenly feeling someone malevolently watching you. Again, this brings an echo of an earlier song: the unreleased *I Wanna Be Your Lover* from 1965–6 (when Bob Dylan knew a great deal about malevolence), in which

> Rasputin he's so dignified
> He touched the back of her head an' he died.

On top of that, there is another echo – and one which, when it strikes home, spectacularly turns around the whole way we visualize the image: this echo is of that painting by Magritte where the man staring into the mirror sees the back of his own head through it.

No Time To Think carries on to deal with the futility, in the salvation-quest, of regrets and yearnings for lost true loves or entrancing future lovers:

> Wild dancin' sorrow and queens of tomorrow
> Will offer their heads for a prayer
> They can't find no salvation have no expectation
> Any time, any place, anywhere . . .

and Dylan is swift to telescope this down for himself into the plain facts of the predicament he's been examining throughout the album:

> You know you can't keep her and the water gets deeper
> It's leading you on to the brink . . .

> You've murdered your vanity burdened your sanity
> For pleasure you must now resist.

On and on goes the struggle:

> The bridge that you travel on goes to the Babylon
> Girl with the rose in her hair

but in prospect at last there is

> Starlight in the east, you're finally released

(the obvious echo there, of course, being of 'I see my life come shinin'/From the west unto the east/Any day now, any day now, I shall be released' plus, from *Isis*:

> I came in from the east with the sun in my eyes
> I cursed her one time, then I rode on ahead . . .

After that, we are back at once to the Christ-Dylan, and it is the Last Supper:

> You turn around for one real last glimpse of the meal
> 'Neath a moon shinin' bloody and pink

The re-birth is coming closer, and the song ends on the theme of sacrifice and life-through-death:

> Bullets can harm you and death can disarm you
> But no you will not be deceived
> Stripped of all virtue as you crawl through the dirt
> You can give but you cannot receive:

> No time to choose when the truth must die
> No time to lose or say goodbye
> No time to prepare for the victim that's there
> No time to suffer or blink
> And no time to think.

This final journey is the 'journey through dark heat' and out the other side that constitutes the album's final song, *Where Are You Tonight?*

He has asked her to make the same pilgrimage alongside him; she has declined; he has gone alone.

As the song opens, Dylan is *on* the slow train:

> There's a long-distance train pulling through the rain
> Tears on the letter I write
> There's a woman I long to touch and I'm missing her so much
> But she's drifting like a satellite.

The second verse is a glancing reflection back to the old New York days. In 1965 we had that scathing song *Positively 4th Street*; this time it is Greenwich Village's Elizabeth Street that is used to place that past camaraderie – and thus to serve as a precursor for those lines on the 'Slow Train Coming' album: 'My so-called friends have fallen under a spell'. Here, Dylan is anticipating the sneers of his New York world at the news of his desertion to Christ:

> There's a neon light ablaze in a green smokey haze
> And laughter down on Elizabeth Street

– followed at once by this terrific characterization of New York City as the valley of death in whose shadow he and his lover have walked too long:

> There's a lonesome bell tone in that valley of stone
> Where she bathed in a stream of pure heat

– the effectiveness of which resides partly in the pure beauty of calling New York City a 'valley of stone' and partly in the strange double-take of juxtaposing cold stone and pure heat in one and the same place: the death and hell, the chill and the furnace at once.

Then Dylan's travelling reflections pause to dwell on the divorce, and the inexpressible gulf between the public story and the inner reality of what he feels went down:

> ... a woman in a rage ...
> As she winds back the clock and she turns back the page
> Of a book that nobody can write ...

> The truth was obscure, too profound and too pure
> To live it you had to explode.

This leads directly to the recollected split-up and his new embarkation:

> In that last hour of need, we entirely agreed
> Sacrifice was the code of the road
> I left town at dawn, with Marcel and St John
> Strong men belittled by doubt

(a great phrase, that) and then come these excellent lines admitting that while he could claim his own agony to be inexpressible, she could still pierce through any aggrandizing mystification he might be putting up around himself:

> I couldn't tell her what my private thoughts were
> But she had some way of finding them out.

From there, the song shows Dylan's thoughts ranging through the whole spectrum of the leaving and its why and wherefores. His irresolution is recollected here:

> She could feel my despair as I climbed up her hair

and, invoking the knowledge of his Gemini nature, again here:

> I fought with my twin, that enemy within
> Till both of us fell by the way.

Recollected too, and confessed, are the betrayals of each other:

> The man you are lovin' could never get clean
> It felt out of place, my foot in his face
> But he should have stayed where his money was green

and

> I bit into the root of forbidden fruit
> With the juice runnin' down my leg.

No wonder Eden is burning.

In the penultimate verse we return to the idea of sacrifice: there is

> . . . a pathway that leads up to the stars;
> If you don't believe there's a price for this sweet paradise
> Just remind me to show you the scars.

The last verse of the song—and of the album—announces Dylan's final arrival at re-birth. He has made it at last. Yet what is most striking here is the humanity, the generosity of feeling. There is no ending on any note of glee or superiority. There is only a gladness which Dylan admits to, while admitting also that it is lessened by the final loss of love:

> There's a new day at dawn and it finally arrived
> If I'm there in the morning baby, you'll know I've survived
> I can't believe it! I can't believe I'm alive!
> But without you it doesn't seem right—
> Oh! where are you tonight?!

So there is 'Street Legal'—indisputably a major album, and indisputably a clear explanation of Dylan's move to embracing Christ.

It is therefore only the *tone*, one of uncompromising certainty, that should surprise us on coming to 'Slow Train', after all the struggle between his twin selves so brilliantly documented by 'Street Legal'. The initial shock should properly be at the leap having *succeeded*—and so the tone of voice switching from the 'oh! but . . .' of 'Street Legal' to the severe certainty of

> You either got faith or you got unbelief
> And there ain't no neutral ground.

The substance of what Dylan has to say on 'Slow Train Coming' and 'Saved', tone of voice aside, is not so very different from what he's been saying before.

The import of that last verse of *Where Are You Tonight*

> ... it finally arrived ...
> I can't believe it! I can't believe I'm alive!

is restated on 'Saved' in *Saving Grace*, which must stand as a direct, careful and courageous summary of his new position:

> By this time
> I'd have thought that I would be sleeping
> In a pine box for all eternity:
> My faith keeps me alive.

Dylan's brain, moreover, shows no sign of having been softened by his change of spiritual home.

There are some bad songs – songs where the lyrics are inadequate because they're content to parrot scripture or to insist, rather than creatively render, a point. But some of these are, regardless of that, terrific gospel music; and in any case, there are good songs too – ones which seem to me to indicate that Dylan is still alert and sharp.

The songs that stand out are *You Gotta Serve Somebody*, *Precious Angel*, *Slow Train Coming*, *Man Gave Names To All The Animals* and *When He Returns* (on 'Slow Train Coming') and *Saving Grace*, *What Can I Do For You?* and *Pressing On* on 'Saved'.

There is also the excellent song released only as the B-side to the single of *Precious Angel* but recorded during the 'Slow Train Coming' sessions – the nuggety little *Trouble In Mind*, which alone would be sufficient to prove that Christian faith, despite one's fears to the contrary, has not dulled Dylan's cutting edge.

It's a great little song – gospel with a real blues slouch to it – and the Dylan burn is here, delivered with as much italicized sarcasm as anything from the mid-60s repertoire:

> Well the deeds that you do
> Don't add up to zero
> It's what's inside that counts
> (Ask any war-hero)
> You think you can hide
> But you're never alone
> Ask Lot what
> He thought
> When his a-wife turned to stone
>
> Trouble in mind, Lord
> Trouble in mind!

Dylan's humour is also a crucial ingredient in *Man Gave Names To All The Animals*, which works on several levels.

It's a good children's song; it invites us to smile at the very idea of Bob Dylan writing one; it's also a gentle mocking of the more fundamentalist brethren the Born Again Dylan finds himself coming across these days, as it tells the Garden of Eden story up to the Fall in ludicrously simplistic terms.

It's interesting too, that Dylan chooses to omit blaming Eve for the Fall, stopping the song on a beautifully hungover note at the arrival on the scene of the serpent.

The repetitive structure and the outrageous casualness of the rhyming also add up to a joke we're invited to share. The representative tone and humour are here:

> He saw an animal leavin' a muddy trail
> Real dirty face an' a curly tail
> He wasn't too small and he wasn't too big
> Mmm – think I'll call it a pig
>
> Man gave names to all the animals . . .

Dylan doesn't lose his sense of humour either when he comes to explaining how, after all that questing and yearning documented by 'Street Legal', he was touched by a new woman's Christian faith. In fact there's an admirable comic self-mockery about the way he tells it on the title-track of the 'Slow Train Coming' collection:

> I had a woman
> Down in Alabama
> She was a backwoods girl but she sure was realistic
> She said 'Boy without a doubt
> You gotta stop your messin',
> Straighten out –
> You could die down here, be just another accident statistic'

Neither is there anything brain-softened about the skilful way that Dylan treats the new woman/old lover themes. On *Precious Angel* he can be speaking to *either* of them, depending how you care to take it, in the opening verse of what is a strongly confident song:

> Precious Angel, under the sun
> How was I to know you'd be the one
> To show me I was blinded
> To show me I was gone
> How weak was the foundation
> I was standing upon . . .

On the other hand there is no mistaking the direct venom, despite his casual tone, on 'Slow Train Coming', when he refers to the as-it-were secular lover of his past:

> Well my baby went to Illinois
> With some bad-talkin' boy she could destroy
> A real suicide case
> But there was nothin' I could do to stop it.

There is another, and much more obviously biographical, reference back to that past relationship, in *You Gotta Serve Somebody*. Those who remember pictures of the Dylans' white-elephant Malibu home, with its ostentatious dome of copper at the top, will get a flash of recognition here:

> You might be living in a mansion
> You might live in a dome . . .

It's a quietly slipped-in but honorable self-rebuke.

Underneath it, though, there remains plenty of smouldering rebuke for other people too, and as Dylan comes back, on these albums, to the *Street Legal* themes of wavering resolve and of betrayal, it rises to the surface.

> My so-called friends have fallen under a spell

begins one of *Precious Angel*'s verses — and he returns to this notion almost obsessively again and again:

> They show me to the door
> They say don't come back no more
> 'Cause I don't feel like they want me to . . .
> Oh! though the earth may shake me
> Oh! though my friends forsake me
> Oh! even that couldn't make me go back
> (*I Believe In You*)

and from *Slow Train Coming*:

> Sometimes I feel so low-down and disgusted
> Can't help but wonder what's happenin' to
> My companions

and again (same song):

> I don't care about economy
> I don't care about astronomy
> But it sure does bother me
> To see
> My loved ones turnin' into puppets.

But in his own wavering of resolve, he can turn for help both to his new 'covenant woman' and to Jesus:

> You know I just can't make it by myself
> I'm a little too blind to see
> (*Precious Angel*)

> Don't let me drift too far
> Keep me where you are
> Where I will always be renewed
> (*I Believe In You*)

and

> How long can I listen to the lies of prejudice?
> How long can I stay drunk on fear
> Out in the wilderness?
> (*When He Returns*)

The same confessions of a faltering spiritual self-discipline are made, though without any of the personal touches of the above, in *Solid Rock*, where Dylan's language becomes at once generalized and scriptural:

> It's the ways of the flesh
> To war against the spirit
> Twenty-four hours a day . . .
> Never give up
> Till the battle's lost or won.

It's a typical Dylan flash to insert into that scriptural mode of writing that playfully modern phrase 'twenty-four hours a day'.

Dylan resumes the personalized statement of this theme on *Saving Grace* with the slightly mournful simplicity of

It gets discouraging at times
But I know I'll make it
By the saving grace that's over me.

It might be relevant to that wavering, too – or indeed to the idea of the intrusive pressures on Dylan from wayward friends and/or the world – that there is a marked decrease in the sort of Dylan-Christ identification which was so clear and prevalent on 'Street Legal'. The only example of it, really, on the Born Again albums is here, from *In The Garden*:

The multitude wanted to make him king
Put a crown upon his head
Why did he slip away
To a quiet place instead?

Plainly, Dylan is drawing a parallel there, and is acknowledging that he at least knows exactly why Jesus should have 'slipped away'.

Dylan's own need to seek the quiet place, the refuge, is a major theme of the 'Saved' album. Not, as on 'Street Legal', from the vantage-point of standing on the edge, still seeking, but from the new 'saved' position of looking back. So it is a kind of fundamental gratitude for his salvation – for his very survival, in fact – that is being expressed.

We have it recurrently in many songs, from

You have given everything to me
What can I do for you? . . .
Pulled me out of bondage
And you made me renewed inside

and

Well I don't deserve it
But I sure did make it through
(*What Can I Do For You*)

to

I've been broken
Shattered like an empty cup
I'm just waiting on the Lord
To rebuild and fill me up
(*Covenant Woman*)

Only occasionally does this get de-personalized and, as it were, philosophized into this sort of bible-thumping creed:

I was blinded by the devil
Born already ruined
Stone cold dead as I stepped out of the womb
(*Saved*)

That has a discomforting sense of insistence whereas when he states it in personal terms, it is as plausible as it is plain:

I've escaped death so many times
I know I'm only living
By the saving grace that's over me
By this time I'd have thought I would be sleeping

In a pine-box for all eternity
My faith keeps me alive
(*Saving Grace*)

Expressed that way, it's utterly convincing. The most casual reflection on how unimaginably great the pressure on him of *being* Bob Dylan must have been, argues for the truth of those lines. Just surviving the 1966 period was more than most of us could have managed, let alone the cumulative pressures of all the years since then. Eighteen years now, the man has been standing up and doing what he does. It isn't hard to see the appeal of a respite in Christ.

And the opting for this refuge has not signalled any abnegation of his intellect either. There is a lot of intellectual, and emotional, honesty in these albums.

First, there is the acknowledgement of that susceptibility towards religious belief inside all of us:

How be it we're deceived
When the truth's in our hearts
And we still don't believe?
(*Precious Angel*)

There's also a sharp look at the way we rationalize away morality under the pressures of the modish and of peer-group approval:

You say everybody's doin' it
So I guess it can't be wrong
The truth is far from you
So you know you got to lie
And you're all the time defending
What you can never justify
(*Trouble In Mind*)

On the 'Slow Train Coming' album there is also this admirable flash of cynicism:

They talk about a life of brotherly love
Show me someone who knows how to live it

and elsewhere Dylan's sharp focus is equally unblurred. I think this line, from *Saving Grace* is an astonishing piece of dark honesty, of which few of us would be capable:

But to search for love – that ain't no more than vanity.

On the other hand, there can be no doubting Dylan's religious passion and his happiness to have it fixed so firmly in conventional, traditional Christianity. Nor can there be any disputing the fact that when he expresses this religious passion, he does so with huge power and skill. Listen to the *tour-de-force* performance on *When He Returns,* and to the vocal delivery, in *Precious Angel*, of the line 'to the judgement hall of Ch-rist!!'.

The same skill and power is there, too, in this marvellous verse from what is the best song on 'Saved' – namely, *Pressing On*, which builds triumphantly and shows as authoritative, agile and compelling a Bob Dylan as any other song you could pick from any year:

Temptation's not an easy thing
And I'm giving the devil rein
Cos each sin I got no choice
It runs in my veins
But I'm pressing on . . .

The hit on that 'veins' is artistry of the highest sort, and the implicit analogy between the addiction to drugs and the grip of sin is a very fine touch, especially placed in the context of Dylan's own druggy history.

That is not the only instance, on the 'Saved' album, of Dylan's using his old secular skills in a new devotional context. The other outstanding example comes in *What Can I Do For You*. That not only gives us, out of nowhere, the most eerie, magnificent harmonica-work Dylan has done since the stoned, majestic concerts of 1966 (check out the harmonica solos on *Mr Tambourine Man* live in Liverpool, for instance) but also applies all Dylan's enviable seductive gifts.

It is the same knowlingly disarming tone of voice that yielded:

> Lay lady lay
> Lay across my big brass bed

back in 1969 that is turned on, in *What Can I Do For You*, to disarm Jesus. This is nothing less than devotional seduction – just listen to the voice:

> I know all about poison
> I know all about fiery darts
> I don't care how rough the road is
> Show me where it starts

The ability to pull off *that* audacity shows us as well, I think, that there has been, in the Born Again process, no drastic excision from Dylan's personality of the restless romantic fascinations he's always attested to in his work.

'Slow Train Coming' shows this too. It takes the same Dylan who has always loved hoboes and the road to deliver these images

> You may be living in another country
> Under another name
> (*You Gotta Serve Somebody*)

and

> Like a thief in the night
> He'll restore wrong to right
> When He returns.
> (*When He Returns*)

Jesus as thief-in-the-night is distinctly a Dylan idea.

Similarly it takes the same artist who seizes name-sounds like 'Delacroix' (on 'Blood On The Tracks') and 'Panamanian moon' (on 'Blonde On Blonde') to alight with such relish and panache on 'Nicodemus' (on *In The Garden*). And it evidences the Dylan of all those romance-of-the-road leaving songs of 1964, when we note the lingering affection he bestows, in 1980, on the notion in these lines:

> You know that we are strangers
> In a land we're passing through
> (*Covenant Woman*)

Again, Dylan's capacity for aphorisms that pass into common currency – the ability to coin those much-loved phrases like 'to live outside the law you must be honest' (1966) – is still alive and well on these religious albums. It would be hard to quarrel with the impact and panache of

> Soon as a man is born
> You know the sparks begin to fly
> (*What Can I Do For You*)

and hard not to remember those lines after even one's first hearing of the 'Saved' album. Similarly, it comes as a pleasurable surprise, on *Pressing On*, to find Dylan using in song in 1980 a motto he had made his own as the title of a film in 1965:

> Shake the dust off of your feet
> *Don't look back*

(my italics)

Yet another welcome element to be found in these albums is the attack Dylan makes on what is essentially a Californian modishness. Dylan's America was always the mid-West and New York, and it always seemed wrong when he moved to California in the early 1970s. One remembered, at the time of his move, how it conflicted with the excellent sentiments he'd expressed on the unreleased mid-60s song *Going Down South*:

> San Francisco is fine
> You sure get lots of sun
> But I'm used to four seasons –
> California's got but one

and when, around 1974–5, Dylan was starting to put himself back on the streets, it was only right and logical that it was the small clubs of New York City to which he returned for a series of unannounced guest appearances at gigs by Jack Elliott, John Prine, Muddy Water and so on. Just as he was never seduced by the hippie milieu of the late-60s, so he has proved himself unimpressed also by the Marin County-hunters. 'Slow Train Coming' makes this crystal clear, from the somewhat obvious barbs of:

> Spiritual advisors and gurus to guide your every move
> Instant inner peace
> And every step you take has got to be approved
> (*When You Gonna Wake Up*)

to the beautifully trademarked Dylan bite of

> Don't wanna amuse nobody
> Don't wanna be amused
> (*Do Right To Me Baby* [*Do Unto Others*])

and

> I don't know which is worse
> Doin' your own thing or bein' cool
> (*Gonna Change My Way of Thinking*)

There is also that polite chastisement given in *Precious Angel*:

> You were tellin' him about Buddah
> You were tellin' him 'bout Mohammed in one breath
> You never mentioned one time the man who came and
> Died a criminal's death

And I suspect that it is as much California as anywhere that Dylan celebrates being spiritually rescued from on *Saved*:

> . . . saved me from the pit
> The emptiness and wrath
> And the fire that burns in it

Dylan's scorn of that West Coast milieu – where people cannot go any further west without falling into the ocean, and so pursue their eternal quest of the American dream through a cocooning consumerism, not just of things but of philosophies and people and where people no longer have lives but have lifestyles instead – Dylan's contemptuous impatience is bound up with an essential seriousness of purpose that he has always evinced. In 1963 he was writing about the need to conduct one's life in the light of one's expecting death:

> I will not go down under the ground
> Cos somebody tells me that death's comin' round
> Let me die in my footsteps
> Before I go down under the ground

and in the mid-60s he's quoted as saying that you have to decide how you behave in the face of the certainty that you will die.

His conversion to Christianity has prompted what is essentially a re-statement of that earlier agnostic seriousness. It is now re-stated as 'Prepare To Meet Thy Maker' and it is one of the basic, major themes of 'Slow Train Coming' and 'Saved' – and it is a message Dylan is urging on us regardless of our religious tenets. It is a message about not wasting our time in this world, regardless (effectively) of whether we believe there is another world to come.

For himself, currently, he chooses to concentrate on this theme with a conventional Christian focus, but essentially it is a re-statement of the same conviction as to the dignity of life and the individual's responsibility for controlling its quality and worthiness as he was expressing in the 1960s.

Dylan comes back uncannily close to echoing William Blake here (and no one knocks *him* for believing in Christ). From a letter by Blake:

> Christ is very decided on this Point: 'He who is Not With Me is Against Me.'
> There is no Medium or Middle state.

From Dylan's *Precious Angel*:

> You either got faith or you got unbelief
> And there ain't no neutral ground.

And from *Gonna Change My Way Of Thinking*:

> Jesus said 'be ready
> For you know not the hour which I come'
> He said 'who's not for me is against me' –
> Just so's you all know where he's coming from

and this clear call to self-examination is representative of the whole stance of these collections:

> When you gonna wake up
> And strengthen the things that remain?
> (*When You Gonna Wake Up*)

It recurs in the title of the 'Saved' song *Are You Ready?* and most pressingly – especially in the contemporary context of the new cold war, reminiscent as it is of the earlier era than produced the Cuban Missile Crisis and thus to Dylan's *A Hard Rain's A Gonna Fall* (which was the same message again, of course) – here:

> When destruction comes swiftly
> And there's no time to say fare thee well
> Have you decided whether you wanna be

In heaven or in hell?
Are you ready? . . .
Are you ready for Armageddon?

The trouble is, of course, that pressing and central as that theme might be, there is no disguising the fact that *A Hard Rain's A-Gonna Fall* is an infinitely better song than *Are You Ready?* – and that what makes these Born Again albums so flawed and shallow in the context of Bob Dylan's whole catalogue is that he has been satisfied, on these records, to assert and argue and declaim but he has hardly bothered anywhere on them to fulfil the more important tasks of the artist: he has not created worlds here, he has only argued about them.

In this sense, Dylan comes full circle, with 'Slow Train Coming' and 'Saved', back to the polemical, creatively-sparse mode of writing that marked his early protest period. (There is even the same radicalism – but of a sort that is, for rich Americans with no grasp of politics, an easier option than activism. Christianity allows you to be radical without arguing for any concrete, worldly attack on the status-quo of the system. Thus Dylan can rail: 'You may own guns and you may own tanks' and 'You got gangsters in power and law-breakers makin' the rules' and 'But the enemy I see wears a cloak of decency' without any necessary corroborative political analysis.) We are light-years away, here, from the creativity and genius of 'Highway 61 Revisited' or 'Blood On The Tracks' or 'Street Legal' or 'John Wesley Harding', or even from the more minor treasures of 'Nashville Skyline', 'Planet Waves' or 'Desire'.

Spiritually Dylan may, for the time being, have arrived. Artistically, he is coasting. And the history of Bob Dylan's output should have taught us that he not only doesn't stay in one place too long – he doesn't coast for long either. A creativity that has survived two decades is not going to disappear next week. The future will include this great artist.

Acknowledgements

The author and the publishers wish to express their thanks to the undermentioned copyright owners for the use of material written and composed by Bob Dylan. Quotations are taken from Bob Dylan recordings and may, in some cases, differ from the printed sheet-music versions.

Copyright by W. B. Music Corp., USA: **Desolation Row,** © 1965; **A Hard Rain's A-Gonna Fall,** © 1963; **I Shall Be Free,** © 1963; **Just Like Tom Thumb's Blues,** © 1965; **Ballad Of A Thin Man,** © 1965; **With God On Our Side,** © 1963; **Ballad of Hollis Brown,** © 1963; **When The Ship Comes In,** © 1963; **Don't Think Twice, It's All Right,** © 1963; **It Ain't Me, Babe,** © 1964; **Restless Farewell,** © 1964; **All I Really Want To Do,** © 1964; **Only A Pawn In Their Game,** © 1963; **It Takes A Lot To Laugh, It Takes A Train To Cry,** © 1965; **Bob Dylan's Dream,** © 1963; **Rocks And Gravel,** © 1963; **Sitting On A Barbed Wire Fence,** © 1970; **Love Minus Zero/No Limit,** © 1965; **To Ramona,** © 1964; **Let Me Die In My Footsteps,** © 1963, 1965; **Positively 4th Street,** © 1965; **The Gates Of Eden,** © 1965; **Subterranean Homesick Blues,** © 1965; **Tombstone Blues,** © 1965; **Bob Dylan's 115th Dream,** © 1965; **Talkin' World War III Blues,** © 1963; **Can You Please Crawl Out Your Window?,** © 1965; **It's All Over Now, Baby Blue,** © 1965; **Motorpsycho Nitemare,** © 1964; **The Chimes of Freedom,** © 1964; **Highway 61 Revisited,** © 1965; **Mr Tambourine Man,** © 1964; **I'd Hate To Be You On That Dreadful Day,** © 1964; **Masters Of War,** © 1963; **Train A-Travelin',** © 1963; **Eternal Circle,** © 1963; **Spanish Harlem Incident,** © 1964; **Paths Of Victory,** © 1964; **Ballad In Plain D,** © 1964; **It's Alright Ma (I'm Only Bleeding),** © 1965; **Like A Rolling Stone,** © 1965; **Farewell, Angelina,** © 1965; **Maggie's Farm,** © 1965; **Lay Down Your Weary Tune,** © 1964; **Sign On The Cross,** © 1971; **The Lonesome Death of Hattie Carroll,** © 1964; **California,** © 1964; **Quit Your Low-Down Ways,** © 1963, 1964; **Watcha Gonna Do,** © 1963, 1966; **Masters Of War,** © 1963.

Copyright by Duchess Music, USA: **Talkin' New York,** © 1962, 1965; **Song To Woody,** © 1962; **Talking Bear Mountain Picnic Massacre Blues,** © 1962; **Man Of Constant Sorrow,** © 1962.

Copyright by Dwarf Music, USA: **All Along The Watchtower,** © 1968; **The Ballad Of Frankie Lee And Judas Priest,** © 1968; **Visions Of Johanna,** © 1966; **John Wesley Harding,** © 1968; **Pledging My Time,** © 1966; **Absolutely Sweet Marie,** © 1966; **Tears Of Rage** (Words by Bob Dylan, Music by Richard Manuel), © 1968; **Too Much Of Nothing,** © 1967; **Open The Door, Homer,** © 1968; **Temporary Like Achilles,** © 1966; **Most Likely You Go Your Way (And I'll Go Mine),** © 1966; **Leopard-skin Pill-Box Hat,** © 1966; **Million Dollar Bash,** © 1967; **Drifter's Escape,** © 1968; **Nothing Was Delivered,** © 1968; **I Pity The Poor Immigrant,** © 1968; **The Wicked Messenger,** © 1968; **Just Like A Woman,** © 1966; **Please, Mrs Henry,** © 1967; **Memphis Blues Again,** © 1966; **Rainy Day Women Nos 12 and 35,** © 1966; **Sad-Eyed Lady Of The Lowlands,** © 1966; **One Of Us Must Know (Sooner Or Later),** © 1966; **Yea! Heavy And A Bottle Of Bread,** © 1967; **You Ain't Goin' Nowhere,** © 1967; **As I Went Out One Morning,** © 1968; **Dear Landlord,** © 1968; **I Want You,** © 1966; **4th Time Around,** © 1966; **Obviously 5 Believers,** © 1966; ***I Shall Be Released,** © 1967; **I Dreamed I Saw St Augustine,** © 1968; **I Wanna Be Your Lover,** © 1971, 1976.

Copyright by Big Sky Music, USA: **Lay, Lady, Lay,** © 1969; **Country Pie,** © 1969; **Tonight I'll Be Staying Here With You,** © 1969; **I Threw It All Away,**

It's Late (reproduced by permission of United Artists Ltd and Eric Music Inc.)

Finally, we also wish to acknowledge permission from the following to quote from copyright works: Hutchinson Publishing Group for permission to quote from *The Pop Process* by Richard Mabey; to Steven Goldberg and to *Saturday Review* for permission to quote from his article 'Bob Dylan and the Poetry of Salvation' (© 1970 *Saturday Review* Inc. All rights reserved); to Allen & Unwin Ltd and Houghton Mifflin Company for permission to quote from *The Lord Of The Rings* by J R R Tolkien; to Cassell & Company Ltd and Da Capo Press Inc., for permission to quote from *Conversations With The Blues* by Paul Oliver; to Cambridge University Press for permission to quote from 'English Tradition and Idiom' by Adrian Bell, which originally appeared in Volume II of Scrutiny, 1935, and was subsequently reprinted in *Selections From Scrutiny* No 2; and for permission to quote from an interview with Bob Dylan which appeared in *Rolling Stone* magazine (© 1969 Straight Arrow Publishers Inc. All rights reserved).

Index

Page numbers in italic refer to illustrations.

Abba 8
Absolutely Sweet Marie 43, 45, 95, 106, 149–151
'After Bathing At Baxter's' 120
Ain't Gonna Grieve 42
Ain't Got No Home 94
Alice In Wonderland 75–6
Alice Through The Looking-Glass 75–6
All Along The Watchtower 13, 18, 79, 161, 192
All I Have To Do Is Dream 94
All I Really Want To Do 10, 43, 166
All The Bright Foam Of Talk 85
Allsop, Kenneth 75
Ancient Mariner, The 195
Anka, Paul 104, 110
Annie's Bin A-Workin' On The Midnight Shift 106
'Another Side Of Bob Dylan' 10, 11, 113, 128
Anyplace Is Paradise 101
Are You Lonesome Tonight? 102
Are You Ready 228–9
Armatrading, Joan 114
Arnold, Kokomo 101
Arnold, Matthew 56, 197
Arrow And The Song, The 81
As I Went Out One Morning 59
Asylum Records 14, 15
At The Hop 99
Atkins, Chet 92
Augustans, the 48

Baby I Don't Care 93

Baby Let Me Bang Your Box 57
Baby Let's Play House 100
Baby Stop Cryin' 188–9, 208
Back In The USA 96
Baez, Joan 13, 45, 85, 145, *160*, 189
Baker, Ginger 111
Ballad In Plain D 132–7
Ballad Of A Thin Man 12, *16*, 18, 69–70, 130, 144
Ballad Of Davy Crockett, The 32
Ballad Of Davy Moore, The 181
Ballad Of Frankie Lee & Judas Priest 30, 98, 182, 200
Ballad Of Hollis Brown, The 26, 28, 49, 126–7, 143
Band, The 14, 16, *53*, 58, 87, 106, 165
Barbed Wire Fence 42, 97, *147*
Basement tapes, the 14, 98, 102, 177, 202
'Basement Tapes, The' 16–17
Bateson, F. W. 62
Baudelaire 122, 196
Baxter, Les 88
Bay Of Mexico, The 25
BBC, the *34*, 89, 90, *95*, 110, *193*
Beach Boy Blues 102
Beat generation/beat poets, the 84, 122
Beatles, The 8, 92, 98, 116, 130, 151
Beautiful You Are 85
BeeGees, The 8, 111
'Before The Flood' 11, 15
Bell, Adrian 53, 54
Belle Isle 13, 27, 167–8
Bells Of San Blas, The 81
Bennett, Tony 100
Beowulf 47
Berry, Chuck 56, 92, 93, 95, 96–8, 99–100, 101,

105, 113, 122
Big Brother & The Holding Company 119
Big Hunk O'Love 99
Billy 103
Bishop Blougram's Apology 69–70
Black Cross 81
Black Diamond Bay 17, 181
Black folk music 25, 36–42
Blackbushe concert 1978 109, *109*, 186
Blake, William 57, 59–66, 68, 174, 190, 228
Bland, Bobby 93
'Blonde On Blonde' 12, 13, 16, 17, 32, 53, 69, 72, 76, 78, 93, 98, 114, 119, 120, 130, 145, 147–160, 161, 167, 169, 171, 174, 176, 177, 183, 191, 200, 226
'Blood On The Tracks' 15–16, 17, 18, 59, 82, 103, 108, 126, 127, 137, 168, 176–180, 181, 182, 189, 200, 201, 202, 205, 207, 210, 226, 229
Blowin' Down The Road 36–7
Blowin' In The Wind 9, 18, 23, *95*, 113
Blue Moon 94, 166
Blue Moon Of Kentucky 32, 102
Blue-Belles, The 94
Blueberry Hill 101, 102
Bo Diddley 105
Bob B. Soxx & The Blue Jeans 94
'Bob Dylan' 9, 46
Bob Dylan & The Poetry of Salvation 190–192
Bob Dylan's Dream 45
'Bob Dylan's Greatest Hits' 12, 18
Bob Dylan's 115th Dream 97, 102, 114, 144
Bonds, Gary US 93
Boots Of Spanish Leather 10, 143, 167

Bosch, Hieronymus 147
Bound For Glory 22, 37, 40, 55, 205
Bowie, David 114, 122
Boxer, The 166
Brando, Marlon 98, 189
Breaking Up Is Hard To Do 93, 94
'Bringing It All Back Home' 10, 78, 97, 114, 207
Brown-Eyed Handsome Man 105
Browning, Robert 57, 68–75
Bryant, Boudleaux & Felice 94, 166
Buckets Of Rain 40, 180, 207
'Budokan (Bob Dylan At)' 18, 131
Bunyan, John 8, 48–9, 53
But I Do 94
Butterfield, Paul, Blues Band *112*, 114
B'Wa Nina 94
Byrds, The 119

C'est Si Bon 90
Calendar Girl 93
Can You Please Crawl Out Your Window 14, 79, 130, 144, 145
Cannon, Freddie 93
Cannon, Geoffrey 163, 165
Canonization, The 59
Can't Help Falling In Love 104
Cardinal And The Dog, The 72
Carlyle, Thomas 80
Carroll, Lewis 76
Carter, Ruben "Hurricane" *180*
Cash, Johnny 10, 30, *34*, 92, 92, 107, 165
Catch-22 49
Cathy's Clown 94
Chambers, Aidan 55
Chandler, Raymond 80

Chanel, Bruce 94
Changing Of The Guards
75, 187, 207, 212–5
Chapel Of Love 172
Chaplin, Charlie 73, *208*
Charles Carville's Eyes 84
Charles, Ray 94
Chaucer 47–8
Chesterton, G. K. 68, 72
Chimes Of Freedom 10,
114, 82, 85, 129, 213
Clapton, Eric 111, 170
Clarke, John Cooper 121
Clash, The 121
Clayton, Paul 29
Cleave, Maureen 116, 119
Cleveland Plain Dealer, the
110–111
Cline, Patsy 92, 107
Coasters, The 93
Coburn, James 103
Cocaine Blues 165
Cochran, Eddie 93, 94, 100
Cohen, Leonard 64, 184
Cohn, Nik 47, 88, 90, 93
Cold, Cold Heart 107, 167
Coleridge, S. T. 58, 64, 80,
195
Collins, Judy *118*
Columbia Records (UK) 99
Columbia Records (US) 9,
14–5, 23
*Come All You Virginia
Girls* 25
Come On Ev'rybody 101
Como, Perry 58
Confessions 80
Connif, Ray 110
Contours, The 94
*Conversation With The
Blues* 38, 39
Cooke, Sam 19, 93, 94
Copper Kettle 13, 27, 166
Cornell, Lyn 94
Corso, Gregory 87
Costa, Sam 90
Costello, Elvis 7, 58, 114,
122, 150
Cotton Candy Land 102
Cough Song, The 108
Country Joe & The Fish
119, 131
Country Pie 29, 72, 102,
162
Covenant Women 224
Cowboy folk tradition 25,
27–36
Crackers, The 87
Cramer, Floyd 92, 93, 102
Crawdaddy magazine 120
Credence Clearwater
Revival 98
Crickets, The 93
Crosby, David 170
Crudup, Arthur 'Big Boy'
98
Crystals, The 94
cummings, e. e. 84
Curfew 82
Cut Across Shorty 93

Dali, Salvador 147
Damon, Bill 165, 166, 167
Dance With The Guitar

Man 94
Danny & The Juniors 93
Davis, Skeeter 92
Day Is Done, The 81, 82
Day Of The Locusts 13, 43,
80, 172
Days Of '49 13, 25
Dear Landlord 143–4
Decca Records 90–1, 94
Deck Of Cards 173
'Desire' 17, 49, 82, 84, 87,
147, 168, 181–2, 201,
202, 206, 207, 211, 229
Desolation Row 8, 12, 23,
70–1, 80, 82, 130,
138–142, 158, 161, 215
Dickens, Charles 157
Diddley, Bo 105
Dion (& The Belmonts) 93,
94
Dire Straits 122
Dirge 57, 60, 75, 85, 176,
200
Dixie Cups, The 172
Dixieland Rock 101
*Do Right To Me Baby (Do
Unto Others)* 43, 227
Do You Love Me 94
Doe, Ernie K. 94
Domino, Fats 88, 93, 95–6,
101, 102, 167
Donne, John 57–9
Donovan 9, *20*
Don't Be Cruel 88
Don't Look Back (film) 43,
64, 110–1, 121, *193*, 227
*Don't Think Twice It's All
Right* 9, 18, 30, 50, 104,
107, 174, *185*
Doors, The 119
Dos Passos 80
Down Along The Cove 13,
120, 167
Down In The Flood 14
Dr. John The Night-
Tripper 119
Dramatic Monologue, the
68
Drifter's Escape, The 73,
76, 106
Drifters, The 93
Drive In Show 100
Dryden 58
Duncan, Johnny & The
Blue-Grass Boys 113
'Dylan', 14–5, 18, 108
Dylan, Sara 202–214

Each And All 81
Eager, Vince 89
Earl's Court concerts 1978
7, 18
Early Morning Rain 13, 166
East Virginia 26–7
Eat The Document (film)
64
Eddy, Duane 90, 93, 94,
131
El Paso 181
Elemental 50
Eliot, George 73, 190
Eliot, T. S. 56, 57, 64, 66,
76–80, 81, 126, 142
Elliott, Ramblin' Jack 23,

205, 227
Ely, Joe 122
E.M.I. Records 90–1
Emergency Civil Liberties
Committee 59
Emerson, Ralph Waldo 80,
81, 199
Encounter magazine 75
'English Tradition And
Idiom' 53
Erie Canal, The 25
Eternal Circle 128–9
Eva, Little 94
Everly Brothers, the 92,
93, 94, 105, 166
Evers, Medgar 25, 37
Every Day 104
Exciters, The 94

Farewell Angelina 130,
145–7, 176
Ferlinghetti, L. 87
Festival (film) 114
Fire Of Driftwood, The 81
Fireballs, The 106
Fitzgerald, Ella 88, 100
Fitzgerald, F. Scott 7, 54,
71, 80, 155
Flatt & Scruggs 107, 108
Fleetwoods, The 93
Foggy Dew, The 25
'Folk-Rock' 76, 113
Fool Such As I, A 104
Fools Like Me 167
Ford, Tennessee Ernie 32,
88
Forever Young 15
Fortune, Lance 89
Four Aces, The 88
Four Seasons, The 94
4th Time Around 58–9, 72,
97, 151–3
Francis, Connie 93
'Freewheelin' Bob Dylan,
The' 9, *118*
Freight Train Blues 43
Freida Florentine 108
From A Buick 6 12, 97,
130, 144, 154
*Fugitive, The (Wanted
Man)* 166
Fuller, Jesse 9
Fulson, Lowell 101
Fury, Billy 89, 94

Garden Of Love, The 62
Gates Of Eden 10, 50, 60,
65–8, 71, 130, 138
Gell, David 90
Genet, Jean 173
Gentle, Johnny 89
George, Barbara 94
George Jackson 14, 173–4
Gibson, Don 92, 107
Ginsberg, Allen 47, 82, 84,
87, *87*, 182
*Girl From The North
Country* 9, 143, 180
Girl Of My Best Friend 100
Give All To Love 199
Give Me The Right 100
*Going Down South
(California)* 43, 227

Going, Going, Gone 174,
176
Goldberg, Steven 174,
191–2, 197, 198
Goldstein, Richard 161,
182
*Gonna Change My Way Of
Thinkin'* 40, 200, 227,
228
Good Hearted Man 95
Good, Jack 89, 94
Good Morrow, The 58
Goodbye 81
Goodchild, Gaye 85
Goodman, Steve *134*
Gospel Plow 20
Gotta Travel On 29, 166
Grapes Of Wrath 25
Great Balls Of Fire 167
Great Gatsby, The 155
Greenwich Village 9, 19,
20, 23, *40*, 64, 218
Grossman, Albert *113*
Guardian, the 56, 163
Guthrie, Arlo *118*
Guthrie, Woody 9, 21–3,
37, 47, 53, 55, 80, 127,
165, 199, 205
Guthrie, Woody, Memorial
Concert 1968 *118*

Haley, Bill 88, 89
Hammond, John 9
Hammond, John Jnr. *125*
'Hard Rain' 18
Hard Rain (film) 13
*Hard Rain's A-Gonna Fall,
A* 8, 9, 82, 123–6, 199,
228–9
Hard-Headed Woman 101
Hardy, Thomas 197
Harrison, George 111, 170
Hats Off To Larry 93
Hawks, The 87, *107*, *147*
Hayter, Alethea 75
Hazel 15, 162–3, 175, 176
He Was A Friend Of Mine
84
Heartbeat 104
Heartbreak Hotel 88, 98,
101, 119
Hemingway, Ernest 25, 30,
57, 80
Henderson, Joe 94
Henry, Clarence 'Frogman'
94
Hiawatha 81
High School Confidential
167
Highway 51 Blues 46
'Highway 61 Revisited' 12,
16, 23, 53, 65, 76, 78,
97, 108, 120, 154, 176,
177, 191, 207, 229
Highway 61 Revisited 97,
144
'His Hand In Mine' 165
Holly, Buddy 93, 94, 95,
100, 104–6, 113
Holmes, Sherlock 75
Hoots Mon! 89
Horowitz, David 123–4,
127
Hound Dog 58, 88, 99

233

Houston, Cisco 21
How Long? 23
'How The Poor Die' 42
Howl 82, 87
How's My Ex Treating You 107
Humble Pie 111
Hurricane 84, 181
Hurt, Mississippi John 39
Huxley, Aldous 190
Hymn To The Night 81

I Ain't Gonna Go To Hell For Nobody 203
I Believe In You 223
I Don't Believe You 105, 114, 143
I Dreamed I Saw St Augustine 13, 17, 62, 80, 216–7
I Feel So Bad 93
I Forgot More 94, 163, 165
I Go Ape 93
I Got A Woman 102
I Got My Eyes On You (And I Like What I See) 93
I Got Stung 99
I Hope I Think I Wish 90
I Know 94
I Love My Love 25
I Love You Porgy 141
I Pity The Poor Immigrant 13
I Shall Be Free 21
I Shall Be Free No. 10 7, 21, 58
I Shall Be Released 14, 195, 200, 217
I Sold My Heart To The Junkman 94
I Threw It All Away 31, 101, 201, 207
I Wanna Be Your Lover 217
I Want You 14, 18, 106, 148, *185*
I'd Hate To Be You On That Dreadful Day 124
I'll Be Your Baby Tonight 13, 72, 73, 106, 120
I'll Keep It With Mine 74
I'm A-Ridin' Old Paint 29
I'm Blue 94
I'm Yours 102
I've Got You Under My Skin 100
Idiot Wind 18, 75, 78–9, 179, 205, 206, 210
If Not For You 169, 171
If Up's The Word; And A World Grows Greener 84
If You Gotta Go, Go Now 14, 99, 144
If You See Her Say Hello 137, 180
Ikettes, The 94
In Search Of Little Sadie 165
In The Garden 224, 226
In White America 141
Incredible String Band, The 9
Introduction To The Study Of Blake, An 66

Iron Butterfly 119
Is A Bluebird Blue? 90
Is It So Strange? 102
Is Your Love In Vain 187, 210
Isis 17, 43, 181, 206–7, 217
Island In The Moon 65
Isle Of Wight concert, 1969 112–3, *186*
Isle Of Wight press-conference 111
Isley Brothers, The 94
It Ain't Me Babe 10, 30, 31, 57
It Doesn't Matter Any More 93, 104
It Feels So Right 101
It Hurts Me Too 154
It Takes A Lot To Laugh, It Takes A Train To Cry 42, 45–6, 84, 101, 130
It Won't Happen With Me 32
It's All Over Now, Baby Blue 11, 24, 43, 50, 79, 144
It's Alright Ma (I'm Only Bleeding) 10, 97, 130, 137–8
It's Late 99
It's Only Make-Believe 90

Jack Munroe 141
Jackson, George 174
Jackson, Jack 90
Jackson, Mahalia 98
Jagger, Mick 58, 98, 114
Jailhouse Rock 99, 101
Jambalaya 88
James, Henry 57
Jay & The Americans 94
Jean, Cathy & The Room-mates: 98
Jefferson, Blind Lemon 9, 19
Jefferson Airplane 119
Jerusalem 60–2
Joey 49, 84, 181
'John Wesley Harding' 12–3, 16, 17, 32, 62, 73–5, 98, 107, 108, 119–20, 161, 167, 177, 191–2, 201, 207, 216, 229
John Wesley Harding 32–6 162
Johnny & The Hurricanes 94
Johnson, Lonnie 19
Jones, Mick 121
Jordanaires, The 165
Joshua Fit The Battle Of Jericho 165
Just Like A Woman 60, 153
Just Like Tom Thumb's Blues 14, 42, 97, 130, 165

Kafka, Franz 142
Kane, Eden 92
Kant, Emmanuel 56
Katy Cruel 25

Katz, Elia 131
Kerouac, Jack 56, 80, 84, 87
King, Carole 58
King, Claude 94
King Creole 99
Knees Up Mother Brown 89
Knight, Gladys & The Pips 94
Knox, Buddy 92

Landau, Jon 120
Lang, Don & His Frantic Five 89
Langbaum, Robert 68
Langland 48
Lanza, Mario 113
Lawdy Miss Clawdy 101, 102, 105
Lawrence, D. H. 49, 50, 57, 62, 64, 80
Lay Down Your Weary Tune 81, 189, 192–8
Lay Lady Lay 94, 102, 161–2, 226
Leadbelly (Leadbetter, Huddy) 19, 21
Leaves Of Grass 82, 87
Leavis, F. R. 48, 54, 64, 84
Lee, Brenda 89, 93
Lennon, John 111, 114
Leopard-Skin Pill-Box Hat 72–3, 153–4, 167, 171
Lester, Ketty 94
Let It Be Me 13, 31, 166
Let Me Die In My Footsteps 228
Let The Little Girl Dance 93
Let's Jump The Broomstick 89, 93
Letter Full of Tears 94
Levy, Jacques 181
Lewis, Jerry Lee 32, 92, 93, 107, 167, 172
Lightfoot, Gordon 166
Like A Rolling Stone 12, 58, 114, 130, 142–3, 163, 166, 168, 191
Lily, Rosemary & The Jack Of Hearts 180, 181
Lindsay, Vachel 81, 83
Lion Sleeps Tonight, The 94
Lipscomb, Mance 39
Listen To Me 104
Little Sadie 165
Little Sister 93
Little Too Much, A 94
Liverpool concert, 1966 112–3
Livin' Lovin' Wreck 172
Living The Blues 167
Lobster Quadrille, The 76
Locklin, Hank 92
Lomax, Alan 22–3, 24, 27, 141
London 60
Lonely Boy 99
Lonely Street 94
Lonesome Death Of Hattie Carroll 25, 40, 58, 137, 143
Lonesome Prairie 32
Long Ago, Far Away 129
Longfellow 80, 81–2

Lord Of The Rings 196–8
Lord Randall 123
Lord Rockingham's XI 89
Lost Generation, the 81
Loudermilk, John D. 92
Love Letters 94
Love Me Tender 88
Love Minus Zero/No Limit 11, 50, 62–4, 130, 144, 183
Love Song Of J. Alfred Prufrock, The 76, 80
Lovelace, Richard 132
Lucille 93

Mabey, Richard 116
Maggie's Farm 11, 182
Magritte, René 147, 217
Mailer, Norman 8, 70, 80, 171
Mailman Bring Me No More Blues 105
Man Gave Names To All The Animals 220–2
Man In Me, The 169, 171, 173
Man Of Constant Sorrow 45
Mann, Mannfred 112
Marcels, The 94
Marcus, Greil 59–60, 105, 106
Mariposa Folk Festival, 1973 *183*
Marsden, Beryl 94
Martin, Dean 88
Martindale, Wink 173
Marvin, Lee 102, 103
Marvelettes, The 94
Masters Of War 9, 23, 126, 128, 138, 199
Matchbox 19
Maybelline 96
MacDonogh, Steve 71
McCartney, Paul 14
McClure, Michael *87*
McColl, Ewan 68
McCormick, Mack 39
McCoy, Charlie 154
McGuire, Barry 124
McLuhan, Marshall 8, 47, 55
Meet Me In The Morning 40, 42, 180
Mellers, Wilfred 37, 40, 47, 119
Melody Maker 111
Memphis Blues Again 85, 97, 155–6, 159, 174, 183–4, 195, 200
Men And Women 74
Mess Of Blues, A 93, 101
Middlemarch 73
Midsummer Night's Dream, A 172
Mighty Quinn, The 102, 112, 166
Milkcow Blues Boogie 42, 101
Miller, Henry 80
Miller, Mitch 88
Million Dollar Bash 58, 73
Minstrel Boy 113
Mitchell, Guy 167
Mitchell, Joni 122

Mixed-Up Confusion *11*, 14, 102
Moby Grape 119
Monster Mash 94
Monument Records 94
Moondreams 105
'More Bob Dylan Greatest Hits' 14
Most Likely You Go Your Way And I'll Go Mine 72, 154, 169, 182
Mother-In-Law 94
Mothers Of Invention 120
Motorpsycho Nitemare 98, 114, 184
Mozambique 181
Mr Tambourine Man 10, 114, 119, 147, 191, 226
Mull Of Kintyre 58
Murray, Pete 90
'Music From Big Pink' 165
Musicians' Union, the 90
My Back Pages 10, 119, 138, 173, 192
My Fair Lady 58, 163
My Father Moved Through Dooms Of Love 84
My Guy 94
My Heart Is Telling Me (Abandoned Love) 23, 205, 213
My Lost Youth 81
My Prayer 88

Nadine 96
Nash, Graham 170
'Nashville Airplane' 108
Nashville Blues 94
'Nashville Skyline' 13, 30–1, 75, 94, 104, 107, 114, 120, *139*, 161–3, 167, 171, 173, 174, 176, 198, 201, 207, 229
Nashville Skyline Rag 108
Nelson, Ricky 90, 93, 94, 99
Never Say Goodbye 15, 43, 128, 176, 200
'New Morning' 13–4, 15, 82, 104, *134*, 168, 169–73, 176, 187, 217
New Morning 171, 173
New Orleans 93
New Pony 40, 187, 207–8
New Yorker, the 111
Newport Folk Festival, 1963 *26*, *34*
Newport Folk Festival, 1964 *51*, *115*, *125*, *160*
Newport Folk Festival, 1965 *20*, 24, *107*, *112*, 114, *204*
Newsweek magazine 111
Night And Day 100
Nino & The Ebb-Tides 98
Nixon, Richard 9, 10
No Time To Think 83, 188, 207, 212, 215–8
North Country Blues 25, 137, 138, 143
Norwegian Wood 151
Nothing Can Change This Love 94
Nothing Was Delivered 102–3

Obviously Five Believers 154
Ochs, Phil *115*
Oh Boy! 89, 94
Oh Sister 74, 181, 201
Old Blue 25
Oldham, Andrew Loog 116
Oliver, Paul 26, 38, 39
On The Rebound 93
On The Road Again 97, 106, 130, 144
On The Street Where You Live 163, 169
One More Night 32, 75, 101
One More Weekend 13, 171
One Night 101
One Of Us Must Know (Sooner Or Later) 17, 72, 114, 154–5
One Too Many Mornings 10, 30, 129, 171
One-Sided Love-Affair 100
Only A Hobo 84
Only A Pawn In Their Game 25, 37, 137
Only The Lonely 94
Open The Door Homer/Richard 58
Opium & The Romantic Imagination 75
Orbison, Roy 94, 165
Ormulum 48
Orwell, George 42
Oswald, Lee Harvey 59
Our Lady Of The Flowers 173
Outlaw Blues 42–3, 130, 154
Oxford Town 23

Paine, Tom 59
Paracelsus 74
Paralysed 99
Parker, Col. Tom *113*
Parsons, Gram 166
Pastures Of Plenty 22
'Pat Garrett & Billy The Kid' 14, *134*
Pat Garrett & Billy The Kid (film) 14, 103, *103*
Patchen, Kenneth 84–7
Paths Of Victory 132
Peckinpah, Sam 14
Peggy Day 58, 102
Peggy Sue 104
Peggy Sue Got Married 104
Penguins, The 57
People Get Ready 46, 205
Perfidia 94
Perkins, Carl 19
Peter Paul & Mary 19, *20*, 23
Petty, Tom 121
Philips Records 90–1
Pickett, Bobby Boris & The Crypt-Kickers 94
Pilgrim's Progress, A 48, 49
Piltdown Men, The 93
Pistol Packin' Mamma 93
'Planet Waves' 15, 43, 50, 82, 151, 162, 174–6, 177, 184, 200, 201, 202, 229

Platters, The 88, 93
Playboy interview, 1966 7, 65, 141
Please Mr Postman 94
Please Mrs Henry 151
Pledging My Time 40–2, 154
Plowman, Max 66
Poe, Edgar Allan 80, 82–3
Pop Process, The 116
Pope, Alexander 58
Porter, Cole 100
Positively 4th Street 14, 57, 72, 75, 130, 144, 176, 179, 218
Pound, Ezra 81
Precious Angel 18, 220, 222–3, 225, 227
Preludes 76
Presley, Elvis 14, 32, 42, 47, 58, 88–90, 92, 93, 94, 95, 98–104, 105, 110, 113, *113*, 119, 165
Pressing On 18, 43, 220, 225–6, 227
Pretenders, The 7, 121
Pretty Boy Floyd 23
Pretty Peggy-O 26, 28
Pretty Saro 25
Price, Lloyd 92
Prine, John 121, 227
Procol Harum 119
Promised Land, The 96
Pump It Up 122
Pye Records 90–1

Quarter To Three 93
Queen Jane Approximately 188
Quit Your Low-Down Ways 27, 199

Radio Luxembourg 90
Raining In My Heart 104
Rainy Day Women Nos. 12 & 35 154
Raven, The 83
RCA Victor studios, Nashville 102
Reconsider Baby 101
Reece, Florence 141
Reet Petite 105
Renaldo & Clara (film) 23, 46, 64, *116*, 205, 206
Restless Farewell 30, 128, 129
Reuben Bright 84
Rhapsody On A Windy Night 78
Richard, Cliff 89, 99
Richard Cory 84
Richard, Little 92, 97, 98, 101, 105
Riddle, Nelson, Orchestra, The 88, 101
Rimbaud, Arthur 122
Ring-A-Rockin' 92
Rites Of Darkness, The 85
Robbins, Marty 92, 107, 181
Robertson, Robbie *87*, 106, *107*
Robinson, Edward Arlington 83–4

Robot Man 93
Rock Around The Clock 88
Rock-A-Hula Baby 102
Rockin' Bicycle 95
Rockin' Goose 94
Rock 'n' Roll Waltz 88
Rocks & Gravel 42
Rolling Stone magazine 56, 106, 120–2, 165, 168, 190
Rolling Stones, The 111
Rolling Thunder Revue(s) 23, *115*, *116*, *164*, *189*
Romance In Durango 10, 17, 181
Ronettes, The 94
Ropewalk, The 82
Ross, Diana 114
Rotolo, Susie *46*, *118*, *133*
Runaround Sue 94
Runyan, Damon 80

St. Marie, Buffy 67
Sad-Eyed Lady Of The Lowlands 79, 155, 158–160
Sahm, Doug *134*
San Francisco Express-Times, the 59
Sara 82, 83, 147, 202, 211
Saturday Club 110
Saturday Review, the 191
'Saved' 18, 30, 43, 49, 139, 140, 163, 165, 168, 189, *203*, *204*, 207, 212, 219–29
Saved 18, 75, 224
Saving Grace 18, 75, 165, 207, 220, 223–4, 224–5
Scott, Jack 107
Scrutiny magazine 47, 53
Sea Of Heartbreak 107
Sedaka, Neil 92, 94
See That My Grave Is Kept Clean 19
Seeger, Pete *38*, *118*
Seger, Bob 121
Selected Poems Of Kenneth Patchen, The 85
Selections From Scrutiny No. 2 53
'Self Portrait' 13, 25, 27, 29, 32, 102, 154, 163–8, 170, 171, 173, 198
Senor (Tales Of Yankee Power) 10, 188, 200, 208, 211
'Sgt Pepper's Lonely Hearts Club Band' 119, 120
Shadows, The 89
Shakespeare, William 48, 49, 73, 151
Shannon, Del 93
Shapiro, Helen 92
Sharpe, Cecil 49
Shazam 94
She Belongs To Me 11, 130, 144, 166
She's Your Lover Now 147
Shelley, Percy Byshe 64
Shelter From The Storm 18, 85, 201, 202–5
Shirelles, The 94

Shondell, Troy 94
Sick Rose, The 62, 64
Sign On The Cross 202
Sign On The Window 170, 171, 172, 173
Simon Legree – A Negro Sermon 81
Simon, Paul 14, 166
Simple Twist Of Fate 179
Sinatra, Frank 88, 100
Singing The Blues 89, 167
6.5 Special 89
Slippin' And Slidin' 106
'Slow Train Coming' 18, 30, 43, 46, 49, 139, 140, 163, 165, 189, *204*, 212, 218, 219–229
Slow Train Coming 55, 220, 222, 223
Smith, Bessie 9
Smith, Patti 122
Snake 64
Snap Your Fingers 94
Solid Rock 18, 223
Somebody Have Mercy 19
Something There Is About You 15, 175, 176, 200
Song 58
Song To Woody 9, 20–2, 23, 28, 127–8
Songs of Experience 62
Sopwith Camel 119
Southern Poor White folk music 25, 26–7
Spanish Harlem Incident 10, 114, 130–1, 132
Spanish Is The Loving Tongue 10, 14
Spector, Phil 94, 114
Springsteen, Bruce 120, 121–2
Staple Singers, The 46, 205
Starr, Kay 88
Starr, Ringo 88
Stax Records 101
Stay 94
'Stealin'' (bootleg tape) 144
Steele, Tommy 88–9, 90, 167
Steiger, Rod 56, 57
Steinbeck, John 56, 57, 80
Steppin' Out Of Line 102
Stick With Me Baby 94
Stills, Stephen 170
Storme, Robb 89
Strachwitz, Chris 39
'Strange Days' 120
'Street Legal' 18, 30, 46, 59, 184, 187–9, 200, 207–219, 222, 224, 229
Stuck On You 100
Studies In Classic American Literature 80
Subterranean Homesick Blues 11, 68, 78, 97–8, 114, 122, 130, 144, *193*
Sugar Babe 39
Sugar Sugar 58
Sullivan, Ed, TV show 99
Sun Records 94, 98, 165
Surrender 94
Swan On The River 95

Sweet Little Sixteen 96
Sweet Nuthins 93

Take A Message To Mary 166
Take Me As I Am (Or Let Me Go) 166–7
Talkin' New York 9, 144–5, 199
Talkin' World War III Blues 96, 123
Talking Bear Mountain Picnic Massacre Blues 22
Talking John Birch Society Blues 23
Tamla-Motown Records 94, 101
Tangled Up In Blue 123, 126, 177–9, *185*
Tarantula 84, 85
Taylor, Edward 80
Tears Of Rage 17, 49
'Technicolour Wasteland, The' 75
Teddy Bears, The 93
Teenager In Love 99
Television (the group) 122
Tell Him 94
Tell Me How 104, 106
Tell Me Mama 188–9
Tell Me That It Isn't True 94, 102
Temporary Like Achilles 70, 148–9, 171
Temptation 94
Tennessee Two, The 165
Tennyson, Alfred Lord 80
Terry, Sonny 21
That'll Be The Day 104
That's All Right Mama 98, 101, 102
That's What They Say 104
That's When Your Heartaches Begin 102
'Their Satanic Majesties' Request' 120
This Time 94
This Train 205
This Wheel's On Fire 42
Thomas, Patrick 168
Thompson, Hunter S. 80
Three Angels 13, 85, 173
Time Out magazine 121
Time Passes Slowly 172
'Times They Are A-Changin', The' 9, 30, 129
Times They Are A-Changin', The 8, 18, 23, 106, 113, 131, 132, *185*, 199
To Helen 83
To Lucasta, Going To The Wars 132
To Ramona 10, 50, 55
Together Again 107
Tokens, The 94
Tolkien, J. R. R. 196
Tom Dooley 92
Tombstone Blues 70, 97
Tomorrow Is A Long Time 14, 104
*Tonight I'll Be Staying Here

With You 31, 45, 162
Too Much Monkey Business 97–8, 122
Too Much Of Nothing 47
Torme, Mel 100
Tough Mama 151, 176, 213
Train-A-Travelin' 127
Transfusion Blues 165
Travellin' Band 98
Travels With Charley 56, 57
Travers, Mary *20*
Treat Me Nice 100
Triple Foole, The 58
Trouble 99, 102
Trouble In Mind 40, 220, 225
True Love Tends To Forget 184–7, 210–1
True Love Ways 105, 106
24th Psalm 71
Twist And Shout 94
Twitty, Conway 90
Tyger, Tyger 63
Tyler, Wat 48

Understand Your Man 30, 107
Up At A Villa, Down In The City 68
Urge, The 93

Valens, Ritchie 93, 105
Van Ronk, Dave *46*
Vee, Bobby 88
Velvet Underground, The 119
Ventures, The 94
Victorian Frame Of Mind, The 73
Village Voice magazine 161
Vincent, Gene 90, 93, 99
Vision Of Piers Plowman 48
Visions Of Johanna 32, 78, 79, 97, 155, 157–8, 159

Wake Up Little Susie 166
Walls Of Red Wing 129
Walrus And The Carpenter, The 76
Wanted Man 97, 166
Wasteland, The 78, 79, 80
Watcha Gonna Do 199
Watching The River Flow 14, 165
Waters, Muddy 227
We Better Talk This Over 184, 211–2
We Shall Be Free 21
We Shall Overcome 138
Weary Of The Railway 25
Weberman, A. J. 59, 67
Wedding Song 50, 74, 81, 175–6, 201
Wells, Mary 94
Went To See The Gypsy 15, 103–4, 171–2, 217
Went Up On The Mountain 25
West, Nathanael 80
What Can I Do For You? 18, 220, 224, 226

What To Do 104
What'd I Say 93
What's A Matter Baby 94
When He Returns 18, 220, 223, 225, 226
When I Paint My Masterpiece 14
When The Ship Comes In 28–9, 106, 131–2, 194, 195, 199
When You Gonna Wake Up 227, 228
Where Are You Tonight (Journey Through Dark Heat) 43, 187, 207, 212, 218–9, 220
Which Side Are You On 141
White, Bukka 9
Whitman, Walt 80, 82, 83
Wicked Messenger, The 13, 17, 80
Wigwam 13
Wild Mountain Thyme (Will Ye Go Lassie) 94
Wild One, The (film) 98, 189
Wilde, Marty 89
Will You Love Me Tomorrow 94
Williams, Hank 23, 32, 43, 88, 106
Williams, Maurice & The Zodiacs 94, 98
Williams, Paul 120
Williams, Richard 165
Williams, Roger 88
Wilson, Jackie 105
Winterlude 15, 169–170, 171, 172–3
Winter's Tale, A 73
With God On Our Side 10, 27, 36
Wolfe, Thomas 55
Wolverton Mountain 94
Wordsworth, William 80, 81, 171, 197
Writings & Drawings by Bob Dylan 165

Yankee Doodle 25
Yankee folk music 25
Yea Heavy & A Bottle of Bread 162
You Ain't Goin' Nowhere 14, 19
You Always Hurt The One You Love 94
You Angel You 184
You Gotta Serve Somebody 27, 220, 222, 226
You Never Can Tell 96, 97
Young, Israel *20*
Young, Neil 170
Your Cheating Heart 107
You're A Big Girl Now 18, 74, 137, 161, 179, 189, 207
You're Gonna Make Me Lonesome When You Go 30, 137, 180
Yuro, Timi 94

Zappa, Frank 119, 120